Rural School Leadership

Rural School Leadership

Lessons from Alaska

Edited by
Christian P. Wilkens
Janice DeVore Littlebear
Robert S. Thompson

ROWMAN & LITTLEFIELD
Lanham • Boulder • New York • London

Published by Rowman & Littlefield
An imprint of The Rowman & Littlefield Publishing Group, Inc.
4501 Forbes Boulevard, Suite 200, Lanham, Maryland 20706
www.rowman.com

86-90 Paul Street, London EC2A 4NE, United Kingdom

Copyright © 2025 by Christian P. Wilkens

All rights reserved. No part of this book may be reproduced in any form or by any electronic or mechanical means, including information storage and retrieval systems, without written permission from the publisher, except by a reviewer who may quote passages in a review.

British Library Cataloguing in Publication Information Available

Library of Congress Cataloging-in-Publication Data
Names: Wilkens, Christian P., 1975- editor. | Littlebear, Janice DeVore, editor. | Thompson, Robert S. (Principal), editor.
Title: Rural school leadership : lessons from Alaska / Edited by Christian P. Wilkens, Janice DeVore Littlebear, Robert S. Thompson.
Description: Lanham : Rowman & Littlefield, [2025] | Includes bibliographical references and index. | Summary: "Rural School Leadership: Lesson's from Alaska provides practical school improvement strategies for leaders in rural schools"— Provided by publisher.
Identifiers: LCCN 2024028141 (print) | LCCN 2024028142 (ebook) | ISBN 9781475874808 (cloth) | ISBN 9781475874815 (paperback) | ISBN 9781475874822 (epub)
Subjects: LCSH: Rural schools—Alaska. | Educational leadership—Alaska. | School improvement programs—Alaska.
Classification: LCC LC5147.A4 R87 2025 (print) | LCC LC5147.A4 (ebook) | DDC 372.9798/091734—dc23/eng/20240821
LC record available at https://lccn.loc.gov/2024028141
LC ebook record available at https://lccn.loc.gov/2024028142

∞™ The paper used in this publication meets the minimum requirements of American National Standard for Information Sciences—Permanence of Paper for Printed Library Materials, ANSI/NISO Z39.48-1992.

Contents

Introduction   vii

1   Rural Alaska Schools   1
Janice DeVore Littlebear, Sean Asikłuk Topkok, and Christian P. Wilkens

2   Being New   25
Robin Jones and Meghan Redmond

3   Cross-Cultural Leadership   43
Robert S. Thompson

4   Adapting Curriculum   61
Carol Thompson

5   Career, Technical, and Subsistence Education   85
Christian P. Wilkens

6   Teaching Through Culture   105
Abby Qirvan Augustine

7   Academic Success: Leadership That Drives Change   123
Robert S. Thompson

8   Small K–12 Schools   141
Evelyn Willburn, Deidre Jenson, and Benjamin Glover

9   School Climate, Safety, and Learning   161
Lesa Meath and Janice DeVore Littlebear

10	Supervision: Recruiting, Improving, and Keeping Good Teachers *Robert S. Thompson and Christian P. Wilkens*	177
11	New Directions: Learning From Others *Janice DeVore Littlebear, Robert S. Thompson, and Christian P. Wilkens*	195

Epilogue	219
Acknowledgments	223
Appendix A: Tribes in Alaska by Location	227
Appendix B: Alaska Standards for Culturally Responsive Schools	233
Appendix C: Alaska Indigenous Languages Map	237
Glossary	239
References	251
Index	259
About the Editors and Contributors	269

Introduction

Figure I.1. *Courtesy of Elizabeth "Putt" Clark.*

This book is about leadership in rural schools. Our context—what we know best—is rural Alaska, especially Indigenous Alaska. If you work in a different context, we think you'll find much or most of this book relevant. We see multiple common threads between school leadership in rural Alaska and school leadership elsewhere. We are particularly hopeful that this book may be useful for school leaders outside Alaska who are working in Tribal schools, First Nations schools, or other schools serving Indigenous students and communities. There are thousands of schools and communities throughout the United States, Canada, and beyond that must navigate the same issues school leaders face in rural Alaska.

We wrote this book because students and schools in rural and Indigenous communities deserve good leadership. Our experience has been that guidance from outside Alaska or from urban contexts often hasn't been useful in the contexts we know. We've rarely seen written discussions of the practical challenges leaders face in rural Alaska, like adapting curriculum and instruction to meet the needs of Indigenous students, leading in schools with small enrollments and few teachers, and learning ways of living respectfully within and alongside diverse cultures. While our discussion of some of these challenges may be unique to Alaska, we suspect that several of our overall themes (*Build relationships! Adapt what you're doing! Have a sense of humor!*) will resonate no matter where you are. Ultimately, we're hoping this book can be one small support as you develop your approach to school leadership and as Indigenous-serving schools everywhere work to become the vibrant places young people need and deserve.

Here is one important note: there is no such thing as a "typical" rural school. The rural Alaska communities we describe here are diverse Indigenous communities. Rural Alaska is not one single thing but many, including more than two hundred Tribal nations with distinct cultures, languages, histories, and ways of being. This diversity is part of what makes living and working in rural Alaska incredible. It also means that a book about rural Alaska—or rural anywhere—can't do justice to the specifics of any single place. While we tell stories rooted in specifics ("This happened in my school," etc.), those specifics may not translate to another school seamlessly, if at all. One theme that you'll encounter in this book and in your own work is that effective school leadership needs to adapt to specific places, communities, and peoples.

Throughout the book you'll see we use the term *Indigenous* (capital *I*) when referring to peoples in Alaska who may also self-identify as *Alaska Native*, *Native*, or by specific tribal affiliations. Our use of the term Indigenous is intended to communicate respect. Here we are informed by Gregory Younging's *Elements of Indigenous Style* (2018), which recommends the use of Indigenous (always an adjective) when referring to people "in a context where their specific identity is not at stake." Authors or those quoted in the book with known tribal affiliations are identified as such; we use the term Indigenous as shorthand when affiliations are not available or are not at the heart of the matter (e.g., the claim above that rural Alaska communities are "diverse Indigenous communities" is true in specific contexts but is also true across Alaska generally).

The terms Alaska Native and Native remain, as of this writing, in wide use in Alaska, although Native has fallen out of favor among First Nations peoples in Canada. Both terms, Alaska Native and Native, have deep historical roots. For example, the Alaska Federation of Natives (AFN) is one of the oldest and most influential groups of Indigenous peoples in Alaska. You'll see the term Alaska Native in many quotations we provide, as well as in reference to organizations like AFN. It is not our intent to question or ignore current terminology; readers are encouraged to learn as much as they can about terms currently used in their communities. One advantage of the term Indigenous is that it avoids the colonial legacy of the term Native and has a direct link to the 2007 United Nations Declaration of the Rights of Indigenous Peoples. We acknowledge that English terminology among Indigenous peoples has evolved over time and will continue to evolve, and we hope that our language choices communicate respect and a commitment to learning.

One risk in using general terms like Indigenous or Alaska Native is that they do not necessarily recognize the cultural integrity and diversity of specific peoples. School leaders working in Kiŋigin (Wales) and Ḵéex̱' (Kake) work in very different contexts, even though both happen to be in Alaska. We urge readers to consider context at all times, wherever you are, as broad or general claims rarely carry the weight or truth of those emerging from specific circumstances.

You may have noticed how we just referred to two places in Alaska: "Kiŋigin (Wales)" and "Ḵéex̱' (Kake)." Throughout this book we will specify place names as first assigned by Indigenous peoples, with their English names in parentheses. The Indigenous place names we use are from the University of Alaska Fairbanks website, Alaska Native Place Names archive (www.uaf.edu/anla/collections/map/names). Readers are advised that although each name has been verified with speakers and language experts, in some cases, there may be disagreement or local variation in spelling or terminology.

We should also clarify what we mean when we use the term *rural*. For us, rural Alaska includes Indigenous villages and predominantly Indigenous hub cities, such as Qikiqtaġruk (Kotzebue) and Mamterilleq (Bethel), mostly off the road system. These communities are not monolithic—we discuss this in the first chapter—but we see enough common ground to consider them rural in this book. We do not discuss schools or students in Dgheyaytnu (Anchorage), Dzánti K'ihéeni (Juneau), or other predominantly urban places in Alaska. While worthy of consideration in their own right, large urban schools are beyond our scope.

We hope you will notice that the various authors use a common lens in their writing: *leadership informed by experiences that bridge Indigenous and Western systems.* This lens shaped how and what we wrote, and we hope it helps hold together a book written by twelve different people who have experiences all over Alaska. We see no true understanding of rural- and Indigenous-serving schools without accounting for the unique crossroads they inhabit between Indigenous and Western worlds. You will almost immediately recognize in your work tensions between the hopes of Indigenous parents and students and the Western-centric school structures you'll be expected to enact. Some schools in rural Alaska are more successful than others at bridging these systems. We attempt to highlight successful schools and leaders in rural Alaska, as well as to provide you some considerations as you shape your own next steps as a school leader.

Each chapter begins with a story. We share stories for multiple purposes. Stories are often memorable, hence they are effective as teaching tools. Stories also help the book be conversational rather than dense or academic. If you don't read this book, we figure it isn't useful—so it's on us to be interesting. The stories we tell raise meaningful questions for school leadership, with parallels to rural places everywhere. In each story we try to show you what's at stake, why the issues might be important, and how you might consider the issues in the context of your own school and community.

This book does not need to be read cover to cover. While that's a fine approach and we applaud your commitment, each chapter can be read alone and in any order. We're not dragging you through particle physics here; we're presenting learned experiences from rural Alaska schools organized in ways that we hope make sense. Feel free to scan the table of contents, find a point of curiosity, and dive in.

Chapter 1

Rural Alaska Schools

Janice DeVore Littlebear, Sean Asikłuk Topkok, and Christian P. Wilkens

Former Alaska poet laureate and professor Richard Dauenhauer posed a quick four-question quiz in his primer, *Conflicting Visions in Alaska Education*, on the early years of schooling in Alaska (1980, p. 5). See how you do:

1. When, where, and by whom was the first bilingual school in Alaska opened?
    Answer: 1824, in Iluulux^ (Unalaska), by Fr. John Veniaminov. The languages of instruction were Russian and Aleut.
2. When, where, and by whom was the last Aleut bilingual school closed?
    Answer: About 1912, Tanax^ Amix^ (St. Paul Island), by the US government.
3. How many of you knew this?
4. Why not?

Dauenhauer's point was that not nearly enough Alaskan educators know the histories of the places where they live and work. This lack of knowledge can harm if school leaders fail to understand that their schools are not isolated from history but operate in contexts entirely shaped by it. Professor Paul Ongtooguk put it in the following way in his 2001 address to the Alaska Native Education Summit:

> We have a challenge, and it's called schools. Alaska Natives have largely embraced the promises of school. The promise was, and has been, to prepare our young people to become contributing members of our communities, our state, and our nation. But schools for Alaska Natives are like a meal laced with an unintended, poisonous effect. Along with the promise of preparing us for the future was this poisonous idea that our Native cultures, our ways of life, our languages, our traditions, our ideas, our understandings of the world, the very

societies that were keys to living here for thousands of years should be stripped from the minds of our children in order to prepare them for a future that will not include Alaska Native cultures. We live with the consequences of this to the present day, and we see the after-effects reverberating through our communities.

Now, I need to emphasize—and we all need to emphasize—that we ask no one in this room to have a sense of guilt. None of us were a part of the policy that told us that, in order to become educated, we had to give up being Alaska Natives. That was a policy that was set in place about a hundred years ago, and it will end hopefully within our lifetimes. And as we are in this room, we need to acknowledge publicly and to accept the fact that that set of policies was a terrible dilemma. It was a poisonous idea that has tainted the promise of education for Alaska Natives. And we have to root it out, sort through it, and redirect the kind of education that our people are going to experience. (Barnhart & Kawagley, 2010, p. 302)

One of your core challenges as a school leader is to meet multiple, sometimes conflicting, expectations with understanding, honor, and respect. You work for a public, state-supported school district; you are expected to help students master Alaska state learning standards, complete assessments, and so on. But you also work for the communities of rural Alaska and are charged with ensuring that your school works in ways that honor and amplify local languages and cultures, ultimately promoting the sovereignty of Indigenous peoples. You do not have the luxury of simply importing so-called best practices from the lower 48. You must also pursue best practices for your community *in rural Alaska*. It may or may not surprise you that notions of what is best for your school are almost always contentious and often in conflict.

You won't find simple answers here. One truly unique aspect of rural Alaska is its diversity; no place is exactly like another and no culture a monolith. This chapter is an introduction, and perhaps the best way to start is with a story. This one is about conflicting visions, but it's also about teachers and teacher aides, the school district, the Alaska Department of Education & Early Development, money, respect, sovereignty, language, and culture.

IÑUPIAQ AT KIVALIÑIQ (KIVALINA) SCHOOL

Doreen Swan (a pseudonym), 63, grew up in the Iñupiaq village of Kivaliñiq (Kivalina) and the nearby hub of Qikiqtaġruk (Kotzebue), on the Chukchi Sea in northwest Alaska. After finishing high school and a 30-credit certificate program, Doreen spent 20 years working as a health aide in Qikiqtaġruk (Kotzebue) for Maniilaq, the regional nonprofit corporation. During her time at Maniilaq, Doreen often served in a dual-aide/interpreter role between English-fluent providers and Iñupiaq-fluent clients, often Elders.

As her family grew, Doreen returned to Kivaliñiq (Kivalina) and took a job at the school as a bilingual aide. As the only fluent Iñupiaq speaker working in the school, Doreen quickly became the entirety of the school's Iñupiaq culture and language program. Each morning, Doreen taught in the elementary grades (1–5); in the afternoons, she supported English-language instruction in the upper grades (6–12). While Doreen taught, the other teachers had time for grading or lesson preparation.

Doreen enjoyed working with students, especially the younger ones, who eagerly learned to count and name local plants and animals in Iñupiaq. She was excited to share traditional knowledge, such as stories of the prophet and healer Maniiḷaq. Although the bilingual coordinator at the (distant) district office provided some resources, Doreen's principal and other teachers left Doreen on her own to make decisions about curriculum, student learning goals, and pedagogy.

At first this arrangement seemed wonderful. Doreen found teaching rewarding, and her students gained important language and cultural knowledge. But Doreen saw that she was treated differently than other teachers; her site leader never asked for lesson plans or observed her teaching. While this may have looked like freedom, it felt a lot like neglect. Did anyone at the school care what she was doing?

Doreen's pay was also an issue—her salary as an aide was less than half what the other (non-Indigenous) teachers made. Her status also meant less generous health, leave, and retirement benefits; fewer professional development and travel opportunities; and second-class treatment among teachers. She was teaching but not treated or paid like a teacher.

When Doreen called the district's human resources department to ask about a raise, the director explained that Doreen needed different qualifications. Doreen had not graduated from a four-year college and did not possess an Alaska teaching certificate. Although Alaska has a Type M certificate for those with Alaska Native language or cultural skills, getting one was expensive and political. The school district would need to sponsor Doreen for the certificate, and doing so would have meant greatly increasing her salary and benefits. The human resources director seemed happy to continue with the less expensive status quo. He suggested that the district might sponsor Doreen for a Type M certificate if her principal agreed to give up one of its other aide positions to cover the cost. Doreen wasn't sure if it was her place to bring these options to her principal, and she had no interest at all in being responsible for a friend losing paid work at the school.

Doreen was left with a range of questions about who really controls rural Alaska schools, how much value is placed on Indigenous languages and cultures, and what her future might be:

- Why is the state of Alaska in charge of deciding who has the proper credentials to teach Indigenous languages and cultural knowledge? Why is it not Indigenous peoples themselves?
- Why do rural Alaska schools pay and respect local people less than teachers from the lower 48?

Although this story is Doreen's, it is also a story of school leadership Consider:

- Why did Doreen's principal and the district treat her differently?
- What would you do if Doreen brought you her dilemma and told you she was planning to retire at the end of the year?
- Whose job is it to fix all this anyway?

The rest of this chapter is intended to briefly outline a history of education and schooling in rural Alaska that may be useful in understanding Doreen's story—and in better understanding how managing multiple, often conflicting expectations is central to your work as a school leader.

HISTORY OF ALASKA EDUCATION

It is challenging to respectfully present a brief history of education among Indigenous peoples in Alaska. This history is long. Indigenous peoples in Alaska have learned through interactions between humans, nature, and the spiritual world from time immemorial (Hensley, 1966; Kawagley, 2006).

Although this book focuses on leadership in school settings, readers should keep in mind that learning is never restricted to what happens at school. Formal schools and schooling in rural Alaska are recent, have been imposed on already-existing educational systems, and have come with ongoing costs. Below we share a modified excerpt of an essay by the longtime director of the Alaska Native Knowledge Network, Dr. Ray Barnhardt, in "Culture, Community and Place in Alaska Native Education" (2005).

Before Western contact, all communities in rural Alaska had systems that preserved and transmitted knowledge—systems that provided an education. Two examples of formal systems were the Qargit and the Qaygiq, which were community gathering places where young people learned about who they were, their places in the world, and how to successfully become adults in a range of family and community settings (MacLean, 1986; Pingayak, 1998). These Indigenous knowledge and educational systems were community led and unified in purpose: to raise young people successfully in place-specific contexts.

The arrival of Russian fur traders in Alaska in the late 18th century also meant the import of Western-style schools. These schools were primarily operated by missionaries and were either segregated (for immigrant students only) or run with explicitly assimilationist goals, such as eliminating Indigenous languages. There were virtually no connections between the goals of Indigenous peoples and the goals these new schools were trying to accomplish. Notably, the impact of these early schools was limited in scope. Through 1900 most Indigenous peoples in Alaska had no contact with Western schools and continued to live traditional, self-sufficient lifestyles (Napoleon, 1996).

Then in the late 19th and early 20th centuries, multiple epidemics killed more than half the Indigenous peoples in rural Alaska, including entire communities. Especially deadly were the Great Sickness (measles) epidemic of 1900 and the Spanish flu of 1918–19. Entire generations of Elders were lost, thousands of young people were orphaned, and Indigenous knowledge systems were devastated.

Following these epidemics, waves of young people in rural Alaska were forced to attend Western schools for the first time. As is now painfully clear, these schools often operated as warehouses for trauma and abuse, the legacies of which we are just beginning to understand (Hensley, 2010; Sharp & Hirshberg, 2005). Although many communities took heroic measures to continue Indigenous knowledge systems, the influence of formal Western schools on the education of young people in rural Alaska became preeminent after 1900. As Barnhart described it, the limited interest that Western schools had in already-existing Indigenous knowledge systems was focused on making them disappear.

From the Great Sickness through Alaska gaining statehood in 1959, rural Alaska schools were segregated by race and ethnicity. There were, by law, separate schools for "white children and children of mixed blood who lead a civilized life" (Nelson Act, 1905). These included church-operated mission schools for Indigenous students, federally operated boarding and day schools for Indigenous students (such as the notoriously abusive Wrangell Institute), and a boarding-home program that sent predominantly Indigenous rural students to live with urban families during the school year. The purposes of these Indigenous-serving schools were removal, assimilation, and worse. Then-superintendent Foster of the Alaska Native Service (in charge of Bureau of Indian Affairs schools in Alaska) commented in 1949:

> We have seen the futility of [keeping children in their communities], and have completely changed our approach to the education problem. We are now setting up a program that will take the boys and girls out of their community, and

we don't care if they ever go back at all. In fact, we urge them not to go back because the communities cannot support them. (Darnell & Hoem, 1996)

It's hard to overemphasize the enduring legacy of these schools and programs. For generations, Indigenous students in Alaska were segregated, taken from their homes, and punished for being who they were. As author Ernestine Saankalaxt' Hayes asked us,

What would we do if . . . this American culture was suddenly subdued by another culture that belived theirs was a superior way of living? Their God was the one true God? Their language the only worthwhile speech? Their history the only one that mattered? What would happen if this young American society—less than 250 years old—suddenly was rocked by cultural trauma? (First Alaskans Institute, 2018, 12:24)

Yupiit Nation chief Mike Williams Sr. commented,

Especially after that 1918 pandemic, the federal government came, and [the] Bureau of Indian Affairs, and they set up schools and they had policies that tried to wipe out our languages. My parents were punished for speaking in our languages in the school. My mom would say that her mouth was washed with

Figure 1.1. Unangax̂ refugees at Wrangell Institute, ca. 1942. This photograph shows a double dose of racism: the seated children are Unangax̂ refugees who were relocated to Sitka during World War II, housed at the Wrangell Institute (background), which assimilated and abused Indigenous young people from all over Alaska (1932–1975).
Courtesy of Alaska State Library, Evelyn Butler and George Dale collection, ASL-PCA-306.

brown soap and my dad said his hands were hit because he spoke in Yup'ik. Those are some of the things that went on.

Kateri Walker (Chippewa of the Thames First Nation and Saginaw Chippewa Tribe) described the horrors of boarding schools:

> Most people don't understand what we went through. They took our land, our homes, our children. They put the kids in these genocidal boarding schools where they beat the Indianness out of you. My grandfather was raped by one of the priests. When he grew up, he went on to hurt his wife and his kids. It gets passed on. Our Elders taught us that our hair is where our memories are stored—so we grew our hair. The first day of boarding school—they cut all of your hair off. They removed your identity and gave you a name like Billy or Sue and told us our grandparents were dead. We were stolen from our families. I was 9 years old, holding on to my mother, I didn't want to leave her. I got in trouble from the nuns for holding on to my mother too long. I took a little piece of fur from her coat, and I got in trouble for it. The nun said to me, "We don't hang on to our mommies here." I thought I would never see her again. They woke me up at 5 a.m. every morning for six weeks and they made me skin the dead animals that white people had left on the back porch. They figured we would eat anything because we were Indians. At my boarding school, we weren't allowed to have emotions. You couldn't laugh, you couldn't cry, you couldn't whisper. If you did, you were beaten. They used to sprinkle flour on the floor of the school because they said the devil could see up from hell and was trying to steal our souls. I would lie awake all night waiting for the devil to come. We were told we were dirty heathens, nobody wanted us, and nobody would ever love us. When you get raped by a priest or abused by nuns and then get thrown into America, where you're treated like a Hollywood stereotype—people expect us to assimilate and lead normal lives, but most of us were traumatized as children. We are a traumatized people. (Nesteroff, 2021, p. 165)

These Western schools, despite their influence, never became the only places of learning for young people in rural Alaska. Indigenous knowledge systems, despite disruptions and loss, were maintained, recovered, and renewed with each generation. It is also worth noting that these formal Western schools were not successful. As the plaintiffs in the educational-equity lawsuit *Tobeluk v. Lind* (1976) argued, students in rural Alaska "experienced accelerated drop-out rates, psychological and social problems, including disruption of family life and loss of sense of identity, and failure to live up to educational potential."

As Alaska moved toward statehood, many Indigenous communities advocated for better schools, especially schools in their home villages. This advocacy led to the construction of elementary schools in most Alaska villages by the early 1960s, as well as the construction of high schools in most villages after the *Tobeluk v. Lind* settlement (often referred to as Molly Hootch for one of the plaintiffs from Imangaq [Emmonak]). In 1976, Alaska's federal- and state-operated education systems were dismantled and replaced by more than 20 new rural school districts, a shift that placed formal school systems serving Indigenous communities under local control for the first time. At least in theory, Indigenous knowledge systems and formal school systems in rural Alaska could now influence each other.

Despite structural and political reform in the 1970s and 1980s, rural Alaska schools have continued to demonstrate a dismal performance record by almost any measure. For example, National Assessment of Educational Progress (NAEP) scores and dropout rates in Alaska are among the worst in the nation. While some cultural elements are now featured in many schools (e.g., basket making, sled building, songs, and dances), such activities have remained largely superficial. Even when schools acknowledge that language and cultural systems give lives purpose and meaning, they are only rarely able to place Indigenous languages and cultures central to the students' experiences. Yup'ik language–development specialist Nita Yurrliq Prince Rearden, who taught for over 30 years in Mamterilleq (Bethel) and Qikiqtaġruk (Kotzebue), noted that by the 1990s, educators from all parts of Alaska were beginning conversations about the potential role Elders could play in revitalization:

> "We discovered that Elders were not being recognized as Elders or teachers! Many Elders said they never used their languages in school meetings, never learned how they could contribute, and never were asked how to do things or honored for their knowledge and skills. There was a time when they cried, real tears coming down from their faces. It was disheartening to watch! We had to do some healing circles to make them know how important their thoughts and their lives were as part of our education. They pushed the Indigenous people on the Alaska cultural standards. They were the founders of our language and culture in our education system. It is still a struggle in some areas for revitalizing languages and even keeping culture alive."
> —Nita Yurrliq Prince Rearden, teacher and Milken Educator Award–winning language-development specialist

An unmet goal for schools in Alaska is what Barnhart called *systemic integration*, where Indigenous knowledge systems and formal Western-style schooling could complement each other in the education of rural Alaska's young people. What are school leaders supposed to *do* with such an aspirational goal? You don't have a reset button; the history described above isn't something you can correct today or tomorrow. The clearest vision for what an integrated model could do is provided by the Alaska Standards for Culturally Responsive Schools (Alaska Native Knowledge Network, 1998). These standards, which cover five areas (students, educators, curriculum, schools, and communities), provide a model for teaching and learning through local culture as the foundation for education. And they can be used to shape two key aspects of your leadership:

- How do you assess your school's educational environment in the context of the community and families?
- How will you integrate the school's and community's values into a plan for growth and improvement?

Importantly, these cultural standards are written into Alaska law. All districts must evaluate teachers and administrators on culturally responsive work, just as they must for English Language Arts (ELA) and math content. Some guidance about how you can supervise and evaluate culturally responsive teaching are found in the book *Culture in the Classroom*, produced by the Southeast (Alaska) Regional Resource Center (2015). Perhaps the best use of the standards is for clarity of direction. Good school leaders must ask themselves the following questions:

- Are we doing a good job with young people?
- What does a good job mean in this community?

Education and schooling in rural Alaska will continue to evolve. Districts and schools aiming at an integrated model can be found throughout Alaska, including the Lower Kuskokwim School District, the North Slope Borough School District, the Ya Ne Dah Ah (Chickaloon) School, the Yukon Kuskokwim School District, and the Nikaitchuat Ilisaġviat Iñupiaq immersion school. (This is not an exhaustive list; see the Alaska Native Language Center in the resource list below for more information.) Spend some time exploring what they do, and consider the possibilities in your own school.

ABOUT RURAL ALASKA

Effective school leaders in rural Alaska learn about where they are and what makes their families and students unique. You may work in a village off the road or a ferry system, or a larger hub, such as Mamterilleq (Bethel), Curyung (Dillingham), or Utqiaġvik (formerly Barrow). Wherever you are, you're in a geographically large place that spans roughly 395,000 square miles, including over 240 villages and cities. Most communities in rural Alaska are predominantly Indigenous, but communities are never homogenous. Keep in mind, as experienced Sugpiaq educator Gguitka Sperry Ash commented, "being a teacher is being a servant. You are a guest, you are not called to boss people around. Allow students to be Native. Allow students to see themselves as part of the classroom, the school."

The challenge for all of us in positions of leadership is one of continuous learning and cultural humility:

- Who are the people here?
- What do they want from their school?
- What is my role in serving them?

FAMILIES AND STUDENTS

There is no "typical" village in Alaska. Each village has unique history, governance, language, and cultural traditions. Learning about your community is key for understanding the people you work with and for your effectiveness as a school leader. A good place to start learning about your community is the Tribe; most communities will have a Tribal hall or office in the village where you work. There's no substitute for speaking directly with the people in your community. Try to connect with Tribal leadership, and make arrangements to meet as soon as schedules permit—ideally not at school but at the Tribal hall or neutral site. Limit meetings at school because getting out of the building puts you in the community and avoids the complex colonial legacies still attached to school structures. Invitations to meet outside school are an opportunity to learn about your community and the families you will serve; accept them readily, and bring along a small thank-you gift to anyone who invites you to their home or place of business.

LOCAL ECONOMIES

Your work in schools connects to the economies of communities. Families need stable and sufficient resources to be whole, and struggles of any sort can impact what schools accomplish. Village economies in Alaska are different from urban economies. Here's a quick rural Alaska economics 101 lesson from the University of Alaska, Institute for Social and Economic Research (2008, p. 1):

- Combining cash-paying jobs and subsistence activities is the way most households in remote areas get along.

- Per capita personal income in most remote rural areas is 25%–50% below the state average; under standard measures, poverty is widespread.
- The locations and types of jobs available in remote areas often don't match the local labor supply—which means many local residents are unemployed, while, at the same time, about 40% of workers are nonlocals either from other areas of Alaska or outside the state.

Rural Alaska operates three distinct economies: *subsistence*, *market*, and *transfer*.

SUBSISTENCE ECONOMIES

Subsistence is defined in law as "customary and traditional uses" of wild resources (Alaska Department of Fish and Game, 2022). Subsistence includes hunting, fishing, berry picking, plant gathering (for food and other uses such as dyes), wood gathering, and the collection of other resources for medicinal or artistic use. Subsistence activities are tied to specific places by tradition and ecology. Perhaps most importantly, subsistence activities are also cultural, linking people to the land and to others, including ancestors. How subsistence is done matters a great deal, and its successful practice is critical. Notably, while traditional foods are necessary for many families, subsistence practices are important beyond calories—they are one aspect of cultural continuity that stretches back generations. You will also quickly learn that most school calendars were not created with subsistence activities in mind. For many of your families, subsistence may conflict with school attendance—a tension you and your district will need to address regularly and resolve in ways that support your community.

Subsistence resources are often shared within and among families and communities—either due to the nature of the resource (a single successful whale hunt, for example, can provide resources shared broadly beyond the whaling crew) or to cultural and community traditions (successful hunts are often first shared with Elders). Additionally, subsistence does not necessarily mean there's no cash; subsistence harvests can yield a direct payment for food, clothing, or art that is created using wild resources. Many village residents combine cash payments and trade with subsistence activities in what is called a "mixed" economy.

MARKET ECONOMIES

Market economies in rural Alaska include cash economies in which residents earn income by working for wages or by buying and selling goods

Figure 1.2. Woman picking blueberries near Uŋalaqliit (Unalakleet). *Courtesy of the University of Alaska Fairbanks, K–12 Outreach.*

and services. The vast majority of working-age village residents in Alaska earn some sort of cash income each year (Goldsmith, 2008). Sources of income may include the school, commercial fishing, the Tribe, the health clinic, the post office, airlines, public safety, and local businesses such as stores. Schools are often the largest employer in rural Alaska. It is important to understand that your role as a school leader in rural Alaska includes managing one of the most substantial sources of wages in your community, and this cannot be taken lightly. Your decisions about hiring and retention directly impact individuals, often entire families. Perhaps not obvious in Doreen's story is that her wages do not just impact her alone (as they might for a young single teacher from the lower 48). Doreen's wages impact her and her household (husband, children, grandchildren) and relatives throughout the village. While you must make good employment decisions on behalf of the school, you must also understand that what you do resonates within a community context. Be prepared to anticipate and manage resulting challenges.

Figure 1.3. Tuyuryaq (Togiak), Alaska. *Courtesy of Emily Hendricks.*

TRANSFER ECONOMIES

Transfer economies are the third leg of the rural Alaska economy. Perhaps the most widely known component is the Permanent Fund Dividend, which is distributed from petroleum revenues to each state resident in the middle of fall. Another transfer payment for many families comes from Alaska Native corporation shareholder dividends (more on Alaska Native corporations below). Transfer economies also include noncash services provided by Alaska Native Claims Settlement Act and regional nonprofits; these may include social, education, and health services for Indigenous peoples in their regions. The Alaska Native Tribal Health Consortium is the largest network for health care in rural (and parts of urban) Alaska, as well as a substantial employer in many communities. Lastly, transfer economies may take the form of pension or welfare payments from former employers, typically for retirement, housing, medical care, energy assistance, or nutrition.

TEACHER SUPPLY, RETENTION, AND QUALITY

Rural Alaska schools have long faced challenges with attracting and keeping teachers. Most Alaska teachers come from outside Alaska (commonly referred to as *Outside*); most leave within two years. The supply of home-grown teachers in Alaska has always been small; the University of Alaska system graduated only about 20% of the teachers districts have needed over the past two decades (DeFeo et al., 2017). Worse still for rural schools is the fact that less than a quarter of these Alaska teacher graduates seek work in rural schools (Hill et al., 2013; DeFeo & Hirschberg, 2020). Your school is likely to have a high percentage of teachers who neither grew up in the community nor were prepared to teach in Alaska. One of your most important tasks each year will be helping teachers engage with and learn about the community where they live and work. One irony in Doreen's story is that she was the *only* person who grew up in Kivaliñiq (Kivalina), who knew Iñupiaq and local customs, and who was likely to stay for many years—yet she was paid and valued less than those cycling in and out.

Teacher turnover is high throughout rural Alaska, averaging 25%–36% annually, which is substantially higher than Alaska's Big 5 urban districts and three times the national rate (García & Weiss, 2019).

In rural Alaska, teacher retention and stability are among the best predictors of student achievement (Roehl, 2010). You need to develop or attract good teachers who are effective in rural Alaska, and you need to keep them. But you don't need just any teachers—you need those who will succeed in rural Alaska. There is evidence that the most effective teachers in rural Alaska may not be the academic all-stars or even those with the most teaching experience but, instead, those who best fit the communities they serve (Tetpon et al.,

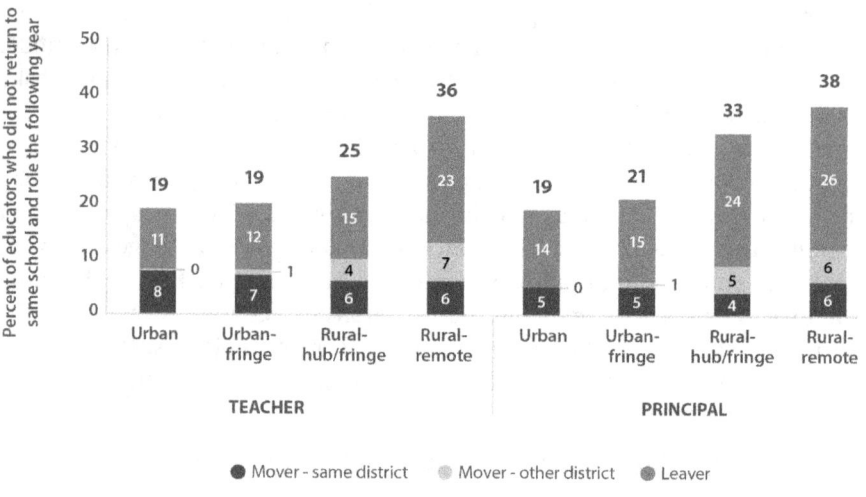

Figure 1.4. **A higher percentage of teachers and principals in rural-remote and rural-hub/fringe schools in Alaska did not return to their school or role the following year, compared to those in urban and urban-fringe schools.** *Courtesy of Vazquez Cano et al. (2019, 13).*

2015; Amarok, 2014; Hirshberg, 2019). Once you've found a good teacher, it is critical to help them stay. High teacher turnover harms student achievement, drains district resources, and disrupts community relationships (DeFeo et al., 2017; Hill et al., 2014; Hirshberg et al., 2014).

How can you keep teachers? While you will not be able to do much about salary, benefits, or teacher housing (all predictors of attraction and retention), you can influence other factors that teachers cite in stay-or-leave decisions. Teachers in rural Alaska indicate that school-community relationships, administrative support, and community characteristics are the biggest influences on their decisions to stay (DeFeo & Hirshberg, 2020). Wherever you are, you can build a school culture where teachers feel a sense of belonging and accomplishment in their professional and personal lives (DeFeo & Tran, 2019). And you can make the decision to stay yourself, another factor that helps retain teachers and boost student achievement (Vazquez Cano et al., 2019). We discuss teacher recruitment, supervision, and retention at more length in chapters to come.

STUDENT OUTCOMES

Parents and guardians in rural Alaska, like parents and guardians anywhere, want their children to grow up safely and become successful adults. Because rural Alaska is predominantly Indigenous, there are additional common hopes for the future: that young people grow up knowledgeable and fluent in the cultural practices and language(s) of their communities (Amarok, 2014; Green, 2010).

Yet there's often a divide between what we say we want from schools and what we measure. Schools in rural Alaska often unwittingly demonstrate Campbell's law: they distort the value of things that are *easy* to measure (such as ELA and math scores) over things that are *important* to measure (such as cultural knowledge and wellness). Don't forget that your charge as a rural Alaska school leader is very broad: to grow young people who are not only healthy and grounded in their culture(s) but can also be adults that are successful in the years following school. To meet this charge, you must learn what success means to the people in your community. You need to talk to parents, guardians, and Elders about what they want for their children. As Nita Yurrliq Prince Rearden shared, "I remember asking an Elder, 'What would you like your grandchildren to learn in school?' He answered, 'I want my grandchildren to learn to become human beings.'"

You will also need to talk to your students and listen to what they tell you about their hopes and dreams. Many of your students may tell you they don't want to go to college. That's okay. What's important to them and to their families? Your students may become Tribal leaders, pursue commercial fishing or aviation, or go into health care or business. Rural Alaska schools should help students become leaders in rural Alaska. You will undoubtedly need to be creative in shaping how your school responds to local needs.

Talking to people without preexisting relationships can be difficult. But don't put it off. The most natural places to start conversations are where parents and Elders already spend time. This might include school (e.g., at basketball games), but it's important to leave the bubble of school. You might say hello to families and students walking in the village or in church or at community meetings. You can always ask relatives about students. Who are their children or grandchildren? What do they think about school? Be prepared to listen. Your role is not to argue or to defend; it's to listen and learn. And in these slowly building relationships, you can model what you want teachers to do.

In Doreen's story, Iñupiaq language and culture were taught separately from other subjects and other teachers, hence devalued. In a real sense, your work as a school leader may be to advocate for programs that do not generate quarterly data. Some outcomes are measured in lifetimes.

Rural Alaska school leadership includes academic leadership, of course. You and your teachers absolutely must ensure that graduates can read, write, and have meaningful options for the future. You can find up-to-date information on your school's attendance, graduation, and ELA/math data at the Alaska Department of Education & Early Development. One useful question to ask as a new school leader is about where your school stands compared to others in your district. If your school stands out for better or for worse—why? What can you identify that it is doing well or poorly?

Overall, rural schools in Alaska have struggled academically compared to their urban counterparts. A quick look at the Big 5 school districts in Alaska (Anchorage, Fairbanks, Juneau, Kenai Peninsula, and Matanuska-Susitna) reveals sizeable student achievement gaps in ELA and mathematics (see Figure 1.5).

Student achievement in Alaska is clearly a statewide challenge; NAEP data consistently show that only about one-third of Alaska students demonstrate grade-level proficiency in reading, math, or science, and that this level of (under)performance has existed for many years. Turning academics around is not an overnight task; we will simply note here that improvements are possible if and only if your school is safe, welcoming, and dedicated to the outcomes valued by your students and the community as a whole.

RELEVANCE OF CURRICULUM

The curriculum your school uses must be relevant to the goals of your community, your students, and your teachers. "Curriculum" isn't limited to

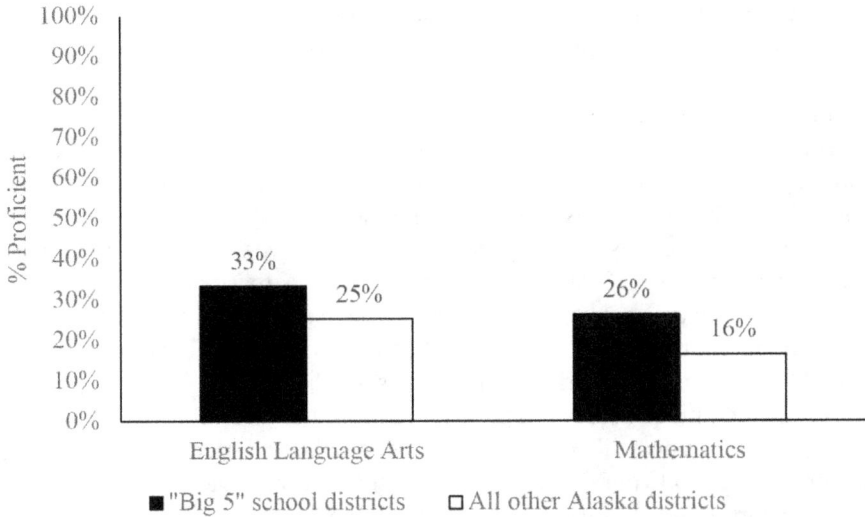

Figure 1.5. 2021–2022 Alaska System of Academic Readiness (STAR) data, grades 3–9, for each school district in Alaska (n = 54). The Big 5 districts include the Anchorage, Fairbanks North Star, Juneau City, Kenai Peninsula Borough, and Matanuska–Susitna Borough School districts; enrollment in Big 5 districts in 2021–2022 was 86,415 students (K–12); enrollment in all other districts was 41,094 students (K–12). *Author's analysis of publicly available data from the Alaska Department of Education & Early Development.*

textbooks but should be considered as the broad set of experiences students have in school. While the state of Alaska specifies requirements to graduate from high school (e.g., four units of ELA, three units of math, etc.), these requirements often do not account for the knowledge and skills valued in rural Alaska or by Indigenous peoples. The failure of curriculum to account for place, to respond to culture, and to be relevant is a nationwide problem (National Congress of American Indians, 2019). If students are all sound asleep during English class, even if your school uses nationally recognized textbooks or programs, those are lost hours. The salient questions are not whether you have purchased the right materials or whether your teachers are delivering curriculum with fidelity. They are the following:

- How well do my teachers know their students?
- How well have we aligned the school's pedagogy, materials, and instructional experiences with the goals of this community?
- How well do my teachers include and teach Alaska cultural standards?

One note of caution—you will need to consistently set high academic expectations in your school. Too many educators in rural Alaska confuse relevance with downgraded academic expectations. Simply replacing challenging texts with easier ones that mention hunting or gathering may engage students in the moment but do long-term academic damage. Your charge is to ensure both relevance *and* challenge. Always make sure you regularly evaluate outcomes.

The existence of an Indigenous language or culture program tells you nothing about quality. As with any academic program, you need to define success, measure outcomes, and seek continuous improvement. How will you know if an Indigenous language program is effective? Again, you can't do all this work yourself. You will need to talk to experts (many of whom will be local) and listen to what they tell you. One useful resource for expanding curricula in your school is the Alaska Native Knowledge Network (ANKN). The ANKN publishes curricula that your school may find does a better job meeting community goals than publishers from the lower 48.

Importantly, you will never be alone as a school leader in rural Alaska; either in or beyond your district, there are fellow school leaders who can help. A good starting place is the Alaska Council of School Administrators, which offers substantial networking and professional development opportunities along with an annual school conference, including sessions specific to rural Alaska schools.

SOVEREIGNTY, TRIBES, AND LEGAL ISSUES IN RURAL ALASKA COMMUNITIES

Meaningful relationships with people in rural Alaska lie at the heart of school leadership. Although there are some common features and challenges, it's important to remember that each community in Alaska is distinct. There are (at the time of this writing) 229 federally recognized Tribes in Alaska, as well as dozens of actively used Indigenous languages and dialects. Unless you are from the same community where you lead, you are a guest. It is critical that you approach the work of school leadership with respect and a willingness to learn from those whose ancestry and history have shaped the place where you work.

TRIBES IN ALASKA

Alaska is not just a state. It is also a region where hundreds of Tribes exercise sovereign national rights. In Alaska the term *Tribe* refers to a federally recognized nation that has "a permanent population, a definite occupied territory, a government, and the ability to enter into relations with other nations" (Seventh International Conference of American

States, 1933, p. 25). Tribes in Alaska include a range of peoples with distinct histories, cultures, and languages. Tribal membership is not placebound; a Tribal member can live in a rural village, a city like Dgheyaytnu (Anchorage), or in another state. Tribal members are dual citizens of a Tribe (or Tribes) and of the United States. Like citizens of any nation, they have rights that vary by Tribe, which are different from the rights of non-Tribal members. As the leader of a school in rural Alaska, you must understand that you will work and live with people who have sovereign rights that may be very different from your own.

Although Indigenous peoples have been in Alaska since time immemorial, denial and rejection of Tribes date back to the days of colonization and treaty making. Indigenous peoples in the United States were only recognized as citizens in 1924; Tribes in Alaska have only been recognized by the federal government since 1994. For many years the state of Alaska claimed Tribes simply did not exist or that if they did, there was just one, in Maxłakxaała (Metlakatla). The state of Alaska only recognized Tribal sovereignty in 2017; its legal opinion about the sovereign status of Tribes is worth a review by all school leaders (see Lindemuth, 2017). One highlight from Alaska's attorney general Jahna Lindemuth: "What we know definitively is that Alaska [T]ribes are sovereign governmental entities with authority over a myriad of matters regardless of whether there is Indian country" (2017).

What does sovereignty mean in Alaska? Below, we share a story.

SOVEREIGNTY: TEEŁĄY (TETLIN), ALASKA

In fall 2020, schools began preparations to reopen across rural Alaska in the middle of the COVID-19 pandemic. Alaskans had adjusted to new realities of quarantines, masking, and social distancing. One school, Tetlin School (in Teełąy, population roughly 130), faced a vulnerability common to many rural Alaska schools: most of its teachers would be coming from outside the village, where virus exposure might be high. The Tribe (the Native Village of Tetlin) and school leadership were concerned: How could they keep students and staff safe?

Unlike much of rural Alaska, Teełąy is connected to the road system. In ordinary times, teachers, administrators, service providers, and visitors can simply hop in a car and drive into the village. In 2020, however, anyone trying to leave the Alaska Highway and head toward Teełąy came upon a roadblock, stopping them in their tracks. At the roadblock, officials from the Tribe ordered any visitor (including teachers) to turn around and quarantine for two weeks before being allowed in.

How, you might ask, was this possible? A roadblock? Didn't the teachers need to go to work? The answer is simple: sovereignty. The Native Village of Tetlin is a sovereign nation with the authority to control access to its land. Leaders need to understand this authority and help their non-Tribal staff understand as well. A good overview of sovereignty in Alaska is Attorney General Jahna Lindemuth's 2017 letter to Governor Bill Walker, "Legal Status of Tribal Governments in Alaska" (https://law.alaska.gov/pdf/opinions/opinions_2017/17-004_JU20172010.pdf).

School leaders in rural Alaska must understand that they serve Indigenous communities. There are boundaries that you must respect, as well as resources and opportunities that can support schools and students. At this moment in Alaska, the precise relationships between local, Tribal, and state governments are evolving. We encourage you to find ways to open and strengthen relationships with Tribal authorities as soon as possible and to continue to invite, listen, and learn in the years ahead (examples of how others have done this are explored in the chapters ahead). The more experience and ideas you can bring in, the better the odds are that the school will be able to meet the needs of young people and the broader community.

ALASKA NATIVE CORPORATIONS

Alaska Native corporations are regional for-profit corporations holding land and business interests in and beyond Alaska. They were formed in 1971 under the Alaska Native Claims Settlement Act (ANCSA) as a partial resolution of land-use disputes following the discovery of oil at Prudhoe Bay in 1968. Members of an Alaska Native corporation are called shareholders. There are 13 regional corporations and more than 200 affiliated village corporations. You should become familiar with the corporations operating where you work:

- Regional corporations: ANCSA Regional Association, https://ancsaregional.com
- Village corporations: Alaska Native Village Corporation Association, https://anvca.biz

Alaska Native corporations are unique in the United States. In the lower 48, Tribal lands have been defined through treaty making and include trust and reservation lands. The federal government took a different approach with Indigenous peoples in Alaska, establishing just one reservation in 1944: the Metlakatla Indian Community on Annette Islands Reserve. Following statehood, Alaska delayed resolving land-claim disputes emerging from its colonial histories until the 1960s. The proposed 800-mile Trans-Alaska Pipeline

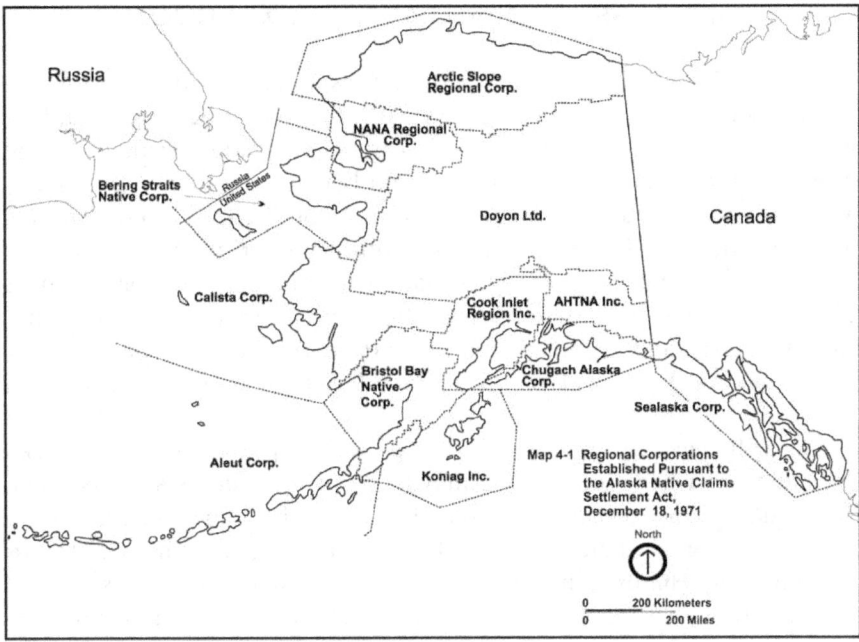

Figure 1.6. Alaska Native Corporations. *Courtesy of the National Park Service (Norris, 2002, p. 47).*

that would carry North Slope oil out to tidewater in Valdez highlighted dozens of competing land claims needing resolution with Tribes throughout the region.

The Alaska Native Claims Settlement Act (1971), commonly known as ANCSA (Publ. L. No. 92-203), has been described by former Cook Inlet Tribal vice president Lydia Hays as "the most unique settlement of aboriginal land claims and the largest land conveyance in United States history" (Hays, 2019, p. 56).

ANCSA resolved, at least in part, who controls the land in Alaska. Alaska has 424 million acres of land. In 1959, 101 million acres were alloted to the new state. In 1971, ANCSA assigned land title for 44 million acres to 13 newly-created Alaska Native corporations, which were also allocated $1 billion in startup cash. These corporations were charged with using lands as assets for the operation of for-profit businesses. Although Alaska Native corporations replicate some functions of Tribes elsewhere—such as the creation of economic opportunities, transfer payments, employment, and training—these corporations are not Tribes. They are businesses. However, Alaska Native corporations influence the villages and communities in which they operate, so educators need to learn what they are and what they do in rural Alaska.

LEGAL ISSUES IN VILLAGES AND SCHOOLS

Hundreds of sovereign nations exist in Alaska, each with differing languages, belief systems, and histories with the land. You may be able to do some self-education before arriving in a new place, yet the best way to learn is by directly meeting people and listening to what they tell you. Who lives here, and how does governance work? How do laws, norms, or expectations differ in this village from your prior experiences? As the school's leader, how can you make sure nonlocal staff are respectful and knowledgeable? Consider sending new hires links to information about the Tribe and village before they arrive, or you could perhaps send them a general book such as the *Rural Alaska Teacher's Moving Guide* (Rose, 2014).

You will need to comply with legal issues specific to rural Alaska. Depending on where you are, you may be subject to federal, state, borough, city, and/or Tribal jurisdictions, possibly all at the same time. There are many dry villages, where alcohol and marijuana (legal elsewhere in Alaska) are outlawed. Hunting, fishing, and other subsistence activities may be restricted to Tribal members or have seasonal and geographic restrictions. Property ownership and family structures—and the authority to make decisions about young people—may work differently in Rural Alaska compared to elsewhere. For example, educators must report child abuse or neglect to the state. But the state does not have unlimited authority over Tribal members (citizens of sovereign nations). Under the (federal) Indian Child Welfare Act (1978), Tribes have decision-making authority concerning Indigenous youth, and it may be that the state and the Tribe differ in how to handle a report. Your personal feelings when it comes to the law are moot; all educators in rural Alaska need to understand the general guideline of working in Indigenous Alaska: "As a general matter, sovereign governments have authority, or jurisdiction, over citizens, over land, and over people who enter their land" (Lindemuth, 2017).

We opened this chapter with a story about Doreen, who was teaching Iñupiaq and struggling with second-class treatment. We hope it has become clear that finding solutions as a school leader in rural Alaska means understanding how to operate within systems that often conflict. Your work responds to broad requirements (federal, state, local, and Tribal) yet remains distinctly human. You will always need to meet the needs of specific students, teachers, and parents. You will always need to comply with requirements you did not create. And, we hope, your work will always be informed by a commitment to understand, honor, and respect.

TAKEAWAYS

- Rural Alaska is most often Indigenous Alaska.
- Tribes in Alaska are sovereign nations.
- School leaders must integrate Indigenous knowledge systems and Western education.
- School leaders in rural Alaska must inform, develop, and keep good teachers.
- School leaders must always listen to and act respectfully with members of the community.

RESOURCES

- Alaska Council of School Administrators: professional association for school leaders in Alaska. www.alaskaacsa.org
- Alaska Department of Fish and Game: overview of subsistence activities in each region in Alaska, along with harvest information, regulations, and research. www.adfg.alaska.gov
- Alaska Federation of Natives: largest statewide Alaska Native organization; promotes sovereignty, cultural, and language education, as well as economic development. Organizes a large convention annually. www.nativefederation.org
- Alaska Native Knowledge Network: curriculum publisher and knowledge base focusing on Alaska Native knowledge systems and ways of knowing; located at the University of Alaska Fairbanks. www.ankn.uaf.edu
- Alaska Native Language Center: highlights school and other programs focused on teaching Alaska Native languages. www.uaf.edu/anlc
- Alaskool: archive of school-focused Alaska Native history, education, languages, and cultural information. www.alaskool.org
- Center for Alaska Education Policy Research: education policy research unit and clearinghouse for education-related research; located at the University of Alaska Anchorage. www.iseralaska.org/caepr
- Institute for Social and Economic Research: research group at the University of Alaska Anchorage; conducts and publishes research on public policy in Alaska. iseralaska.org
- SERRC/Culturally Proficient Schools: Alaska-based education resource center; developed indicators for the Alaska cultural standards. www.culturallyproficientschools.org
- State of Alaska, Department of Education & Early Development: profiles of each school and district in Alaska, including attendance, graduation, and achievement data. education.alaska.gov/data-center

- State of Alaska, Division of Community and Regional Affairs: community profiles and extensive data on each village in Alaska; maps for each community, including governmental, Tribal, business, religious, and other community features. www.dcra-cdo-dcced.opendata.arcgis.com
- US Bureau of Indian Affairs: Tribal government and leadership contact information for all tribes in Alaska. www.bia.gov/regional-offices/alaska/tribes-served
- US Census Bureau: population statistics for each village, including demographics, employment, housing, economy, and education. www.census.gov/tribal

Chapter 2

Being New

Robin Jones and Meghan Redmond

Meghan Redmond

When I got my first school leadership job as a lead teacher in Ingricuar (Twin Hills), Alaska (Population: 80), I was so excited. I packed my entire home and school life into Rubbermaid totes and shipped them up before getting on a plane. And then I did not have a single day off for weeks.

That first school year started with a 10-day in-service workshop in Curyung (Dillingham), the hub for villages in Southwest Alaska. When the in-service workshop concluded, I boarded the first bush plane I'd ever taken and flew to Ingricuar. My brain was awash with information about curriculum and instruction, insurance, salmon, and arctic survival. I had a classroom to set up, lessons to write, a mountain of Amazon boxes and Rubbermaid totes to unpack, and an apartment to organize.

On the first day of school with students, the returning staff organized a clamming trip. That meant a group of 20 students (every student in the school) and 10 adults were riding four-wheelers miles down a dirt road to the beach. And then down more sandy, rocky miles to the clamming grounds. That first day, I felt more exhausted than I ever had in my life, and I really didn't have the proper gear for that kind of trip. And I had never driven a four-wheeler before. All I wanted to do was get unpacked. I had every reason to say no: fatigue, stress, and no small amount of fear.

But instead, I said yes. I had a big cup of coffee and told myself I could nap when the weekend came. I borrowed a pair of rain boots (mine had not yet arrived in the mail). I ignored the mountain of unpacked boxes and the messy classroom. And I listened with undivided attention as the Elder who had worked at the school longer than I had been alive gave me a crash course in driving a four-wheeler. He made sure I knew to never slow down if I felt like I was about to get stuck, especially when crossing any moving water.

I can absolutely guarantee that I did not teach a single academic thing that day. Instead, the students and community members spent the entire day teaching me. And the connections we made that day carried us through the next six years. That day became the foundation for relationships built on trust and respect, where everyone had something valuable to offer.

That first day, my classroom remained a mess; my boxes, unpacked. Instead, I had the most incredible afternoon driving a four-wheeler miles and miles, crossing a stream and nearly being washed out into the ocean, hiking out to the edge of the low tide, digging clams with a butter knife, and breathing in the salty breeze off the Bering Sea. I was 4,000 miles from everything I'd ever known, and yet I was finding a place in my new home.

PRACTICAL WISDOM
Meghan Redmond

There is no road map for school leadership in rural Alaska. But that doesn't mean the work is unknowable or impossible. Just keep in mind that rural Alaska schools and people aren't a single, unified whole. They are shaped by specific places and histories. It would be a mistake to approach your work in Southwest Alaska the same way you might on the North Slope. Before we dive into guidance about the work, here are a few notes about taking good care of yourself throughout. A comfortable, happy you means you'll do a better job and be more willing to take the kinds of risks that reward in rural Alaska.

Figure 2.1. Bush plane cockpit, rural Alaska. *Courtesy of Emily Hendricks.*

Whether you're a lead teacher in a small school or running a department in a rural Alaska school district, you'll find that the clearest direction for what to do can only come from the people and place where you work. You may feel the need to fix everything and solve every problem. You may feel the need to fill every silent moment and answer every question. Don't. In all aspects, humility and respect will prove reliable companions. You'll need to listen and learn before making changes. This means listening to your community and Elders. It means listening to teachers and staff. And most importantly, it means listening to your students. You may find that your students have different needs, interests, goals, and responsibilities than you anticipated, but only by getting to know them will you be able to support them on their paths to adulthood. It will take time—time that you might feel you do not have—to gain trust. But that trust, as well as the relationships it makes possible, are at the heart of effective school leadership in rural Alaska.

ADVICE FOR NEW SCHOOL LEADERS IN RURAL ALASKA

- Say yes the first time you are invited by a community member to go do something. If you say no, it is likely to be the last invitation you'll get.
- Find partners in all things. Being new is hard. Partners ease burdens by sharing time and stories, introducing you to new people, and showing you prior practices.
- Love your students—all of them, especially the ones who make you think hard and grow. But remember your role. You are neither a parent nor a fixer of everything.
- Get out of your office. You need to be in classrooms, in the hallways, and in the village.
- Bring treats. Friday morning mailbox chocolate, a bowl of fruit for a meeting, or whatever. Pay particular attention to your building plant operator/maintenance crew.
- It's okay to go home, even when your to-do list at school is not completely done. (Note: it will never be completely done.)
- Call your mother. This is just as true in rural Alaska as anywhere.
- Splurge on good rain boots and a winter coat. Bring a rain jacket and a warm hat no matter where you go, no matter the weather. You will be terrible at predicting weather.
- Never pass up the opportunity for fresh produce or ice cream. Ignore the price.
- If the pilot says the weather is too bad to fly, the weather is too bad to fly.
- Get used to waiting at airports, sleeping on school floors, and hosting visitors. Rural Alaska requires patience and caring for each other.
- You cannot adopt all of those dogs.

Below are three checklists that you may find useful in getting oriented to the community and the operations of the school during your first days on the job. They are certainly not comprehensive, and should be adapted as you see fit—but hopefully will help you think through many of the areas you might need to explore and consider as the school year begins.

	Before First Day of School			
Instruction	• Find, read, and distribute to teachers the adopted curriculum and assessments	• Plan teacher/staff in-service days	• Review academic and behavioral data	• Review HS class schedules to ensure students graduate
Community	• Meet advisory school board and Tribal, city, or other government leaders	• Write welcome letter to send home	• Find community/Tribal center, health clinic, post office, store, church, etc.	• Identify custodial issues (who can pick up students), and court orders
Facilities	• Review major systems and maintenance needs (HVAC, water, sewer, etc.)	• Determine system for issuing school keys	• Review teacher housing assignments and conditions	• Set up staff workroom and office, including staff mailboxes
School climate	• Review discipline plan and district or school handbooks	• Review procedures for common areas, transitions, etc.	• Review school safety plans and practice with staff	• Plan for first day, first week, and first month celebrations
Technology	• Review technology inventory, network, and curriculum or other logins	• Confirm sufficient copy/print supplies for the first quarter	• Confirm network access for all staff and any filtering/access routines	• Identify cell or walkie-talkie use protocols for communication
Administration	• Meet incoming staff, show them their housing units	• Review district policy manuals and negotiated teacher/staff contracts	• Review prior year budget and district budget process	• Review schedules with staff, work out conflicts

First Week of School

Instruction	• Administer screenings required by district or RTI/MTSS system	• Review evaluation tools with teachers, develop observation schedule	• Identify/hire substitute teachers and staff
Community	• Review prior practices for Elder and parent presence at school	• Identify protocols for community building use (e.g., after-school recreation)	• Establish regular communication with parents/guardians
Facilities	• Verify cleaning schedule and expectations with staff	• Verify meal preparation and expectations with staff	• Review school exterior and maintenance process, including trash removal
School climate	• Offer a staff potluck, movie, or outing	• Review School Climate and Culture Survey data on your own and with staff	• Visit each classroom, provide brief positive feedback to all staff
Technology	• Identify school internet/social media presence	• Establish systems for announcements and communications	• Post or share a first-week summary note
Administration	• Finalize schedules, rotations and coverage of hallways, gym, etc.	• Review plan for airport arrivals/departures during the year	• Establish/review chain of command (especially if you will be off-site)

First Month of School

Instruction	• Create schedule for data analysis and goal setting	• Administer benchmark exams, review data with staff
Community	• Attend advisory school board or other community meetings and events	• Spend time in the community and outside the school; be visible
Facilities	• Review school vehicles: condition, age, maintenance, and fuel storage	• Review HVAC, water and fuel storage/systems, and roof and exterior windows before winter
School climate	• Review sports and activities schedules; hire coaches/advisors	• Plan first open house

(Continued)

	First Month of School	
Technology	• Identify and plan for heavy-use periods (benchmark or state testing)	• Identify hardware replacement or software purchasing needs
Administration	• Plan start of the year school-wide assembly for the student body	• Complete paperwork (ASAA eligibility lists, payroll, dues, etc.)

BUILD RELATIONSHIPS
Meghan Redmond and Robin Jones

This chapter opened with Meghan's story—a new school leader immediately navigating fatigue, time pressures, and the disorientation of doing new work. It's ultimately a success story, as Meghan got coffee, went clamming, and started to develop relationships with the students, parents, and Elders in the village. But notice how easily this story could have gone the other way. No one would have argued with a decision to stay home and unpack or take a long-overdue nap. Consider what would have been missed: a sharing of boots, four-wheeler advice, and shared laughter. The seemingly small decision to suck it up and go gave both Meghan and the community a first chance to learn about each other, and importantly, it was a chance that took place outside school walls. Venturing beyond the bubble of school is a critical step for any school leader to take, and such opportunities almost never come when you are well-rested, have nothing on your desk, and are looking for something to fill the hours.

You'll find that some relationships are easier to develop than others. For example, you will get to know a small set of teachers and staff at school very well. You'll see them every day and solve common challenges together (instructional, operational, logistical, etc.). Shared work is a good foundation for professional trust. This is as true in rural Alaska as it is everywhere. Keep in mind that building professional relationships with teachers and staff isn't your only charge. There's just no way to be effective in rural Alaska school leadership without deep knowledge of the people in the community. If you don't know about the local languages and cultures, how will you figure out if the bilingual program at school is successful? If you don't know parents or Elders, how can you expect them to support your efforts to improve the school?

Nearly everyone in rural Alaska communities is connected, daily or occasionally, to what happens at school. As such, you don't just go to work, put in a day, and go home—school hat off. In rural Alaska you are *always* a school leader. At the post office, at the airport, and out fishing. You *always* have a responsibility to make positive, respectful connections. And not to make you paranoid, but in close communities, every interaction you have carries a signal function. Are you spending time with just a few people at school? Do you seem interested in meeting Elders? Do you treat people differently because they are teachers or custodians? It's important that you develop relationships with as many people as you can and across multiple parts of the community. There's no such thing as reaching out and listening too much.

You will need to dedicate time to get to know each member of the school community, ideally in and beyond classrooms. This knowledge will help you get through challenging times (many of these people will become your friends) and will demonstrate your commitment to the broader school community. In your work as a school leader, it's a good idea to learn as much as you can about school staff, from their professional strengths and weaknesses to personalities, backgrounds, interests and families. It's not a bad idea to figure out their favorite foods; virtually all humans in rural Alaska can be wooed, at least in part, with food.

When you invest in the lives of the community, you gain a better understanding of how everyone can best support the school's mission and how you can meet their needs as a leader. The relationships you develop can become a support (working in rural Alaska schools can be hard), can promote a collaborative environment, and can encourage partnerships in- and outside school. If you learn, for example, that there are staff members who enjoy sewing, you might help organize time during or after school when they can work with students or community members. The same goes for those who enjoy hiking, fishing, or tinkering with small engines. Every chance you have to bring people together is worth considering.

Josh Purkeypile, who taught in Alarneq (Alakanuk), remembers his first year in rural Alaska:

> I think one of the best things [my principal] did was use school funds to pay for a fishing/berry-picking trip for all the teachers, or at least the new ones. We spent the day out with each other and members of the community, and it really opened our eyes. I think an orientation at each school site would be great before teaching took place. Simple things like how you say the students' last names, more about the history of the village, culture, etc., a kind of a teaching in rural Alaska 101 course.

In a rural Alaska school, you may work with just a few teachers and staff. This can prove helpful in forming relationships, as there just aren't that many people to get to know. However, small schools are universally busy; there's almost never unstructured time where relationship building happens without something else getting done. You will have to set conditions for people to work on shared goals that are positive and comfortable, where people can learn with each other, and where strong relationships can help the school make better decisions for students. Intentionally and deliberately taking time to build trust establishes a strong foundation for guiding school improvement. You may want to consider a "Did you know?" time in each staff meeting, where you discuss an Indigenous leader or community event, making sure to alternate and include as many families in the community as possible.

Another way to build relationships is to help your team get connected to the area and to each other. Rural Alaska is a big place that is full of adventure but also risk (social, weather, terrain, bugs, carnivorous mammals, etc.). It's definitely not a place where individual trial and error is advised. Rural Alaska is best explored with others. You can be particularly helpful in acclimating new teachers and staff to an area by seeking connections to local people willing to share their time and experience. You don't want to push yourself onto others, but as Meghan's story showed, you can be open to invitations when they come. There's no substitute for connecting to the community and learning from them. And once you have formed relationships and gained some knowledge of the area, be sure to invite others to share experiences!

We can always strive to be engaged in community activities. It is critical for the community to see you outside school, whether picking berries on the tundra or picking up mail at the post office. This will require patience; it takes time for people to get to know each other and to develop mutual trust. But it's absolutely worth it; building relationships matters.

BE PATIENT
Meghan Redmond

Working in rural Alaska may be unlike anything you have experienced before, and every place is unique. Rural Alaska is Indigenous Alaska. There are hundreds of Tribal nations in Alaska, as well as distinct languages, histories, and cultures that are all specific to the peoples and places where you might work. Be cautious about taking advice from any source—this book included—that suggests a simple approach. Developing relationships in your work as a school leader is best understood as an ongoing responsibility and reward, one that involves cross-cultural work every day. You must get to know the people and the place where you work, and you'll have to find ways to bridge them to your own background and skills. Throughout, you'll answer to parents and students, you'll answer to Elders and community norms, and you'll answer to Western educational demands. Often, you, as a school leader, will be held responsible for addressing conflicting expectations, especially when there's friction. No matter what experiences you have had in the past, and no matter what advice you may have been given before taking on a rural Alaska school leadership role, I promise you there will be times when you will have to make decisions without clear answers.

And you may not have a long line of people eager to help you right away. Many communities in rural Alaska have seen teachers and leaders come and go over and over again. It's hard to fault anyone for getting burned out by welcoming yet another new educator. So, too, can longtime district employees get less enthusiastic over new people with each passing year. It's not their fault, and it's not yours either. Just try not to be insulted when it takes time to earn trust. Remember that taking advice and saying thank you to those trying to help you goes a very long way.

It's probably also true that as a new school leader, you are unlikely to have the luxury of an extended transition period where you get to learn the ins and outs of the job before making decisions that matter. You will be asked to dive in and get going quickly. You will have to be flexible and think on your feet. And you will have a lot of learning to do. All of us have been asked to make quick decisions without perfect information or experience. All of us make mistakes and have to go back and try again. All of us need to apologize. The goal isn't immediate perfection; it's to start building positive relationships that grow over time.

ADVICE FROM COMMUNITY MEMBERS

Throughout this book you will find the advice to listen to community members. Below we share responses to questions about school leadership from four community members in Cetuyaraq (New Stuyahok) and Teełąy (Tetlin):

- Tatianna Andrew, Yup'ik studies instructional aide, Chief Ivan Blunka School
- Matushka Pauline Askoak, St. Sergius Church, Cetuyaraq
- Eva Thomas-Churchwell, instructional aide, Tetlin School
- Dorothy Wonhola, community school council chair, Chief Ivan Blunka School

What do you think the community is looking for in a new leader?

Tatianna Andrew: "Somebody that will care about and respect the students. Also, someone who will be open to new experiences and meeting new people."

Matushka Pauline Askoak: "Leaders that are not afraid to go into the community to interact with the students and parents."

Eva Thomas-Churchwell: "Someone who is friendly, respectful, and outgoing. Also, someone that has a strong willingness to learn about the local culture and traditions."

Dorothy Wonhola: "A lot of them are really shy when they come in. So I encourage our new teachers and our new principal: Don't be like that! I want you to be open and be around the community. Don't hide yourself."

If you had one tip for new leaders in your community, what would it be?

Tatianna Andrew: "Communication is the number one priority! Introduce yourself to all of the staff and the different members of the community. Try to be as outgoing and friendly as possible and not be too shy to miss out on new experiences."

Matushka Pauline Askoak: "Be as friendly as possible and [. . .] interact with the community, teachers, and classified staff alike."

Eva Thomas-Churchwell: "Be willing to help others and to learn about the culture and what the community values."

Dorothy Wonhola: "Every school is different. Every culture is different. There are some things that you can't do, and then there's some things that you can do. Keep an always-open mind."

How can new leaders connect to the community?

Tatianna Andrew: "By attending dances, community events, and church. Also, by participating in outdoor activities and finding the best fishing spots."

Matushka Pauline Askoak: "Visit homes, attend sporting events, and participate in outdoor activities."

Eva Thomas-Churchwell: "Be open to new experiences and welcoming to the people in the community. Subsistence activities are also a great way to connect!"

Dorothy Wonhola: "Our former principal brought us in—the community—and we talked to them about the background of what our people do and the history of our village."

TAKE CARE OF YOURSELF
Robin Jones

Building relationships and saying yes to new experiences are essential, but taking care of yourself and others is what will keep you healthy and successful over the long term. Although you are a school leader, you're not *only* that.

You should find activities beyond school that fill your soul and encourage staff to do the same. On my end, I find exploring the outdoors with my husband is the best way I know to recharge my batteries, and it helps me navigate ongoing school challenges with a clear head and heart.

Taking care of yourself is not as simple as just identifying hobbies; it also involves finding small ways during each day or week to recharge or plan for the same. You may love camping, for example. But clearly, you can't just leave school and sleep under the stars every night. Your responsibilities to the school are ongoing and grow just about every waking hour. What you *can* do is learn your schedule inside and out and plan for your own time as you would plan for school. It may make sense, for example, to map out several weeks at a time in detail. So if you want to go camping on a Friday, you may need to set aside a brief time each night of the prior week to pack and prepare. If you wait until Friday, you may be too tired to go or too overwhelmed to make the experience enjoyable.

You will also need to pay close attention to the well-being of your teachers and staff, and if you are hiring new people, pay attention to their mental and emotional status. Sometimes we all need a reminder that the long, hard days are worth it. Experienced principal (now associate vice chancellor for Alaska Native Programs at the University of Alaska Southeast), Ronalda Cadiente Brown (Aantooxu.aat) reminds us that nonschool recalibrations can help:

> [O]n those horrible days I always sought the innocence and positive energy of great nieces and great nephews . . . to create opportunities to seek them out and play by nurturing their health and well-being. Recognize that that's not the life that a lot of students have the opportunity to experience. Find a healthy outlet where you can re-energize, however you can, to find your footing again on those hard days.

One way to take care of yourself, your students, and the entire school is to share leadership responsibilities. Effective school leaders build leadership capacity throughout the school. Of course, you will need to make some decisions on your own, but especially as a new leader, the more inclusive you can be about how decisions get made (and who makes them), the more likely you'll approach *good* decisions at your site and with the people in the community. Sharing responsibilities is the only practical way to position the school for sustainable improvement. Rural Alaska schools have historically had much higher leadership turnover than schools elsewhere; concentrating responsibilities on any single person puts the schools at risk for disruption each time a position turns over.

When leadership becomes more than just you, you can work out a schedule with others in the school to cover responsibilities (e.g., after-school and extracurricular work) while allowing everyone to find a semblance of work/life balance. This may involve formal roles (e.g., I'll lead the scheduling committee; you lead the ELA curriculum review team), sign-up sheets (e.g., we need gym coverage Thursday and Friday nights this quarter), or some creative budgeting. For example, I spent over three years sacrificing a lot of precious weekend time being an on-call shuttle driver for student activities before realizing I could budget for someone to be compensated for that position through an extra duty contract (*Note*: you may need to get them trained and licensed). You cannot possibly manage everything yourself, so finding innovative ways to share leadership responsibilities and opportunities will be key to maintaining your health and well-being.

Something else our entire school does every year is establish accountability partners. These partners help each of us set relationship, personal, or professional goals. We have, for example, paired staff members with a shared professional goal of elevating student voice. They wrote prompts into their weekly plans and met regularly to review progress. Partners can also connect about entirely nonacademic goals, such as taking a hike together each week for the first quarter, or speaking with one parent each week. Accountability partners meet formally multiple times a year (e.g., after school, during staff in-service time) and also informally on a weekly basis. The idea of an accountability partner is simple yet powerful: most of us find leaving our desks and getting outside easier when a friend knocks on the door than when we're on our own.

Taking care of yourself is not selfish. It's fundamental to a compassionate school community. Taking time every now and then away from professional responsibilities lets us refocus and reengage. This is not a lack of love or commitment. As others have said about families, they deserve the best from us, not what's left of us—so, too, do our schools, our staff, and our students.

YOU CAN DO A LOT, BUT YOU CAN'T DO EVERYTHING
Meghan Redmond and Robin Jones

Your contract specifies some of your responsibilities as a school leader. It may also assign you responsibility for "other duties as assigned." There are few places in the world where that phrase covers as many possibilities as in rural Alaska. You could end up being any of the following:

- A *landlord* of multiple housing units, dealing with doors that stick, boilers that fail, and pipes that freeze
- An *athletic director*, running basketball tournaments where visiting teams need housing and food in the school and where bad weather can extend trips indefinitely

- A *shuttle driver* when planeloads of frozen food (or people!) need to be picked up
- A *security guard* when bears or moose wander near the playground during school hours

In rural Alaska you are not just your official role. You may also be a counselor, testing coordinator, carpenter, custodian, cook, bus driver, secretary, nurse, and/or coach. And you also need time to be a spouse, parent, sibling, student, friend, and all the other things that make you, you. School leadership in rural Alaska largely cannot get done well in eight hours per day. Many leaders regularly put in 12-hour days. The work itself could occupy 20. *Do not work a twenty-hour day, no matter what is going on.*

The feeling of needing to get everything done and to make everything perfect can be overwhelming, especially in your first years. You should be dedicated to doing the best you can for students all the time, but it will be necessary to go home with undone things on your to-do list. It is okay to say no. It is okay to delegate. Trust your team. You cannot be the expert at everything, and you cannot do everything, even though you will feel the weight of expectation. It also helps to, at some level, become okay with not being able to make everyone happy.

Being a principal is challenging anywhere, and in rural Alaska, the work is compounded by complexity and pressures on your time and energy. I (Robin) remember directing a middle school basketball tournament during my first year as a principal. We were hosting twelve teams; they traveled midweek, played basketball for the next seven days, and then were weathered in the following week. The tournament doubled the number of students and adults normally in the building for two straight weeks. And tripled our issues. We spent hours and hours every day extinguishing one problem after another. We were doing our best to provide meals, friendly smiles, showers, love, and conflict resolution to all these extra people—all of whom were quite ready to be back home. The last Saturday before everyone left, we had an awards ceremony. We recognized our most valuable volunteers and tried to honor all the work everyone had invested in the tournament. Sunday morning, dropping the last team off at the airport, I felt like I needed a month off.

I didn't get a month off. Instead, I got immediate criticism from a staff member—one who had not shown up to cook or shuttle or organize, who had been largely invisible for two weeks. And who had no problem telling me I hadn't done enough while hosting the tournament. I remember feeling so frustrated, so completely misunderstood . . . and all of our good and positive efforts, unvalued.

Ultimately, you won't make everyone that you serve happy. That's not the criterion for success in rural Alaska schools. Your job is to work with the community to help young people grow up whole and become successful adults with legitimate options ahead of them. You should expect to work incredibly hard. You should enjoy your work with students and families—there's joy in ample measures in what we do—but you'll also need to find ways to take care of yourself. What felt damaging after the basketball tournament wasn't the stress or lack of sleep. That's something we can all recover from over time. It was a sense that we weren't fully together at the school. Perhaps the most important goal that I'm working on in my own school now is nurturing an environment where people are inspired to take care of each other in ways big and small.

ON MAKING MISTAKES

"Mistakes? Ah, where to begin. We all make mistakes. I remember there was a principal who complained to the community about teachers being underpaid, that *we* were the poor ones. This is fairly true in many places in the lower 48, but in the villages, we were the rich ones to a certain extent. Just being naive. Not realizing our privilege, our power, and that school for many of these families brings up a lot of hard feelings from the past—that is, boarding schools and assimilation."

—Josh Purkeypile, elementary teacher
in Alarneq (Alakanuk)

STAY
Robin Jones

Relationships aren't built overnight. Great schools can't be developed in a year. In rural Alaska school leaders come and go. Year after year. This means that you may be starting work in a community that isn't going to invest deeply in getting to know you simply because you've taken a job. Any of us who have been burned in relationships understand this; people get cautious. It will be on you, over time, to prove your worth.

Naturally students will occupy the center of your decision making, but don't neglect staff, parents, and Elders. They are a resource—not because they'll all agree with you or value what you value but because they've been in the community the longest. They know the culture, the recent history of the school, and the students you serve.

In order to do a good job during school hours, you'll need an understanding of what happens beyond. The community is the context for young people, so staying disconnected or holed up in the building will create huge gaps in your understanding. During the early days of your time in a position, you will be constantly learning and regularly surprised. Ask: Why is this student acting out? Where is that staff member today? What's going on with all this teasing? The more connected you are to the community, the more you can prepare for issues and better support students. This student's father may have left to work a two-week rotation at a mine. That staff member may be hunting. This teasing may be coming out of something that happened over the weekend at church.

Everyone wants to improve at their job; it's part of why we stay. Just committing to another year is a good first step. But how do you keep growing and stay long term? For me, two key supports have been other leaders in my district and mentors at the local and state level. One of your most important sources of local knowledge is other school leaders in your district. Likely, there will be structured times when you'll be together (for in-service or regular meetings), but it's often informal discussions that are most critical. Don't be afraid to pick up the phone when you're wondering or stuck. Being a school leader can be isolating, but you have colleagues who would love to help and who have almost always faced similar challenges. Your questions may be a welcome break from their own challenges.

For experienced school leaders, conversations about school where someone else's problems are at issue are almost always welcome. They're a venue for reflection on their end too. They might share stories about things they've tried, things that have failed, or things you might think about. They might just listen and ask you questions. But perhaps most importantly, you'll feel what it means to not be alone in the work, and the door to staying for at least the next year might stay open.

It's often a good idea to connect with school leaders *outside* your district as well. There may be politics involved in the areas you're working on (employment, supervision, contracts, etc.), so sometimes a neutral third-party view is the best way to have an honest discussion. You might consider joining the Alaska Association of Secondary School Principals, the Alaska Association of Elementary School Principals, or the Alaska Council of School Administrators, or you might take advantage of the professional development support of the Alaska Staff Development Network. Peers and mentors can provide guidance, support, and encouragement while often assuring you that you are making a difference, even if the impact is not immediate or obvious.

Here is a last note on staying: one way to lay the groundwork is to find an enjoyable life beyond school. No one we know (well, okay, no one *healthy*) lives a full and complete life in the triangle between home, school, and the store. They become disconnected and then leave. Getting beyond school takes a willingness to extend yourself into places where your role is not clearly defined. For my husband and me, fishing, hunting, and berry picking are enjoyable and have helped me learn a great deal about local cultural traditions. And we never get bigger smiles or warmer receptions from community members than when passing each other on the water or out on old trapping trails.

I remember a few years into my tenure as a principal, I had spent the summer away and returned to the village in August to get ready for the school year. Greetings from families changed from "Welcome back!" to "Welcome home!" The word shift was small, but the meaning, vast. My first years as a school leader were extremely difficult. It was challenging to find balance, avoid burnout, and make connections. But as the months and years have passed, I've been able to find confidence in the work and in connections to community and place.

In rural Alaska schools, you getting better at your job helps people trust your competence. You staying in your job and in the community proves that you care. We hope you will find it all—competence, community, and connection—over time. We hope you stay patient with yourself and open to growing as a person and leader. If you do, you will find yourself at home in rural Alaska, a place like no other.

TAKEAWAYS

- Build relationships within and beyond the school.
- Say yes to new experiences, especially with community members.
- Take care of yourself.
- You can do a lot, but you can't do everything.
- Find reasons to stay in rural Alaska.

RESOURCES

- Alaska Association of Elementary School Principals: professional association focused on elementary school leadership in Alaska. www.aaesp.net
- Alaska Association of Secondary School Principals: professional association focused on secondary school leadership in Alaska. https://alaskaprincipal.org
- Alaska Council of School Administrators: professional association for school leaders in Alaska. www.alaskaacsa.org
- Alaska Department of Education & Early Development: profiles of each school and district in Alaska, including their attendance, graduation, and achievement data. https://education.alaska.gov/data-center

- Alaska Department of Health and Social Services: statewide agency promoting wellness statewide; connections to agencies and Tribes. http://dhss.alaska.gov
- Alaska Native Health Consortium: Alaska's largest health care provider in rural Alaska, focused on services and advocacy for Indigenous peoples in Alaska. https://anthc.org
- Alaska Staff Development Network: nonprofit focused on professional learning and support for schools across Alaska. www.alaskaacsa.org

Chapter 3

Cross-Cultural Leadership

Robert S. Thompson

William was a young minister and had recently accepted a position at a church in Alaska. There were only 20 members of the congregation, but they were a dedicated bunch. The father in one family was a man named David, a member of the Dena'ina Nation. David was also a member of the board of trustees of the church.

William and David became good friends. When they spent time together, there would often be long, silent pauses. David would visit and sit on the sofa, smiling pleasantly, saying nothing. These silences were uncomfortable for William. Feeling obligated to entertain his guest, William would ask endless questions and tell personal stories. David would politely answer, but most of the time, he was content to sit, watch, and listen. After a while David would say good-bye and leave. William and his family were baffled by these experiences.

One day David came to William and told him that he was resigning from the church's board of trustees. William asked why. David explained that whenever he began to speak in a meeting, he would often pause, sometimes midsentence. Before he could continue, others would jump in and finish his sentences for him. David felt like he was not being heard.

William asked David if he would come to another meeting and explain this to the board. At the meeting, David tried to explain that in his experience it was customary to pause while speaking. David spoke about the value of silence, of slowing down, and of showing respect by letting someone finish their thoughts. Some board members had a hard time understanding. They said, "Yeah, but . . ." or said that they were concerned with finishing on time. During the meeting David just smiled and waited, letting their impatience speak for itself.

Later David explained to William how silence had been his teacher when he was young. One time he'd watched his uncles sew sealskins for a baidarka. When it was David's turn to sew, his uncles watched without comment. Then one of his uncles said, "That is an interesting way of sewing. My grandfather did it *this* way." David shared that his uncles never corrected him, never scolded him, and never told him he was wrong. Instead, they all took turns watching each other and offering different ways to complete the job. It took a long time, but the learning was thorough.

David explained that it was not necessary to talk just to fill the void. People could be together and observe without judgment. People could begin to understand in ways that speaking does not allow. When people were allowed to finish a thought after a pause, it often resulted in deeper understanding.

These lessons proved to be enlightening for William. He became a better listener and less impatient. He began to understand some of the difficulties children of Indigenous peoples had in school. He began to spend more time in silence. More importantly, he began to bridge the gap of understanding between different cultures.

DIFFERENT WAYS OF KNOWING, DIFFERENT WAYS OF LEARNING

A new school leader is often thrust into a situation of public trust and accountability with which they are not familiar. The path from classroom to office is the path most often traveled, but upon arrival at the destination,

Figure 3.1. Church in Manuquutaq (Manokotak). *Courtesy of Emily Hendricks.*

the person that chose that path, despite months of preparation and learning, may arrive without any of the tools or the experience necessary to handle the complexities of the job itself. This is never truer than when someone arrives as a leader in a school or district office in rural Alaska.

In addition to the challenges presented by staffing, schedules, budgets, in-service trainings, management plans, and myriad other responsibilities, rural Alaska adds the requirement that school leaders successfully operate in cross-cultural contexts. In the story above, David taught William a very useful lesson about leadership and learning in one Indigenous community. Ways of communicating and learning can be drastically different between cultures. The best possible advice for you as a new administrator, whatever your background, is to observe and listen and to encourage other staff members to do the same. David taught William a new way of communicating, learning, and showing respect. As a school leader in rural Alaska, you must seek out opportunities to better understand the same.

WHAT IS A CULTURALLY RESPONSIVE SCHOOL?

There are different ways of knowing and different ways of learning, but there are also universal elements of learning that apply to nearly all situations. One of those elements is relevance. Another element is connection to personal experience. A third element for students is gaining self-knowledge to set meaningful goals. How can you ensure that these elements are addressed for predominantly Indigenous students in rural Alaska?

When looking at the curriculum for your school, in what ways do you see relevance? What connections are there to personal experiences? What does the curriculum teach students about themselves, their communities, and their cultures? I can confidently say that if you have an adopted curriculum in your school that's been purchased from an outside publisher, when looking for relevance, connections, and self-knowledge, you will find none. In fact, not only will these elements not be there, there will be elements that confuse all of these things for students in rural Alaska.

The following is a case in point: Not knowing yourself or the community and culture where you live can create a huge divide in your understanding of how to fit into the larger world. A story shared in a talk to the Sealaska Heritage Institute by Shgen George, a Tlingit teacher from Aangóon (Angoon), describes how she did not learn about the oppression and racist treatment of Indigenous peoples until she was a sophomore in college at the University of Puget Sound. She found the book *Bury My Heart at Wounded Knee* (Brown, 1970) and was astounded to find out about the systematic annihilation of Indigenous peoples across the western United States in the late nineteenth century. Only later did she learn about the US naval bombardment that destroyed her own village in 1882 (Sealaska Heritage Institute, 2020). Students in rural Alaska need to know this history. Learning about the Napoleonic Wars, while they are important world history, is far less relevant, less connected, and less meaningful to Indigenous students in rural Alaska than what happened to their ancestors in their own communities.

> "Educators in rural Alaska are often teaching about the greater world, yet the students are living in a microcosm of that world. The challenge is that we must teach students how to operate in both of these worlds."
> —Rick Luthi, administrator, Lake and Peninsula School District

Though precise terms have varied over the years, Dr. Gloria Ladson-Billings originally defined a culturally relevant education as one "that empowers students to maintain cultural integrity, while succeeding academically" (Ladson-Billings, 1995). Something often overlooked when calling for culturally relevant or culturally responsive education is the need to support educators in their efforts to understand and work effectively and sensitively with students within their local contexts. Research shows that schools can have strong positive effects on student learning when they make connections to students' prior knowledge (Neuman et al., 2014). Most Western educators do not share the same prior knowledge as their students in rural Alaska. The good news is that there's a framework for you to use. The state of Alaska has adopted the Alaska Standards for Culturally Responsive Schools, which administrators have been required to use since 2013–14 during evaluations of certified staff (4 Alaska Administrative Code § 19.010).

To see how this can work in practice, let's consider a science lesson about ecosystems, where the curriculum included readings and questions about a Western prairie. Could teachers replace the prairie example with a more familiar ecosystem, such as a rainforest in Southeast or tundra on the North Slope? Lessons could explore local rivers, fish, mammals, or plant life, as well as include discussions of how students' families harvest plants, animals, or other resources for subsistence. Making such changes regularly is a lot of work but can create opportunities for rural Alaska students to make connections and provide opportunities for deeper learning. A helpful resource for integrating Indigenous knowledge into mathematics and science lessons is the Alaska Native Knowledge Network (www.ankn.uaf.edu).

How do you help teachers create lessons that "empower students to maintain cultural integrity, while succeeding academically" when teaching in rural Alaska? It is not easy, and it will take time. Just like William did, the first thing you need to do is learn to observe and listen. The most valuable information will be gleaned from local Elders and others familiar with the local environment and history of the area. The effort will be worth it because creating a culturally responsive school or school system will pay dividends in community/school relationships, academic success, and healthier students.

> "If we are serious about truly working to incorporate culture and language into the schooling process, then we, as educators, parents, and [the] community, need to envision a different kind of education that incorporates culturally appropriate ways of thinking and behaving."
> —Tarajean Yazzie-Mintz, 2000

A culturally responsive school is one where the teaching and learning are in sync with the local, Indigenous ways of knowing. It is one that includes local history and teaches current laws and policies that affect local people. It is one that creates connections to local events, systems, livelihoods, and organizations. It is one that creates relevance by connecting subsistence activities, cultural knowledge, languages, and local skills to curriculum. It is one that helps students develop self-knowledge. Creating a culturally responsive school is a big undertaking. It cannot be done alone. You will need assistance from local Indigenous people, from teachers, from other administrators, and especially from local Indigenous leaders. It will take time.

A CULTURALLY RESPONSIVE SCIENCE LESSON

Background

A village on the banks of the Tuluksak River, a tributary of the Kusquqvak (Kuskokwim River), depends on annual king salmon runs for sustenance. In the last decade, salmon harvests have steadily diminished as the number of king salmon entering the river has declined. The Alaska Department of Fish and Game has severely limited these harvests for Indigenous peoples along the Kuskokwim, even to the point of confiscating nets.

Science/Math Lesson

Local people informed a teacher at Tuluksak School about a fish weir on the river near the village. The Department of Fish and Game monitored the weir and collected data on fish returning to their spawning grounds. The teacher contacted the Department of Fish and Game biologists to gain access to the data being collected. The teacher asked students to begin charting the data using spreadsheets, eventually creating a large hallway chart that showed historical escapement and catch rates for king salmon from the Tuluksak River. As the lesson continued, the students concluded that harvesting female king salmon was contributing to the diminished resource. Since a single male salmon can fertilize thousands of eggs from several different females, harvesting males had a negligible effect on fish populations.

Results

This information was shared with both the Department of Fish and Game biologists and local harvesters. The results assisted in changing policies with changes to policies that resulted in limited harvests of king salmon for the villagers.

Figure 3.2. Drying fish in Manuquutaq (Manokotak). *Courtesy of Emily Hendricks.*

YUUYARAQ: THE WAY OF THE HUMAN BEING

Yuuyaraq is the Yup'ik term for how the Yupiaq view their place within the world. In English, Yuuyaraq is described as "the way of the human being." Among the Yupiaq it means much more than that. It is the definition of who people are as humans living on this planet. It governs all aspects of a human being's life (Napoleon, 1996).

According to Harold Napoleon, Yup'ik author from Naparyaarmiut (Hooper Bay), Yuuyaraq defines the correct way of thinking and speaking about all living things for the Yupiaq. The late Angayuqaq Oscar Kawagley, Yup'ik anthropologist and teacher from Mamterilleq (Bethel), said that the Yupiaq worldview consists of three equal elements: the natural, the human, and the spiritual realm. The human is a key figure but does not stand apart from or above the natural or spiritual realms (Kawagley, 2006).

To begin to understand how best to work with any population, some level of understanding of basic beliefs is necessary, at least enough to be able to honor ways of knowing and learning. The Yupiaq way of learning involves observation, experience, social interaction, and listening to the conversations and interrogations of the natural and spiritual worlds with the mind. The person is always a participant observer (Kawagley, 2006).

Angayuqaq Oscar Kawagley points out that "the holistic approach to teaching and learning of the Native people represents a significant difference in perspective from the incremental and componential ways of Western education" (Kawagley, 1992). School leaders in rural Alaska need to recognize ways of teaching and learning that depart from compartmentalizing content and then demonstrate the ways that content is interconnected.

School leaders carry the responsibility to direct instruction in such a way that student learning is maximized. You must be adaptive, innovative, and flexible (Barnhardt, 1977). When you identify something that is not working, look for ways to change. Try something new. Ask people in the community. Talk to other leaders. Bring people together to look for solutions. Perhaps most importantly, be willing to ask questions of people who are knowledgeable about the community's ways of thinking and of doing things. You must turn this knowledge into actions that reflect the community's values. You must also work with your staff to instill these values and to integrate Indigenous and non-Indigenous ways of learning to maximize opportunities for students.

"As Yupiaq people assert greater influence on the educational system, there will begin to emerge a Yupiaq educational philosophy and theories that give cultural and cognitive respect to the Yupiaq learner. Students can first learn their language, learn about themselves, learn values of their

society, and then begin to branch out to the rest of the world. . . . Given such a foundation, they can fearlessly enter any world of their choice, secure in their identity and abilities and with dignity as human beings."
—Angayuqaq Oscar Kawagley, 2006

COMMUNITY/SCHOOL DISCONNECTS

Creating a more cohesive relationship between the school and community is a task littered with obstacles and pitfalls. Not only are there cultural differences that need to be understood, there are also many historical events involving Indigenous peoples in Alaska that have created cynicism and discontent with Western schooling.

Many of the Indigenous peoples in rural Alaska today were educated in Bureau of Indian Affairs (BIA) boarding schools that attempted to eliminate Indigenous cultures. Children were removed from their villages and families at young ages and were punished for speaking Indigenous languages. They were taught that their traditions, beliefs, and ways of living were wrong and to be forgotten. The stated goal of BIA schools was to assimilate Alaska Native children into Western society. It is hard to overstate the trauma this caused to individual children, to families, and to entire communities, languages, and cultures—or the aftereffects still visible in current generations.

It is no small task for you to try and overcome some of this historical mistrust and to create an atmosphere of inclusiveness that connects the school to the people that live in the community. However, ignoring it will not make the situation better. Openly and honestly acknowledging mistakes of the past is one of the first steps. Try asking yourself the following questions, and ask others the same questions:

- How does being in the school feel different to you than being in the rest of the community?
- In what ways can the school project openness and friendliness while ensuring the safety of staff and students?
- In what ways can the school be made more inviting to community members?
- What systems can be put in place that would encourage and reward parent and community visits to the school?
- Who are the leaders in the community, and how can they also be involved with decision making in the school?
- What cultural elements can be included in the school environment that would make it more culturally responsive and feel more like a welcoming place?

- What ways of communicating would better reflect community values and honor traditional ways of learning, both with community members and, most importantly, with students in classrooms?

BUILDING COMMUNITY RELATIONSHIPS

Strong school-community connections are essential to effective schools (Haupt et al., 2020). Just as William learned from David that ways of speaking and listening can be vastly different between cultures, you will find that in many rural Alaska communities, life in the village and life in the school can be vastly different as well. Parents can be intimidated by visits to the school; school staff can be intimidated by visits to homes. Parents and community members are often talked to or given advice without ever being asked for their views. Some people avoid the school for these reasons. Learn how to ask questions, and do not just tell people what you think and what you propose to do. Learn to ask, not tell.

School/community disconnects are real and have deep roots. An excellent goal for all school leaders in rural Alaska is to connect the community and school in positive, mutually supportive ways. A good place to start is with your local advisory school board. Alaska law requires the establishment of local advisory boards in communities with more than fifty people. Principals are in charge of setting up meetings and an agenda for the board. These boards can be great advocates and an earpiece to the community. But don't stop there. Reach out to others.

An easy way to create interactions between the school and community is to invite the community to the school and ask questions of them in a roundtable atmosphere. You can gain far more than just information from these meetings. Community members will learn to trust you over time and will appreciate the opportunity to voice their views.

QUESTIONS TO ASK AT OPEN HOUSE (OR ANY TIME)

- What do your kids like about school?
- What do you and your kids do for fun?
- What would you like your kids to learn about traditional ways of living?
- In what ways can I help you and your family be successful in school?
- What do you look forward to when you come to school?

You should conduct discussions with your staff about ways to engage with the community. They should introduce themselves when meeting people and make sure people know who they are. They should ask people they meet about their families and try to remember family connections through generations. The post office and a community store often present the best opportunities for these friendship-building interactions.

A way to get you and the school's teachers out into the community is to distribute report cards in person. One time we did this in Cetuyaraq (New Stuyahok) on a Saturday, when it was pouring rain. The added benefit of getting thoroughly soaked was that many families invited us in to warm up as they shared warm drinks and treats with us. Sometimes opportunities to interact present themselves in unexpected ways.

Do not neglect local staff members. Custodians, cooks, coaches, paraprofessionals, and office personnel can be your go-to people when it comes to learning and understanding community issues and beliefs. Involving these people in decision making and the flow of information can be one of your greatest assets in building trust and support from a community. These staff members usually have the most longevity in the school. They have understanding and knowledge that can inform you of needs, ways of doing things, and ways of not doing things that may be difficult to learn from others in the community. Involving classified staff means spending time in meetings with them. This is best done in small groups, not individually (where a staff member may feel uncomfortable without the support of others). Plan to schedule meetings at different times for different employees, ensuring meetings are always during scheduled work hours. Do not expect hourly employees to attend meetings on their free time. They have families and homes to attend to and often have busy schedules.

COMMUNITY LIFE

There is vibrant life happening outside the school, in the community. What do you and your staff know about those happenings, and how can you get involved?

The first step in community involvement is to participate in the community. That may seem obvious, but it is astonishing how many teachers and administrators live in a small community and hardly ever attend anything beyond school walls. Cross-cultural relationships cannot happen in isolation.

It is important to respect others when making attempts to become involved in community or family activities outside the school. Don't necessarily wait for invitations (that may not come), but if you are aware of events in the community, it is respectful to ask before showing up. Show an interest in learning about the goings-on in the community. Offer to have meetings at the school and maintain an open-door policy. Try to

Figure 3.3. Community celebration, Curyung (Dillingham). *Courtesy of Emily Hendricks.*

make a habit of only asking open-ended questions instead of making statements. It is always better to ask, "How can I help?" than to assert: "I can help by . . ."

VILLAGE ACTIVITIES (NOT A COMPLETE LIST)

Church services or activities	Health care meetings
Informal church gatherings	Informal community gatherings
ATV and snowmachine trips	Regional school advisory meetings
Beading	City council meetings
Dances	Birthday parties
Bingo	Weddings
Holiday celebrations	Subsistence activities
Regional corporation meetings	Skin sewing
Tribal organization meetings	Sports gatherings

It is also important to be an observer and not always ask for verbal explanations, especially with Elders. It is much better to ask, "Can you show me?" than to ask, "Can you tell me how?" Asking to observe can lead to far more learning on your part than listening to an explanation. Try asking, "The next time you work on your baidarka, would it be okay if I came over and watched?"

Too often school teaching staff will self-isolate and spend most of their leisure time with other teaching staff in the confines of their housing units. You cannot correct this separation from the rest of the community by merely telling staff to go to bingo on Wednesday nights. As the school leader, it is important for you to set up interactions between the community and your teaching staff. Have your staff brainstorm and plan events that will invite the community into the school, such as movie nights, game nights, local sports competitions, celebrations, and dinners. These relaxed social activities will help to build relationships. Here's an example of one such event that you could adapt for your own context:

Math Night in Cetuyaraq (New Stuyahok)

- Invite families with all age groups to attend math night at the school.
- Each classroom teacher or group of teachers designs a group activity using math.
- Attending families can decide which function to attend and can either attend as a group, despite age differences, or split up and go to a variety of activities.
- Teachers should plan together and be given a small budget to purchase supplies.
- The following are examples of types of activities:
  - Measure cubic volume of harvested berries.
  - Tell addition and subtraction stories using manipulatives.
  - Create an algebraic formula for the time it takes to travel between villages on a snowmachine.
  - Use fractions in a recipe to make play dough.
  - Make tagboard digital and analog clocks.
  - Play a card game using money cards.
  - Measure items in the classroom in inches, feet, and millimeters.
- Provide a dessert to end the night's activities. Food is important!

Field trips can also be a great way to bring staff, students, and community members together. You can take students out ice fishing in the winter or berry picking in the fall, or you can visit important places around or near the community. These types of activities provide an opportunity for Elders and other community members to be the experts. You and your staff will undoubtedly learn more on these outings than the students!

INDIVIDUAL RESPONSIBILITY

Bridging community-school divides is a shared responsibility. As a school leader and a community member, it is important that you model how you want others to act. Do not isolate yourself and then ask community members to be involved in the school.

The community needs to accept some responsibility for integrating culture into the school too. After all, local community members are the only people that can share knowledge about local culture, traditions, beliefs, and languages. Many community leaders are willing to help, but you should ask for their help rather than wait for them to come forward. Get to know the Elders and leaders in your community. Visiting homes for coffee or tea is a great way to break the ice.

Understand also that people in rural Alaska are every bit as modern as people anywhere else. You do not have to ask questions about how to set a beaver trap to engage in conversation. Indigenous and non-Indigenous peoples live in the same year, are on the same planet, and share many of the same interests. You can talk about professional basketball or football. You can talk about cooking or travel. You can ask kids about music they listen to and about movies or shows they like. You can just spend time together, without talking at all. People form relationships day by day, and in any case, wouldn't *you* find it a little off-putting if someone you just met kept asking you about how your grandparents did things?

Getting to know Indigenous leaders beyond community boundaries is also important, especially for those of you in district office positions. Alaska Native corporations in many regions have stepped up their support of schools, especially supporting cultural- and language revitalization programs. Find out who these people are, and initiate introductions and communication with them.

Getting community members into the classroom to teach cultural crafts, tell stories, or share histories is a great way to help create a community atmosphere in the school. If you can find ways to pay people who are willing to share their time, do so. Initially, you may find it difficult to convince Indigenous community members to share knowledge in the school. It takes time and trust. Luke Rowley, a former teacher in Isiŋnaq (Shungnak), says,

> [When inviting a community member into your classroom,] do not be discouraged if you are not met with enthusiasm. Remember that there have been many teachers before you, and not all have been as respectful of the culture. Just as important as who you ask, and possibly even more, is how you ask. When possible, have someone introduce you to the person you want to talk to. Explain why you are interested and why you are asking them specifically.

As Angayuqaq Oscar Kawagley has pointed out, it may be difficult or impossible for the school to meet its goals without community participation: "Elder participation is critical to Yupiaq science teaching. The premise in teaching Yupiaq science is to begin with the environment, ensuring cultural sensitivity and relevancy, because it is something Elders are most intimately in tune with" (Kawagley, 2006, p. 101).

When inviting someone into your classroom, it is important that you consider local ways of doing things. Setting precise meeting times or expecting a local person to keep a presentation to a specific time limit will likely lead to the person being uncomfortable or missing the set time. Be flexible. This is hard for some teachers, but you must let teachers know that their protocols may differ from local protocols.

Often, having Elders or others visit a classroom informally is a great way to start. Have them come in and observe or join in a class activity. It is always a good idea to have some small memento made by the students to present to someone that visits your classroom. You can have some items set aside for impromptu visits, or you can have students make items for a specific person on a planned visit. It can be as simple as a card or pictures drawn by students. If someone does share their knowledge and expertise, be respectful of their personal stories and property. Never share these stories or skills without the explicit permission of the person providing the information.

When looking for where to begin with creating a culturally responsive school or district, the first place to start is with building relationships. The strength that you build with individual relationships will provide the platform for improvement.

CONNECTING CULTURES

Much of this chapter has described what you, as a school or district leader, must do to take responsibility for infusing local culture(s) into schools. However, merely describing the process can be frustrating to those who want a blueprint for change. Unfortunately, that handbook has not been written. Change is a process, not a list of things to do. This is where you come in as a leader: you start that process and nurture it over time.

You cannot expect school staff who have been transplanted to a rural Alaska community to be able to make all of the connections needed to learn about local culture(s). It is important that you reach out to community leaders and let them know that the teachers want to be part of community activities but also that many teachers feel they need to be invited and welcomed before they will feel comfortable outside the school.

Many rural Alaska districts have instituted culture camps or weeklong orientations for newcomers prior to the start of a school year. If your district does not do this, you should look for grant money to support a culture camp and encourage others to get one started. Alaska Native corporations—both regional and village corporations—are often willing to help. The most important part of learning about cultures is experiencing them. Standing on a riverbank and learning how to cut and dry fish, listening to Elders tell stories, or learning to make a beaver hat only reinforces the adage of learning by doing.

INTEGRATING CULTURES IN THE SCHOOL AND CLASSROOM

When attempting to integrate cultures with school curriculum, it is important to teach students what culture is. Too often we make assumptions about what students know. Cultures are complex. To create a deeper understanding of culture, a person must teach it in multiple ways before true understanding begins to develop. Luke Rowley, a teacher in Isiŋnaq (Shungnak), shares the following:

> One of the big barriers, in my experience, is that students do not feel personally responsible for culture. This is not to say they do not respect it or find it important. Rather they take it for granted. Having talked with students from several villages (an admittedly small sample) I have found that the common responses to the question "What is Inupiaq culture?" tend to be along the lines of, "Hunting, trapping, respect for Elders and subsistence living." These answers reflect traditional practices. This is a positive image, but one that is not fully representative of culture.

Rowley, a non-Indigenous fourth-grade teacher, built a foundation for efforts to integrate Isiŋnaq culture within the classroom by reading what he could find, participating in local activities, and observing people in the community. He made friendships with Indigenous people. He adds,

> Often districts or schools will tell teachers to integrate with few suggestions, supports or guidelines. The result can be activities that appear on the surface to be quality but which have very little value. Even if the teachers do recognize and want to provide quality, they may not know how.

Curriculum can be adapted to add cultural connections, such as using blue, red, and black Legos or blocks as math manipulatives to represent blueberries, cranberries, and crowberries. Or practicing local dances with students to enhance gross motor skills. Or using a snowmachine to teach how internal combustion engines work. The addition of cultural connections adds interest, motivation, and engagement. As Angayuqaq Oscar Kawagley has pointed out,

> Curricula can be approached in a way that integrates Yupiaq and Western knowledge systems and the methods by which they are derived. A teacher, whether Native or not, can develop explanations and experimentations by asking Elders, young, educated people, and the students themselves how something studied was or can be applied in village life. (1993, p. 188)

Integrated instruction should go beyond just adding cultural context to lessons; it should include cultural elements as valued learning objectives on their own. The goal of successfully integrated cultural instruction is to enhance students' understanding of the historical or current cultural elements of their communities, including ways of knowing, ways of being human, local and Indigenous histories, current events affecting Indigenous peoples, and subsistence knowledge and skills.

CULTURAL INSTRUCTION PROJECT: COMMUNITY GENEALOGY PROJECT

Create a genealogy tree in a visible public meeting place in your school. Ask students to research their family history by interviewing adults and Elders. Then make a chart, map, or mobile that shows all of the family connections in the village and the family history of every student. Use the information to build a sense of self and place with the students.

Achieving a level where the school is providing integrated cultural instruction requires time, patience, learning, and local help. This will be a multiyear process, but you can initiate the effort, build the foundation, and get others involved who will continue the work. The result will be a stronger community-school relationship that will enhance learning. Isn't that the overall objective?

ENHANCING AND PRESERVING LOCAL CULTURES

What role and responsibility does the school or district have for preserving or teaching local cultures or languages? It is a complex question. There are many elements of culture and of language. There may be different answers, too, depending on where you are. What is the relationship of the community to the school? What role do parents have in preserving local languages and cultures? Are there local dance groups or other culture or tradition bearers in the community? How many adults or Elders are fluent in the local Indigenous language(s)? What community resources exist beyond school walls?

All of these questions point to varying answers about where the school's roles and responsibilities begin and end, as well as how the school can intersect with the roles of parents and the community. The answer lies in the belief that culture and language teaching in rural Alaska is a collaborative responsibility. The goal for educators is—and always has been—student learning. Infusing local languages and cultures into curriculum will lead to better outcomes. Making connections to local and prior knowledge enhances learning. Doing so provides relevance and meaning. In order to prioritize and accomplish these things, collaboration with community members is required. Luke Rowley continues,

> Prioritizing cultural context and cultural instruction involves consideration of where else and how often the students are learning this outside of school. If students are already being taught at home, it may be a lower priority because they will learn it whether or not it is taught in school. If it is a skill that others prioritize because it is diminishing, it would be a higher priority. If the skill spans many topics, then it would be higher.

SOME ROLES AND RESPONSIBILITIES OF SCHOOLS

- They should reflect local cultures in the school and classroom.
- They should reflect local cultures in the curriculum.
- They should assist with teaching local languages.
- They should identify and teach functions of local institutions—that is, Tribal organizations, Alaska Native corporations, and local art or dance groups.
- They should teach local and Indigenous histories.
- They should teach local governance.
- They should teach teachers about local histories and cultures.
- They should teach all staff about Indigenous ways of knowing and being.

MAKING IT WORK

When it comes to building culturally responsive schools, your first leadership responsibility is to learn. This learning will come at times and places where it is least expected, as with David's explanations to William. Just remember to always ask, not tell. Listen and observe. There is a sense of community in rural Alaska villages that supersedes individualism. The community may become standoffish when outsiders come in and offer perspectives focused only on their own ideas or values. If you, as a leader, can help teachers understand the importance of working as a team with local people, you will find a lot more receptivity.

Integrating local cultures with teaching and learning at school takes sustained effort but will pay many dividends. You can succeed by adapting to the community in your village. Become a part of the community, not an outsider. Try not to be discouraged when setbacks occur. Most administrators can tell stories about their mistakes when trying to learn about the cultures in which they have become immersed. These mistakes will be forgiven and forgotten as long as you continue to honor the cultures and the individuals with whom you work. Set goals for yourself and the school along with your school staff and community. Start small and look for easy wins. Build from there. Continue to revise and set new goals. Small steps can lead to big accomplishments. As with most school reforms, there is no blueprint that can be applied to all situations. Local solutions are lasting solutions. There are many experienced educators who can help. Do not be afraid to connect with these people. Share your learning, and ask for assistance when needed.

As rural Alaska leaders, we are all in this together. And we are stronger in partnership than we could ever be in isolation.

TAKEAWAYS

- A culturally responsive school understands different ways of learning and different ways of knowing.
- Every community is unique.
- Trusting relationships are the foundation for building success.
- Learn to bridge Indigenous ways of knowing and Western curriculum.
- Include Indigenous histories, local governance and traditions, subsistence skills, and current local events when teaching both students and staff.

RESOURCES

- Alaska Department of Education & Early Development: state education agency; maintains repository of all learning standards for Alaska schools, including the Alaska Standards for Culturally Responsive Schools. https://education.alaska.gov/standards
- Alaska Native Knowledge Network: curriculum publisher and knowledge base focusing on Alaska Native knowledge systems and ways of knowing; found at the University of Alaska Fairbanks. www.ankn.uaf.edu

Chapter 4

Adapting Curriculum

Carol Thompson

Sandy loved her new job teaching first grade in a coastal Alaskan village. The K–12 school of 95 students had a friendly atmosphere, her principal was supportive, and she had made close friends with her colleagues. So, too, had Sandy connected with the classroom paraprofessional Jasmine, who'd grown up in the village. As the fall unfolded, Sandy realized that her students were not making the progress she expected in math; her class averaged just 45% correct on weekly assessments. Sandy and Jasmine met to discuss causes and solutions.

They looked ahead to an approaching math lesson in the curriculum. The lesson, a standard one for any math program, introduced the concept of *how many more than*. Sandy remembered teaching this same concept to urban students outside Alaska. She had seen them fail to connect the words "how many more than" with the concept of subtraction. She remembered that she'd had to expand her single textbook lesson into multiple concrete mini-lessons for students to understand the math:

1. First, Sandy taught students how to form a simple array out of two groups of objects (e.g., pencils and erasers). Students then practiced forming arrays. See Figure 4.1.
2. Second, students needed to form an array and point to pairs of objects (e.g., one pencil, one eraser). Students would say, "Partners, partners, partners. . . ." Students would point to any leftover objects in half the array and say, "More."
3. Third, students counted the nonpaired objects in one group (e.g., the pencils). Students then said, "(Number) more."

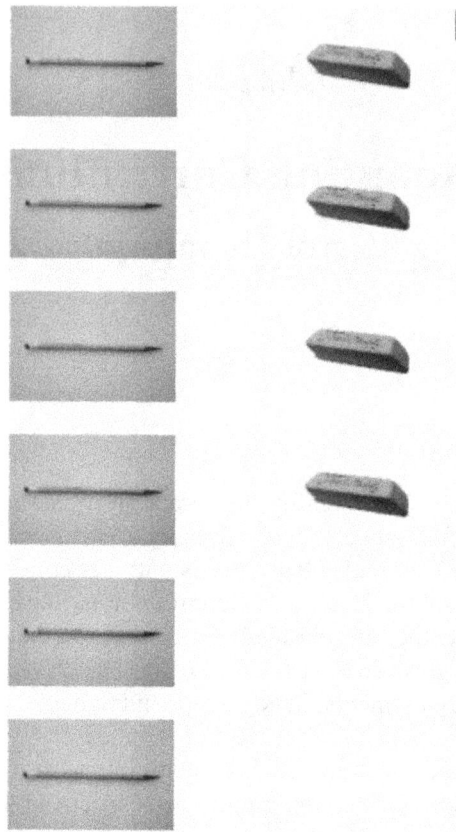

Figure 4.1. Array of pencils and erasers. *"Pencil" by A. Taylor, licensed with CC BY 2.0. "Pink Pearl Eraser" in public domain.*

4. Fourth, students formed arrays, identified and counted "more," stating, "There are (number) more (objects) in this group than (objects) in that group."
5. Finally, students said the matching subtraction sentence—for example, "Six minus four equals two."

This approach had proven effective with urban students, and Sandy wanted to try this same method with her students in rural Alaska. In their discussion Sandy asked Jasmine whether students would know the term *partners*. Jasmine suggested that Sandy instead use the term *same-same*, which students often used while playing games. When Sandy and Jasmine taught the multistep "how many more" lesson using the children's own language (same-same), the students confidently engaged and quickly mastered the concept.

This success led Sandy and Jasmine to think hard about the commercial math program her school used—one widely adopted across the country. Before every lesson, they looked at the language used and tried to ensure they explicitly supported the students' oral language skills before or during each lesson. They provided more practice for almost every skill than textbook lessons provided. These supports worked but notably slowed their teaching pace. Sandy and Jasmine were torn. They wanted to make sure their first graders ended the year ready for second grade, and they wanted to make sure their principal understood what they were trying to do. Sandy looked ahead in her calendar and noted with some anxiety that her principal would be observing her class the following week. She wondered: was their approach the right one?

Although this story is Sandy's and Jasmine's, it's also one of teacher connections, leadership, student support, and decisions about how students engage with content. If you, a school leader, saw what Sandy and Jasmine were doing and agreed that their students might not make it through the entire curriculum for first grade, what would you tell them? Why?

WHAT TO LOOK FOR IN CURRICULUM

In this chapter, curriculum means the materials and resources used to support student learning. This may include published programs, textbooks, and intervention materials, and it can also include contributions from Elders, local resources, and experiences beyond classrooms. It may be tempting to assume that board-adopted curricula from national publishers are of good quality in all regards. They often are not. "Research-based" and "standards-aligned" qualities are not the same as "demonstrably effective in rural Alaska." If you're not sure about whether you have the right curricula, take 10 minutes to review current student performance. If your students are all working at grade level and demonstrating meaningful cultural and Indigenous language skills—awesome. Your curricula are perfect. Quit reading this chapter.

If not, it's worth asking what role your curricula play in student outcomes. Sandy and Jasmine clearly experienced tension in trying to follow a Western curriculum while meeting the needs and building on the strengths of their Indigenous students in rural Alaska. A good first step in exploring curricula is to ask three basic questions:

- Are the curricula in use *complete*? Do your curricula include supports and extensions? Or do teachers find they need to supplement with materials beyond or in place of adopted resources?

- Are the curricula in use *appropriate?* Are curricula aligned to state standards, including the Alaska cultural standards? What do students and parents think?
- Are the curricula in use *effective?* What evidence exists that teachers—including new teachers—are able to teach the curriculum well and as designed? What evidence is there that students are learning what they need to learn?

Schools in rural Alaska mostly use curricula published by a few large companies. In 2020 just three publishers (Houghton Mifflin Harcourt [Massachusetts], McGraw Hill [New York], and Pearson [North American headquarters in New York]) collectively held more than 80% of the US K–12 publishing market (Fitch Ratings, 2020). None of these major publishers has ever produced a curriculum that puts rural Alaska or Indigenous students on center stage. And, to my knowledge, none has proven consistently effective with rural Alaska students without a great deal of adaptation. Keep this in mind as you read the rest of the chapter: *all curricula must be adapted to be effective in rural Alaska schools.*

Below, I outline several common issues with mass-produced curricula in rural Alaska schools. You should review what you are using with teachers and staff, and look for the following:

EASE OF USE

Teacher turnover in rural Alaska is high, averaging 36% annually (Vazquez Cano et al., 2019); it is not unusual to see an entire school teaching staff turn over in a single year. For rural Alaska schools, the *less professional development* needed by teachers, the better. This may seem counterintuitive; don't we all want sophisticated programs for our students? Maybe not. If it takes years for teachers and staff to get the hang of a curriculum package, those years are lost for the students you have *now*. And if teachers or staff leave, you'll need to start over again. Curriculum complexity is not your friend in rural Alaska. Curriculum must be accessible to teachers who are new to the profession or to the district.

It's also true that digital platforms or curricula that rely on a high volume of regularly restocked consumables may be unwieldy or unusable in rural Alaska. The question isn't what's "best" (in the abstract) when it comes to a curriculum. It's what's best for students and teachers *in rural Alaska.* One problem with buying the wrong stuff is that then you can't buy other stuff. At some point textbook dollars become real money that could have been spent on other things for your school or district: professional development, culture camps, squishy chairs for fidgety second graders, and so on.

CULTURAL RELEVANCE

Indigenous students in rural Alaska often enter classrooms and encounter materials that feel foreign to them and may seem totally irrelevant. The Southwest Region School District director of Yup'ik Studies Arnaq Esther Ilutsik commented in a keynote to the Alaska Bilingual/Multicultural Conference (as cited in Barnhardt & Kawagley, 2010, p. 268) the following:

> *We have become the invisible people* [emphasis added]. On the surface, the curriculum looks promising, but investigating further we find that certain textbooks, including the ones for the "core" curriculum adopted by the district and used by the teachers, haven't really changed that much since the Dick and Jane series. Now, instead of a dog named Spot, we have a dog named Bingo. Although animals from our environment may be portrayed, they are often presented with misleading information. One can wonder how our Elders would have presented this information. What would be their focus, and would the information be presented in a culturally local relevant way? Actually, I was shocked to find that none of the stories contained in one of the current reading series portrayed any of the North American Indigenous peoples. There were tales from Japan, China, and even Africa, but nothing from the Indigenous peoples of North America. Again, we have become the invisible people.

LANGUAGE DEMANDS

Many students in rural Alaska use Indigenous languages as a primary language at home (schools classify them as *English learners*). Others use a contact language sometimes called "village English," which can diverge from formal academic English (Kellie, 2017). In Sandy's and Jasmine's story, their students used *same-same* as a comparison. *Same-same* is not an example of lesser English. It is an example of hybridized syntax and grammar from English and local Indigenous languages. Iñupiaq language teacher Suzzuk Mary Huntington noted the following (in Carter, 2008):

> I didn't consciously realize that I felt bad about the way I speak until I took the Iñupiaq grammar class and saw "Oh, that's why we say it this way, versus the other way." I mean, we always laugh about "Sometimes I always" because "sometimes" and "always" in English are conflicting terms. You can't sometimes always do something. But in Eskimo, the way we use always is more "habitually":

"Sometimes I habitually do that." To see the direct correlation between our language that we don't know and the English that we speak, versus just the English we're told to speak—you know, that's a real self-esteem downer to not realize that what we're doing is legitimate for all reasons and not just cultural pride.

The formal academic English of textbooks and classrooms places significant language demands on rural Alaska students. Yet textbook support for academic English is weak to nonexistent in most popular textbooks, no matter what publishers claim. Support components may be vague, general statements of what teachers might do, without the kind of language instruction or practice actually needed by students and teachers. Sometimes textbooks present challenges far more complex than teacher notes might suggest. For example, see Figure 4.2 for a third-grade English-language learner resource page from the popular series *Go Math*.

This activity suggests that English-language learners can improve their speaking, reading, and writing skills, as well as their understanding of important mathematics vocabulary, by showing in writing that they understand the very math vocabulary purportedly being taught! While this may work as an assessment, it's not instruction or practice. The illogical nature of this support strategy apparently escapes many educators. Don't let it escape you. If teachers suggest that they're not finding language supports that work, they're probably right. Sandy's and Jasmine's approach—breaking one math concept into a series of language-supported mini-lessons with local-language integration—is an example of what often must be done by staff as an adaptation of mass-produced curricula.

BACKGROUND KNOWLEDGE DEMANDS

If, as Arnaq Esther Ilutsik pointed out, Indigenous peoples are invisible in most textbooks, so too are the day-to-day experiences of life in rural Alaska. Many textbooks focus on topics unfamiliar to rural Alaska students. This can lead to an understandable lack of engagement, but the real problem is cognitive load. If every page in a book presents unfamiliar concepts, students are never able to rely on long-term memory to support new learning.

Teachers may tell you they find it almost impossible, timewise, to explicitly teach students every word they need to know in order to comprehend textbook passages. These teachers are not exaggerating. Mass-produced teaching strategies provided by textbooks are typically insufficient and not designed with rural Alaska students in mind. To comprehend the text, students must successfully decode, understand the vocabulary, and be able to connect the text to background knowledge they already possess. Background knowledge

Adapting Curriculum 67

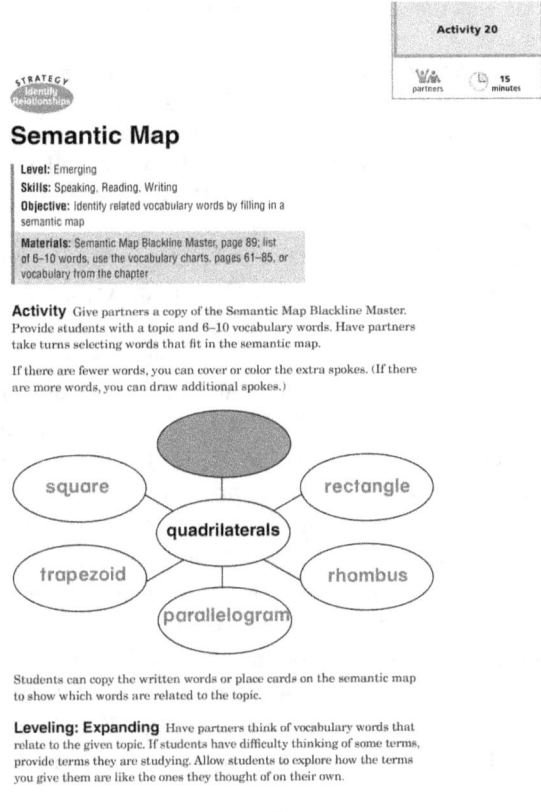

Figure 4.2. Semantic map of "quadrilateral." *From GO Math! ELL Activity Guide, Teacher Edition, Grades 3–6. Copyright © 2015 by Houghton Mifflin Harcourt Publishing Company. All rights reserved. Used by permission of the publisher.*

is one of the best predictors of reading comprehension available—*not* fluency, vocabulary, IQ, or any other measure of reading skill (Willingham, 2006; Lemov et al., 2016). The answer is not simplifying or dumbing down texts, which can do real harm; it's finding appropriately complex texts that take advantage of students' background knowledge *and* that directly teaches unfamiliar concepts and new vocabulary daily.

Here's what this looks like in practice. Take, for example, a popular elementary reading curriculum, *Journeys* (published by Houghton Mifflin Harcourt). Its third-grade reader includes a nonfiction selection titled "You Be the Jury." A portion of that selection reads,

> Citizens of the United States live in a country where they can take part in their government. Good citizens work together in many ways to serve their

government. One way that that [sic] citizens can help their state government is by serving on a jury. A jury is a group of people that decides whether someone is guilty of breaking a law or not guilty. Members of the jury are called jurors. When people are accused of breaking laws, they have the right to have their case heard by juries. In return, citizens also have a duty to serve as a juror, if asked. Citizens take turns serving jury duty. A letter tells a person that it is his or her turn. It tells when to go to court. (Masters, 2014)

Most third graders will have some limited background knowledge of courts and juries, perhaps drawn from television and movies. However, when it comes to comprehending the information in this text, the vocabulary used in this selection may present obstacles from the very first sentence. Many third graders will not truly understand the meaning of the terms "citizens," "state government," "accused," "heard by," or "duty," all of which are found in this paragraph. The publisher includes the terms "trial," "jury," and "guilty" in a list of eight target vocabulary words, and provides brief vocabulary activities with the lesson plans. It is very important to realize, though, that for many students, the amount and quality of vocabulary development found in the textbook is not enough. A teacher can do the recommended vocabulary lessons, and yet students may not comprehend part or all of the text. In order for a student to grasp the meaning of this short selection, much vocabulary work must be done before and during the reading. And notably, every concept presented in the text ignores Tribal citizenship, Tribal governments, and Tribal courts, which may be far more familiar to rural Alaska students than the terms used here.

TEXT COMPLEXITY AND GRADE LEVEL

Grade level and age are often seen as interchangeable in schools. On the surface the concept of grade level texts may seem clear; it involves some measure of readability (teachers can check readability measures of texts using Word or a range of web-based tools; e.g., https://hub.lexile.com/analyzer) and some measure of background knowledge (harder to measure).

One problem with the concept of grade level is that eight-year-olds in rural Alaska (as everywhere) are all over the place developmentally. A second is that many reading programs are intentionally built around core texts written entirely at or above grade level, and these assume background knowledge that ignores the lives of Indigenous students in rural Alaska. Teachers in rural Alaska may find entire classrooms struggling to access grade-level texts. Often, these teachers go into triage mode: they anticipate and attempt to prevent student failure by narrowing the classroom focus to only what's assessed. This is simply teachers trying to survive. And as this happens, students slip further and further behind. Even if teachers manage to get students modestly capable on tests, they're not really teaching the process skills of reading. They are focusing on getting students to remember comprehension questions that were discussed in class. And students aren't becoming readers.

Many proponents of the teach-at-grade-level philosophy insist that it respects students by delivering equity. After all, if a textbook gets good outcomes with students in suburban America, then don't students in rural Alaska deserve the same? Although using the same materials might superficially look like equity, it risks weighing age (or grade level) too heavily in the alignment of students, teachers, and curricula. It does students no good to provide materials they cannot yet access or that teachers cannot yet successfully teach. Importantly, we can't ask students to struggle indefinitely. Though perhaps well-intentioned, insisting that students be taught using grade level texts that assume shared background knowledge can force students to decide that they are just not good at school. Such students are ill-used by an insistence that they learn at a universal pace and with inappropriate materials. In 2010 Dr. Ray Barnhardt pointed out the fallacy of a "teach harder and more" approach in rural Alaska:

> Under the banner of "all students can learn to high standards," teachers will be admonished to teach harder and more of whatever it is that students are determined by the tests as lacking. While this may seem logical on the surface, it ignores the possibility that the real issue may not be low expectations at all (though certainly . . . [these do] exist), but the more fundamental issue of lack-of-fit between what we teach, how we teach it, and the context in which it is taught. Intensifying the current curriculum and extending schooling into the weekend or summer also ignores the inherent limitations to school improvement in rural Alaska. (Barnhart & Kawagley, 2010, p. 338)

ON FIDELITY/NOT ADAPTING CURRICULA

This chapter claims that adapting curricula to meet local needs is critical for success in rural Alaska schools. Not all agree. Many publishers resist the idea of local adaptations, pushing the claim that *fidelity to the curriculum* (strictly following the published program) is the only effective approach. It clearly is not. Many rural Alaska school districts have used "research- based" curricula for decades without sustained success, and yet the pressure to avoid local adaptations persists. Discussions of fidelity can provoke strong feelings and can lead to conflicts between staff and administration that are not productive. Try to avoid devotion to any particular curriculum as a panacea. Be aware that many concerns that you might identify in school (student failure, lack of engagement, classroom management issues, etc.) may be caused or exacerbated by inappropriate curricula. Below, I'll explore some steps you can take to adapt curricula not yet working in rural Alaska.

HOW TO ADAPT AND IMPROVE CURRICULA

This chapter has outlined a lot to look for when you review curricula. You may see a lot of problems. Don't despair! Importantly, there's a lot you can do to make things better.

HIRE AND RETAIN INDIGENOUS TEACHERS AND STAFF

This may not seem like a curriculum fix. After all, it's about people. But, as we saw with Sandy and Jasmine, one of the key steps in getting curriculum right is getting *people* right. There are several interrelated issues. Rural Alaska schools often

- have few or no Indigenous teachers who can directly address curricular problems in their classrooms;
- struggle to connect Indigenous staff members with non-Indigenous teachers in ways that address curricular problems;
- hire a high proportion of their new teachers from the lower 48, who are new to teaching, new to rural Alaska, and new users of adopted curricula; and
- have high teacher turnover, forcing schools into permanent professional development mode.

I noted above the problems with irrelevant and non-adapted curricula. Local Indigenous staff are the people in the best possible positions to adapt curricula effectively. If Sandy leaves (like more than one-third of rural Alaska teachers do annually), the positive relationship she has with Jasmine (a local Indigenous paraprofessional) disappears. Sandy's teaching knowledge leaves with her. And Jasmine is left trying to work with the next teacher, who may or may not address problems as Sandy capably did.

The more you can recruit, hire, and keep local talent, the better. The work is long-term. And when you have good people in place, try to keep them! Some schools in rural Alaska manage to keep teachers and staff for many years. If you identify long-standing employees, ask them what has motivated them to remain for so long. Try to make sure you get to know each employee and meet the needs that might help them stay.

ADAPT MATERIALS OR SUPPLEMENT WITH CULTURALLY RESPONSIVE CURRICULUM

For many students in rural Alaska, Western-oriented curricula will not accomplish nearly enough. The Alaska Standards for Culturally Responsive Schools (Alaska Native Knowledge Network, 1998), adopted by the Alaska State Board of Education in 2010, specify five concrete goals for culturally responsive curricula for which you, as a school leader, are responsible:

- Reinforce the integrity of the cultural knowledge that students bring with them.
- Recognize cultural knowledge as part of a living and constantly adapting system that is grounded in the past but continues to grow through the present and into the future.
- Use the local language and cultural knowledge as a foundation for the rest of the curriculum.
- Foster a complementary relationship across knowledge derived from diverse knowledge systems.
- Situate local knowledge and actions in a global context.

These are not just abstract goals. Culturally responsive curricula work. Yet one fundamental problem you will encounter is a lack of complete curricula for use in rural Alaska. There are bits and pieces. You will need to make decisions about how to adapt what you have and how to find supplements when you identify missing components. Culturally responsive curricula can't be implemented solely by a single well-intentioned school leader. You will need help, and your teachers will need help. Okalena Morgan, a Milken Award-winning Yup'ik teacher in Anyaraq (Aniak), encourages non-Indigenous teachers to reach out to local staff and community members. In most grades and content areas, there's probably a local context or connection that could make teaching and learning more successful. For example, when teachers identify a particular story in their curriculum, they could ask community members if there are appropriately shared stories that echo similar themes. The survival story of Ada Blackjack, for example, is surely at least as compelling as that of Chris McCandless in *Into the Wild*. And both have movies!

One way to start this work (at all levels—classroom, grade, school, or district) is to self-score using the rubrics in the *Guide to Implementing the Alaska Cultural Standards for Educators* (Alaska Department of Education & Early Development, 2012). Each rubric provides examples of evidence and probing questions that can help you decide how to move from where you are to the next level. The rubrics include suggestions for some low-hanging fruit (e.g., recognize local cultural values by displaying cultural posters on classroom walls),

Figure 4.3. Cover of second-grade *Math in a Cultural Context* module. *"Going to Egg Island: Adventures in Grouping and Place Values"* (Lipka, 2019).

along with in-depth, long-term adaptive work, such as delivering all classroom activities, both behavior and content, through local, traditional values. As with all school improvement processes, curriculum adaptation is not a one-time event but a process that can and should be embraced regularly and persistently.

Figure 4.3 provides an example of one set of materials (not, alas, a complete set of grade-level curricula) tailored for Alaska schools: *Math in a Cultural Context*, developed by the National Science Foundation, the US Department of Education, and the University of Alaska. The materials include multiple mathematics modules, storybooks, lessons, tools, videos, and additional resources for students in grades 1–7 that integrate knowledge from Yup'ik Elders, teachers, and academics. These modules have demonstrated positive learning gains among rural Alaska students, and they are available for free use under a Creative Commons license.

ADD PRACTICE

This seems simple but is perhaps one of the most critical adaptations teachers can make. One curricular barrier for students in rural Alaska is the lack of skills practice written into textbook lessons. Many students need a tremendous amount of practice in order to reach mastery. Conventional core textbooks do not recognize this need. No textbook series exists that provides all of the practice needed for all students, whether in rural Alaska or elsewhere. Even robust curricula that provide student textbooks, workbooks, and extensive teacher materials can't possibly anticipate every needed skill for students at a wide range of developmental levels. Practice must be tailored by teachers who know their students well.

To find good practice, your teachers should explore supplementary-, intervention-, and English learner–focused materials. Frequently, these provide explicit direct-instruction programs with scripts for teachers. Some direct-instruction programs have a proven track record of promoting learning in rural Alaska, and yet they may not be loved. Direct instruction with embedded practice may feel old-fashioned, and teachers may dislike teaching with scripted programs. They may get bored. But you can help them. Remember, we do what students need, which may not be the same as what we ourselves want.

Here is one note of caution: the goal is not piling worksheet after worksheet on students. What's needed is targeted, repeated, brief practice that is spaced out through the year and *focused on specific student needs.* The need is to deliberately introduce measured amounts of new content and then provide ongoing repeated practice over time (Willingham, 2009). For example, in second-grade math, students may need many repetitions of just one step in subtraction problems that demand regrouping (e.g., deciding whether digits in the tens place are enough). In language arts (at almost any grade level), students may need repeated practice decoding with a focus phonogram (e.g., reading sets of real and nonsense words, all involving *ai/ay*). The right amount of practice is the amount that gets each student to mastery.

HELP TEACHERS BREAK CURRICULA DOWN INTO SUBSKILLS

Sandy and Jasmine realized the problem of skills complexity when teaching students about *how many more than.* Although the given lesson included manipulatives, nothing in the lesson indicated that students needed to perceive that

- one group of manipulatives had *more than* the other group;
- by pairing the manipulatives, students could *see* the *more than*; and
- the manipulatives left unpaired *were* the *more than.*

The curriculum writers should have identified these subskills and should have built in scaffolds, easing Sandy's and Jasmine's burden. An explicit focus on subskills is often missing from general curriculum, but it is present in intervention materials, or those specifically designed for English learners. This lack is unfortunate, as many students need explicit subskills instruction.

If your curricula don't specify subskills or provide clear teacher guidance, student outcomes will disappoint. It is up to someone (e.g., the district curriculum department, teachers, a coach/consultant) to assess curricula, determine subskills, and write needed teacher and student materials. Hire someone to do it if you do not have that person on staff. If you are lucky enough to have teachers who can do subskill analysis (not often taught in university teacher-education programs), ask them to help and give the team paid time in which to do the following:

1. *Prioritize standards and align with curriculum.* Teachers should identify the focus standards—the skills and knowledge that students absolutely must know—at each grade level, as well as identify where those standards are taught in textbook lessons. Alaska standards are numerous (e.g., grade 2 ELA includes 44 anchor standards). Decisions about how all standards will be taught is a core challenge; there are limited hours each day. Some standards may be worth extended time and practice, while others may be adequately covered in limited time. Additionally, some practices within the school may be nonnegotiable, such as teaching academic vocabulary using a certain strategy, daily oral language practice, or using manipulatives in math.
2. *Do task analysis of each lesson.* What do lessons actually ask students to do? Do students have the knowledge and skills to achieve proficiency?
3. *Break down every lesson* as needed into subskill lessons, practice work, and assessments, in a sequential manner.

SUPPORT ORAL LANGUAGE DEVELOPMENT

Academic English isn't anyone's first language. But it is an important language of school. You should try to find out whether your district has a clear understanding of oral language use among students. Who uses Indigenous (or other) languages at home? What kinds of language assessments does the school have? What supports exist for students, families, and teachers?

Sandy and Jasmine realized that students didn't understand the phrase *how many more than*. They then connected students' current use of *same-same* to the academic English required in the lesson. They asked the students to repeat a sentence using academic English: "This group has ___ more ___ than this group." Talking about academic English does not accomplish much; students must have plenty of actual practice in forming sentences themselves. This need is common in rural Alaska; students often need help with pronouns, verb tenses, and expanded-sentence forms (e.g., those using dependent clauses). It is also common that students in rural Alaska use oral language differently than students elsewhere. They use language at school as they themselves have experienced it.

The issue here is not one of judgment. It's that there is often a mismatch between home and school language and, perhaps even worse, that few teachers (through no fault of their own) are prepared to support oral language development in the ways students need. Students in rural Alaska can absolutely develop solid academic English language skills—they just need practice. Plan explicit time in the schedule for writing instruction and help teachers find ways to build in oral language practice on a daily basis. This does not need to be fancy or purchased. It does need to be a regular part of each lesson and something you should look for when observing classes. Here's a short example of what this can look like:

Teacher: Kids, please repeat after me. Today I yell for my team to win.

Students: Today I yell for my team to win.

Teacher: Yesterday I yelled for my team to win.

Students: Yesterday I yelled for my team to win.

Teacher: Tomorrow I will yell for my team to win.

Students: Tomorrow I will yell for my team to win.

Teacher: Right now I am yelling for my team to win.

Students: Right now I am yelling for my team to win.

Teacher: Today she yells for her team to win.

Students: Today she yells for her team to win.

Teacher: Now I'm going to ask each one of you to make your own sentence with "yell." Brianna, use "yell" with "last week."

Brianna: Last week I yell for my team to win.

Teacher: Brianna, when did you yell?

Brianna: Last week.

Teacher: Is last week happening now in the present, or did it already happen in the past?

Brianna: Past.

Teacher: Right. So we have to use "yelled." Would you please say it again, using "yelled?"

Brianna: Last week I yelled for my team to win.

Teacher: Yes! Everybody, repeat Brianna's sentence.

TEACH VOCABULARY

Students must master frequently used academic vocabulary. This vocabulary needs to be taught differently (repeatedly, over time) than words that only appear in a single text. Does your school have a list of must-teach academic vocabulary words? In early grades, teachers sometimes mistakenly confuse the Fry or Dolch "sight word" or "high frequency" word lists for vocabulary lists, but sight words and academic vocabulary are different. Teachers need to teach frequently used academic vocabulary that appears in the curricula they use. These words can't be identified apart from curricula. If you need a starting place, a useful resource may be Marzano's *Teaching Basic, Advanced, and Academic Vocabulary* (2020).

You will likely be working with new teachers; you can help ensure that they get decent, regular professional development focusing on teaching academic vocabulary and that you look for its use when you observe classes. Professional development does not need to be external or costly. As we saw with Sandy and Jasmine, perhaps the most important resource is time. Sandy and Jasmine needed time to collaborate. They needed time to look ahead in the curriculum and plan for vocabulary instruction.

One key resource can be staff who are already working in the school. Okalena Morgan has said she often needs to relate unknown words in a text to things in students' known environments: "I try to make things relevant to my students. If we are talking about measurements, for example, I might use distances the students are familiar with, like from here to Qalqaq (Kalskag)." For teachers who are not locals, making these kinds of connections can be difficult. Okalena reminds us that it's important for teachers to have a way to reach out to those who have been in the school or area for a long time so they can get help with their many questions. Does your school ensure nonlocal teachers get to work with Indigenous staff?

INTEGRATE SCIENCE AND SOCIAL STUDIES WHENEVER POSSIBLE

Earlier, I shared a third-grade passage about court systems that could pose vocabulary and background knowledge challenges for students in rural Alaska. I am not suggesting that students don't need to learn about courts.

I am suggesting that the passage was incomplete for students in rural Alaska. The Alaska Standards for Culturally Responsive Schools explicitly require schools to "incorporate local ways of knowing and teaching in their work" (Standard A) and to "use the local environment and community resources on a regular basis to link what they are teaching to the everyday lives of the students" (Standard B; Alaska Native Knowledge Network, 1998). Neither of these standards are met without consideration of the local, Tribal, or regional court systems most relevant to rural Alaska.

Meeting standards for culturally responsive schools in rural Alaska is perhaps most straightforward in social studies and science. Indigenous peoples have been in rural Alaska from time immemorial (Hensley, 1966; Kawagley, 2006), so the experience, traditions, and knowledge base of peoples in Alaska are vast. Both the natural and human histories are long-standing and accessible, and they can be a rich resource for teaching and learning in schools.

The passage about court systems should not stop with a Western definition of "court" or "citizen" but should include consideration of how these terms may vary across local governments and Tribal contexts. What is a "court" in Kivaliñiq (Kivalina)? Without such context, the passage about courts is surely somewhat magical—things that happen elsewhere to other people. It's almost always best to start exploring social studies locally. One potentially useful statewide resource is Alaskool, a curriculum resource developed by the University of Alaska in partnership with multiple schools, Tribes, and the United States Department of Education: www.alaskool.org.

The same cross-cultural approach is needed in science. Indigenous peoples in rural Alaska have developed cultures that interact with geographies of place and that inform scientific understandings of environmental health, sustainability, climate change, subsistence, technology, and others. Science has been a huge factor in human and cultural survival in rural Alaska, and it remains so today. Roy Nageak Sr., whaling captain from Utqiaġvik, summarized it well: "What's tradition? Our tradition is to use the best tool available in our time" (Sakakibara, 2020, p. xvi).

It's also true that there's no better place in the world for doing science than in rural Alaska. A good example of a rural Alaska district that has done extensive curriculum adaptation in the Lower Kuskokwim School District, whose multiyear Quyurramta (All of Us Together) project has been creating adapted Yup'ik-English bilingual science and social studies curricula across the K–12 grade span.

The good news is that teachers may not need textbooks or digital resources to meaningfully include relevant social studies and science content. They can simply ask in each unit: How does this connect with or vary from what is already known here in rural Alaska? Elders, Tribal or government officials, and other local people can provide context if they are welcomed into school or if the teachers are able to develop good relationships. The availability of rich ecosystems just beyond classroom walls, coupled with deep local knowledge of seasonal cycles and subsistence activities, lends itself to exploration with students, even if budgets are modest. It costs nothing but some preparation and time to take a hike, and some of the most memorable experiences students can have in rural Alaska involve time spent outdoors. As with social studies, the best scientific knowledge is likely to be local.

TEACH WRITING

In your leadership role, you may be tempted to focus on reading, perhaps thinking that reading must improve before writing. Not true. Reading and writing go together, as do fluency and comprehension. In a disconnect, most modern math (and science and social studies) curricula require a great deal of writing . . . without ever really explicitly teaching students how to write. It's worth reviewing your ELA curriculum, and if you don't see much explicit writing instruction, it needs to be added. You must help teachers find the time in the school schedule to fit writing instruction into the school day—writing *by itself*, not just as an add-on to a literacy block or a neglected part of a weekly reading program.

This is an Alaska problem and a national problem. Writing skills are poor nationwide. Three-quarters of fourth and eighth graders in the United States lacked writing proficiency on the most recent NAEP (Institute for Education Sciences, 2017). Writing proficiency is either unknown or poor in most places in Alaska. Mostly, we don't know because we don't assess, but whenever we do assess writing, Alaska students don't do well. You'll need to help teachers find explicit writing curricula and get the training they need to teach and assess writing consistently throughout the year. It's a good idea to explore writing intervention programs that explicitly teach fundamental thinking and writing skills that may be missing in conventional core writing programs.

One example I'll share comes from SRA's *Expressive Writing* curriculum for students in grades 3 plus (my intent is to show one example, not to endorse any particular commercial product). See Figure 4.4 below for an example adapted from a student workbook. In Part A, students practice finding the "part that names" a sentence's subject. In Part B, students practice choosing the correct past tense of a verb. Part C gives students practice in changing nouns to the matching pronouns.

Students are provided scaffolded instructions and support. Part D (Figure 4.5) provides instructions on a paragraph-writing exercise. Assistance includes illustrations in a sequence, vocabulary spelled correctly, verbs

Part A: Instructions: Put in the capitals and periods. Underline the part of each sentence that names:

A young boy threw a ball the ball went over his friend's head it rolled into the street a big truck ran over the ball the truck driver gave the boys a new ball they thanked the truck driver.

Part B: Instructions: Change each sentence so that it tells what happened.

1. The books fall off the table.
2. Rodney and Mark fix the broken toy.
3. The key is under the book.

Part C: Instructions: Fill in each blank with *he, she,* or *it.*

1. The car broke down.	1. __________ broke down.
2. The dream went on for an hour.	2. __________ went on for an hour.
3. The pen fell off the table.	3. __________ fell off the table.

Figure 4.4. Engelmann, et al. (2004, p. 36). *Reproduced with permission of McGraw Hill.*

Part D

Instructions: Write a paragraph that reports on what happened.

Frisbee	bushes	bark	climb	appeared
growl	heard	caught	threw	field

Check 1: Are there any run-on sentences in your paragraph?
Check 2: Does each sentence begin with a capital and end with a period?
Check 3: Does each sentence tell what the person or thing did, not what the person or thing was doing?
Check 4: Did you tell all the important things that happened?

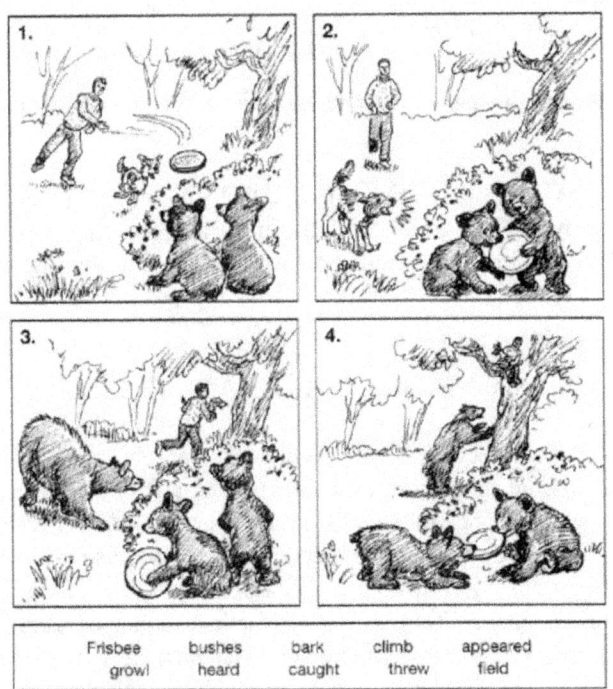

Figure 4.5. Engelmann, et al. (2004, p. 122). *Reproduced with permission of McGraw Hill.*

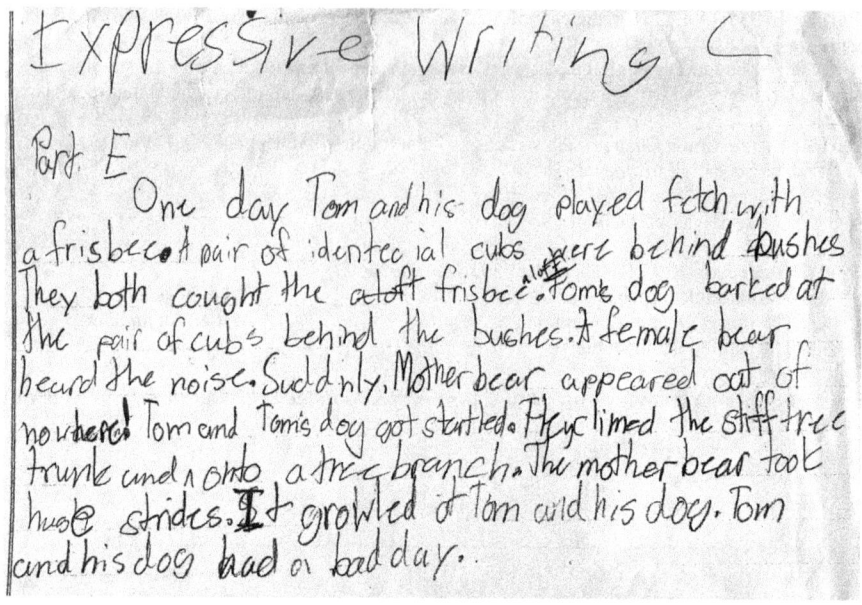

Figure 4.6. Writing sample, response to SRA prompt. *Courtesy of Carol Thompson.*

in the past tense, and self-editing checks. The student writing example above (Figure 4.6, by a fifth-grade student in rural Alaska) shows a possible response. This student had struggled with writing skills before intervention; the paragraph reflects his first draft.

CONSIDER ALTERNATE TEXTS

If your main texts are not useful, you might consider replacement with alternative, intervention, or English learner texts. Such materials may provide more direct guidance for teachers and students, and they often include better skills practice for students. Another option could be to allow teachers to use textbooks off grade level (for example, using a third-grade textbook with fourth graders). This chapter has already discussed the pitfalls of strict grade level adherence, but be aware that jumping down grade levels isn't a clean fix. What happens to those fourth graders next year? Unless the district or school has a coherent plan across grade levels, such an approach may be confusing and counterproductive over time.

What about Response to Intervention (RTI) or multi-tiered system of supports (MTSS) materials? Will they help? Less than most curriculum packages claim. In many rural Alaska schools, the issue is that the groups most often identified for intervention (students below "grade level" in ELA and/or math) can be disproportionately large—sometimes, it's all students in a grade. I will note simply that when an intervention program is necessary for a majority of students, this suggests strongly that there is something wrong with the core academic program. If you find yourself in this last predicament, intervening with virtually all students, you might consider advocating for adoption of different materials. This would be a discussion to have with your district, and it may not be one you can have immediately. But you might gently ask, What evidence is there (from local, state, or national assessments) that students are learning what they need to learn from the curriculum in use?

START SMALL, WITH EARLY GRADES

You can't fix everything all at once. Principals inherit teachers and staff from prior years and are constrained by district decisions; district leaders must follow school board guidelines and so forth. But in all circumstances, your role as a school leader gives you a platform. You can always begin conversations about curriculum and show evidence that demonstrates student learning and struggles. It's often easier for curriculum leaders and district personnel to try a new approach within a defined time period and with data reporting than to simply abandon prior practice wholesale. Try a bite-sized approach first. You will make it easier for cautious district humans by clearly defining what you want to do, what data you'll collect, and how you will report back the progress you make.

Perhaps you can pilot something in your district or school by beginning in kindergarten or first grade rather than overhauling an entire curriculum. Perhaps you can target a grade or subject area that seeks mastery learning rather than externally driven pacing. Maybe you can take one hiring risk that emphasizes local knowledge over formal preparation. Think outside of the box: maybe your first grade could become a two-year grade, where students have ample time to practice and learn the all-important foundational process skills inherent in reading and writing. Whether you are at a school site, a central office, or working in another capacity, it's always, always worth trying to better align curriculum, teachers, and students in rural Alaska. You may surprise yourself with what's possible. It does take courage, and it does take patience. You will be challenged by those around who have accepted (or caused) the status quo. But it's worth it. Be courageous.

ADOPTING NEW CURRICULA

If your district is considering a new curriculum adoption (a typical cycle in Alaska is every five years), then you have an opportunity to improve the materials your teachers use. Curricula should be complete, appropriate, and effective. All curricula need adaptation to be effective in rural Alaska schools. Even if you're not in love with the curricula you have now, it may not make sense to abandon it and start over. You may save time and professional energy keeping what you have and working on adaptations as a best first option.

SPEND TIME IN CLASSROOMS

If you are looking into new curricula, you first need to understand the skills of teachers and staff. There is no such thing as ideal curricula in the absence of the people doing the work. Part of your job in exploring new curricula is to honestly appraise how current materials are used and what teachers and staff are currently able to do. New curricula will not work miracles, and you can't ask staff to do impossible things. You can help both get better incrementally. Please circle this note: *you must spend time in classrooms.* If you are a site leader, you have to do teacher and staff evaluations anyway; part of your time can be spent observing curricula use and in discussions with teachers and staff. Any time you can, ask about their work. They have daily experience with curricula. You do not.

BE SKEPTICAL AND IDENTIFY FEATURES USEFUL IN RURAL ALASKA

In your review of new curricula, be skeptical. This may seem like rookie guidance, but look past publishers' bells and whistles to the issues identified above for rural Alaska schools:

- Is the material culturally relevant?
- What language demands do texts present?
- What background knowledge do texts require?
- How complex are the texts?
- Is explicit daily writing instruction included?
- Is skills practice frequent and useful?
- Is there daily practice in the use of oral academic English?
- Are new skills broken down into subskills?
- Are crucial vocabulary words deliberately and intensively taught and practiced?
- Can teachers and staff learn to use this quickly?

Your team must know the Alaska standards for academics as well as for culturally responsive schools and use that knowledge to evaluate published materials. Otherwise, how could you tell if the curricula are any good? Every publisher will claim to have a good product. But seemingly small details can make large differences.

For example, early reading curricula should focus on reading skills so teachers can address struggles as quickly as possible. But in many reading curricula, the time sequence is backward. You might see that students read texts during the week and are later given assessments on what they read. Such an approach may seem to make sense—read, then quiz—but often fails to tell teachers what they need to know about reading skills. Look at that time sequence: students are tested on content (e.g., about courts) after reading (often together, in class). What does that tell teachers? Mostly about content knowledge rather than reading skills.

Edna Ahmoagak, a veteran teacher in Ulġuniq (Wainwright), notes that effective reading programs take a different approach; they give students new texts in every reading assessment and thus provide valid data on student reading skills.

When reviewing new curricula, don't forget your Alaskan peers! Ask teachers who have been elsewhere in rural Alaska about what they've used. You can also ask school leaders in your district or beyond about programs they recommend and why. Often, peers in rural Alaska will provide the clearest and most practical guidance around.

Above all, know that your work as a school or district leader can make a huge difference in the day-to-day experiences of your students and staff. In Sandy's and Jasmine's story, we saw dedicated, creative professionals adapting materials to better meet student needs. A misguided school leader might have swooped in and demanded that the class get back on track with a published curriculum calendar. But you have an opportunity to be better than that. You can spend time in classrooms, observe student challenges and teacher responses, review existing data, provide teachers with time to adapt curricula, and support approaches that effectively connect students and teachers to appropriate curriculum in rural Alaska.

TAKEAWAYS

- Curricula must be adapted to the needs of students in rural Alaska.
- Use local knowledge to adapt curricula for local relevance.
- Provide additional practice, and teach all necessary subskills.
- Meeting student needs is more important than fidelity to programs.
- Rural Alaska school leaders need to spend time in classrooms to see how curricula work.

RESOURCES

- Alaska Native Knowledge Network: curriculum publisher and knowledge base focusing on Alaska Native knowledge systems and ways of knowing. www.ankn.uaf.edu
- Alaska Standards for Culturally Proficient Schools: especially useful are the standards for curriculum. www.ankn.uaf.edu/publications/standards.html
- Alaskool: a curriculum resource developed by the University of Alaska in partnership with multiple schools, Tribes, and the United States Department of Education. www.alaskool.org/default.htm
- EdReports: a nonprofit that analyzes curriculum from multiple publishers. www.edreports.org/compare
- Guide to Implementing the Alaska Cultural Standards for Educators: rubrics and guide for self-assessments at the classroom, school, or district levels. www.asdn.org/wp-content/uploads/Implementing-AK-cultural-standards-1.pdf
- Institute for Education Sciences: *Practice Guide: Effective Literacy and English Language Instruction for English Learners in the Elementary Grades*. https://ies.ed.gov/ncee/wwc/PracticeGuide/6
- Lexile Analyzer: one cut-and-paste measure of text complexity. (Another useful option is Microsoft Word's Flesch-Kincaid readability and grade level—you can check with spelling and grammar). https://hub.lexile.com/analyzer
- *Math in a Cultural Context*: curriculum developed with the University of Alaska and others. www.uaf.edu/mcc
- WIDA: state consortium focusing on English-learner supports; provides useful assessments and curriculum. https://wida.wisc.edu/resources/oral-language-classroom

Chapter 5

Career, Technical, and Subsistence Education

Christian P. Wilkens

Dog bites, being chased, and poop. Principal/teacher Emma Johnson (a pseudonym) wasn't sure how this afternoon's first session of Alaska Care and Husbandry Instruction for Lifelong Living (A-CHILL) would go for her students, but she *was* clear about their concerns. Almost all of her students were afraid of dogs. Most of them had experience with village dogs, which spend their days outside, often in survival mode, and the students had quite reasonably concluded that dogs were scary. Yet here Emma was, driving a school van to a yard filled with dozens of high-energy racing dogs that might look like ferocious little wolves to her students.

The A-CHILL program, a partnership between the Alaska Gateway School District (AGSD) and the Yukon Koyukuk School District (YKSD), emerged from the Frank Attla Youth and Sled Dog Care-Mushing Program first offered at Jimmy Huntington School in Ts'aateyhdenaadekk'onh Denh (Huslia) in 2012. The program involved 6th- through 12th-grade students in sled dog care and veterinary science. Related goals were increasing community engagement, improving career and technical education skills, and boosting cultural knowledge. But those were long-term goals. In the short term, Emma just wanted to spend time with her students beyond school walls and make sure they got out of the van. This was not a given, especially not with Marvin, one of her 11th graders. Marvin had vocally opposed the dog-yard visit, claiming that all dogs were mean and that snowmachines were faster and less smelly. He'd complained about being in the van, about being outside. Yet he'd come along.

Much to Emma's relief, everyone piled out at the yard into an expanse of barking and wagging dogs, some standing on top of their houses. The musher welcomed the students and waved them over to a harnessed dog. Emma's students watched as he outlined dog anatomy, communication, and nutrition.

She saw one student reach out to pat the dog on the shoulder and giggle. Throughout the two-hour visit, Emma saw Marvin at the back of the group. Sometimes he watched and listened, sometimes not. He didn't pet the dogs or help feed and water them as his classmates did. When the session ended, Marvin was the first one back in the van.

Over the following months, Emma's students returned weekly to help with yard cleanup and dog care. They also caught and dried fish, built dog houses, harnessed and ran dogs, and helped with the school's annual spay/neuter clinic. The dogs showed patience and trust in Emma's students, connecting them to the experiences of generations of Athabascan peoples in rural Alaska. Emma's students listened to stories, old and new, from Tanana Elders. The point of A-CHILL, Emma knew, was not for her students to become mushers or veterinarians. It was, as George Attla Jr. (1933–2015) explained, about acceptance, learning, and pride:

> No matter what kid you get—whether it's a shy kid, or a talkative kid—dogs accept you as you are. They don't care what you look like, they don't care what you sound like. They'll accept you. Our kids have to know their own history in order for us to build pride in them, and in who we are as a people. (Recording by Catharine Axley in Ts'aateyhdenaadekk'onh Denh [Huslia]; as cited in Dittmar, 2018)

Emma could never quite tell what Marvin was learning, though his attendance improved.

Figure 5.1. Nulato School students at a local dog yard, Noolaaghe Doh (Nulato). *Courtesy of Amy Graham.*

In early May, Emma asked her students about their summer plans. Some were traveling; others were doing "nothing." Marvin, after a gentle nudge, announced that he was going to fish with his grandfather on the Tth'iitu' Niign (Tanana River) for a few weeks. And he added, "Maybe I'll bring back some fish for those dogs."

There's a win in this story, but it's a subtle one. Marvin was never going to wake up one morning and tell Emma that—*Eureka!*—he wanted to become a veterinarian or musher. Instead, his comment told Emma that his thinking about A-CHILL was evolving. He was thinking about it as he headed out to do a subsistence activity (fishing) central to the lives of Tanana Athabascan people for generations.

Career and technical education (CTE) programming can often feel like it's heavy lifting up front (relationships, equipment, logistics, partnerships, etc.) to uncertain ends. That may be true. But it's also the case that the success of CTE programs is perhaps most properly judged over lifetimes. How long does it take young people to establish who and what they will become? When do we decide if they're successful, in all the senses that may include?

SUBSISTENCE AND CAREER AND TECHNICAL EDUCATION IN RURAL ALASKA

The federal government defined subsistence in the Alaska National Interest Lands Conservation Act (1980) as:

> Customary and traditional uses by rural Alaska residents of wild, renewable resources for direct personal or family consumption as food, shelter, fuel, clothing, tools or transportation; for the making and selling of handicraft articles out of non-edible by-products of fish and wildlife resources taken for personal or family consumption; for barter, or sharing for personal or family consumption; and for customary trade.

In rural Alaska, people engage in a broad range of subsistence activities outside the market economy—for example, maintaining and repairing boats and gear to fish for immediate- and extended-family member consumption. Much of this work involves no cash, hence subsistence is often not considered a "career" on par with others. Subsistence is almost entirely ignored by the federally defined career and technical education pathways discussed later in this chapter. Yet the skills and knowledge required for subsistence activities are complex, are important for independent living after graduation, continue to evolve over time, and are held in high esteem by rural Alaska communities. Subsistence *is* a career, in all of its senses, and is also substantially more.

Subsistence is often central to Indigenous identities and what it means to live in rural Alaska. Subsistence activities go beyond career and technical education by providing opportunities for sharing traditional knowledge, cultural practices, spiritual beliefs, stories, and language, especially across generations. Through subsistence, young people can learn how to live with respect, how to be self-sufficient, and how to care for others and share resources, as well as about the connections between land, people, and culture. Subsistence activities are among the most powerful means young people in rural Alaska have for learning how to become successful adults. On the topic, Siberian Yup'ik artist John Waghiyi noted the following (National Park Service, 2022): "Subsistence is not a sentimental activity. It nurtures our soul and our bodies. If we can't have (wild, traditional) food, it affects us psychologically and physically. We need to do it every season, every year."

One clear challenge for rural Alaska school leaders is that many of the essential skills for practicing subsistence (e.g., harpooning a whale, towing it to shore, and distributing meat to the community) are absent from published career or vocational education pathways (O'Malley, 2017). One of the most important steps you can take as a school leader in rural Alaska is to bring subsistence into and throughout the school day. Subsistence activities are not just gathering wild resources; they are cultural activities linking people to the land and to others, including ancestors stretching back generations.

The right way to go about ensuring school programs align with local values and traditions is to ensure that connections with the community are strong. Unless you happen to be an Elder in the community, you won't have access to the full range of traditional knowledge and skills that could form a subsistence-based curriculum. What is there to do? A-CHILL is one example. Teachers and schools were not the experts in mushing or local knowledge; instead, they worked hard to make sure students could learn directly from mushers and Elders. The school supported access to knowledgeable communities and people by providing an adjusted schedule, stipends, and transportation along with off-site supervision. To summarize:

- Subsistence is a common postgraduation career path in rural Alaska.
- Subsistence skills are technical skills that are valued in rural Alaska.
- Subsistence education must be connected to the people in the community, especially Elders.
- You must be able to answer the following question: If students want to become subsistence providers for their families and community, what classes and preparation does the school offer?

Career and technical education (CTE) is narrower in scope than subsistence. A general goal for CTE is to prepare "students with technical, academic and employability skills for success in the workplace and in further education" (Association for Career and Technical Education, 2022). CTE programs typically don't touch on culture, spirit, or tradition, instead focusing on more technical matters such as answering, How do I use this equipment? What's my role as an employee?

Yet both subsistence and CTE involve young people in how they will become productive adults in their communities. Both include academic goals (e.g., communication, mathematics, science), general orientations (e.g., inquiry, problem solving, perseverance), and technical skills (e.g., mechanical, medical, services). And both respond to local needs and interests. One opportunity for school leaders in rural Alaska is to demonstrate a commitment to local cultures and values by affirming the academic content of subsistence activities and CTE work. Working with dogs *is* doing science and mathematics. Ensuring that Elders have a role in the transmission of shared knowledge and values *is* social studies. A vibrant language-revitalization program *is* a pathway to ensure young adults find their places in a changing world.

You might have read the overview (in the first chapter) of the three major economies in rural Alaska: subsistence, market (or cash/wage economy), and transfer. Each matters. As such, it would be a disservice to your students to focus school programs solely on packaged CTE programs and the market economy while ignoring the subsistence economy.

While not everyone can or will find jobs linked to CTE coursework in school, every single student in your building can practice subsistence activities for a lifetime. The A-CHILL program, for example, focuses on dog mushing. Is dog mushing a viable career goal for every student in the Alaska Gateway or Yukon-Koyukuk School Districts? No. But all of those students will spend time outside in rural Alaska. All benefit from learning about the landscape around them, about measurements and estimations, and about when it's better to stay inside than to risk traveling. And all can benefit from what George Attla Jr. described as "knowing their own history" by connecting with Elders and learning from their stories (as cited in Dittmar, 2018).

Here are some places to start exploring subsistence education curricula, with the caveat that you will always do best to connect with the people in the community and adapt academic content to local resources:

- Alaska Care and Husbandry Instruction for Lifelong Living: AGSD & YKSD overview. www.achill.life
- Alaska Department of Fish and Game: curriculum resources. www.adfg.alaska.gov/index.cfm?adfg=curricula.main

Figure 5.2. A-CHILL K'ehtthiign (Northway) students at a Yukon River culture and fish camp. *Courtesy of Kathy Turco.*

- Alaska Native Knowledge Network: curriculum resources. http://ankn.uaf.edu/Resources
- Alaskool: curriculum resources. www.alaskool.org/curriculumindx.html
- Attla: film and related curriculum. http://attlafilm.com/educational-materials

CAREER AND TECHNICAL EDUCATION IN RURAL ALASKA

Not all students in rural Alaska want to go to college. That's okay. They don't need to. Alaska has jobs for high school graduates in a wide range of careers. In 2019, just 30% of Alaska's workforce had a bachelor's degree, somewhat lower than the national average of 35% (National Science Foundation, 2021). Your job as a school leader should not be limited to college preparation but should be about finding ways to make learning opportunities in school align with what students and community members value and what employers need.

Importantly, CTE should be for *all* students. Gone are the days when anyone who could fog a mirror could get work on the North Slope oil fields. Many employers in Alaska's largest occupations (mining, fishing, and oil and gas production) need workers with strong technical and academic skills. CTE programs need to be engaging for students, available, and useful in preparation for careers. You don't need to carve out separate academic and CTE tracks as you may have seen in other schools. Instead, rural Alaska schools should ensure every student has the chance to complete a CTE concentration.

A major benefit of CTE for all is that graduation rates are likely to improve; 95% of CTE concentrators in Alaska graduate from high school vs. 78% of non-CTE concentrators (Alaska Department of Education & Early Development, 2020b). As Terri Walker Aviññaq, superintendent for the Northwest Arctic Borough School District, pointed out, exposure to careers during the school years can be pivotal (as it was for her):

> I always knew I was going to be a teacher. Since before I could even remember, there was no doubt in my mind. In high school, I went to an on-the-job training opportunity in Fairbanks that the school provided. For a couple of weeks I worked at a school as a paraprofessional. Students must get exposed to different opportunities ("Hey, I might be interested in cooking!"); that exposure is significant, [and] they get a little bit of a taste of different things.

Superintendent Walker also pointed out the value of including the community in shaping career, technical, and subsistence opportunities:

> It is important to involve the community in your school, so you are aware of what is happening out there. Listening as a leader is vital to understand your community, the challenges they face, what they consider success for their kids, and then, to guide your school in that direction. Every parent wants what is best for their child. Every parent loves their child. Furthermore, everybody wants the same result in the end—what happens is they sometimes disagree on how to get there!

Schools in rural Alaska that focus solely on ELA and math scores will miss the chance to prepare students for life after graduation. Some of Alaska's most popular CTE programs focus on knowledge and skills relevant to life in rural Alaska—for example, health sciences, construction trades, maritime industries, mechanics, and aviation (DeFeo et al., 2014). Many Alaska Native corporations have established internships, scholarships, and shareholder-hire preferences intended to support workforce entry for all students (ANCSA Regional Association, 2022), and many industries in rural Alaska are looking to make local hires. State-funded Alaska performance scholarships dedicate CTE awards for top students seeking additional postsecondary training.

RURAL CAREER AND TECHNICAL EDUCATION PROGRAMS

What should school leaders in rural Alaska think about when reviewing existing CTE programs? Alaska has a statewide CTE plan that identifies several considerations:

Figure 5.3. Student with soldering iron, Tuyuryaq (Togiak), Alaska. *Courtesy of Emily Hendricks.*

FUNDING AND FACILITIES

Does your school have space, money, and equipment for modern CTE classes?

Don't despair here. Few schools in rural Alaska feature shops, up-to-date equipment, and comprehensive insurance. Some options for your students will be discussed in a moment. In the meantime, note that CTE does not necessarily require shop space; it's not all heavy equipment and diesel mechanics. Your school may be able to begin or expand coursework in health care, subsistence, resource management, business administration, or information technology without significant additional funding. If you can't immediately run a metal shop, find something else that could engage students, and start with what's possible in the short term.

Can you partner with community members, Tribes, or businesses? Can distance delivery provide your students access to CTE programs not possible on site? Can small investments over time build an inventory of equipment? Could your district support short- or long-term student travel to locations that have appropriate facilities? No matter what, you will need to work with your district. They have scale that simply isn't possible at the school level, and districts coordinate federal and state CTE funding, such as Perkins grants and residential program stipends.

CURRICULUM AND TRANSITIONS

Do school offerings align with current industry standards and local subsistence, employment, or training opportunities?

You want to make sure that your CTE programs are useful for graduates. Subsistence activities are deeply important and typically have broad community support and student interest. What do those practicing subsistence do for food and income? Is there a way to connect academic curriculum with subsistence activities in the region? You should also speak with tribal officials and representatives of regional and village Native corporations to identify relevant CTE offerings.

What are local employers looking for? You might be surprised by the range of businesses Alaska Native corporations manage. They operate a majority of the most valuable companies in Alaska (Alaska Business, 2020) and consistently win a broad range of government contracts in areas as diverse as tourism, construction, security, facilities management, and information technology. Virtually all regional and village corporations need more talent and have hiring preferences for shareholders. They want to hire your students, and many invest heavily in additional training and scholarships for young people via affiliated foundations.

You should also work with your district to support dual enrollment for students so they can earn college credit for CTE courses completed in high school. Although the paperwork may be a burden, the credit is absolutely worth it for students in terms of reduced tuition and credential progress. Earning college credits while in high school is particularly valuable for students who are the first in their families to go to college. Many students in rural Alaska assume they're not capable of success in college. Earning credits while in high school clearly communicates that they are, as well as having other benefits, such as increased achievement and graduation rates, higher college application and enrollment rates, lower debt, and faster degree completion if they do go to college (DeFeo & Tran, 2019). At the very least, try to ensure that one or more classes each year provides dual credit for students at the campuses your students are most likely to attend (e.g., University of Alaska, Alaska Pacific University, Iḷisaġvik College).

Here's what to look for when reviewing or developing CTE curricula at school:

1. *They expand knowledge of jobs.* Many students in rural Alaska don't have a clear sense of what jobs exist in the world. Most have been to the doctor at some point, so they may consider becoming a doctor or nurse as the only viable health careers. Yet there are dozens of jobs that require brief or on-the-job training. The Alaska Native Health Consortium, for example, regularly lists 20-plus different categories of

job postings, including certified nurse assistants and behavioral health aides, as well as positions in accounting, medical records, information technology, human resources, child care, and many more. Middle and high school students will benefit from exposure to the broad universe of possible work. They don't need to decide whether to be a nurse while they're in high school. Interest in health care should be enough to signal to them that the school will help them find what's out there. This means career exploration that begins in middle school and continues through graduation.

2. *They require career plans.* Many students would struggle if you asked them why they should work hard and graduate from high school. Because . . . they're supposed to? An important no-cost step you can take is to ensure that all students complete a personal learning and career plan. It matters less what the plan is—we all grow and change our minds—than that it exists and that it is connected to each individual student's interests and strengths. Students can set up an Alaska Career Information System (AKCIS) portfolio, take assessments, and explore careers and training opportunities as early as middle school. Students who know why they are doing things and where they want to go are much more likely to invest and persevere through challenges.

3. *They partner with organizations.* Many jobs require relatively brief technical training or internships, and employers or foundations often cover training costs for those willing. Rural Alaska schools can't provide training or certifications in dozens of possible career fields, but they can partner with those who do. A good first point of contact is your district; connect with the CTE director or coordinator, and learn what options exist. Questions to ask include the following: Where is our regional training center, and what do they offer? What's our local University of Alaska campus (UA operates multiple rural and community colleges) or contact at Iḷisaġvik College? What options are there for job training or apprenticeships through the state, Alaska Native corporations, or other programs?

4. *Think local.* Students from rural Alaska can be successful anywhere, but their odds are best if they're not required to abandon everything familiar to them to pursue training or careers. Pushing students to attend four-year colleges or programs in urban settings can backfire. Students who move away from home invariably face cultural adjustments, loneliness, or financial pressures, and they may find faraway programs conflict with family or subsistence needs. Families, intending love and support, may tell them that they can just come home. Finding bridges between lives in rural Alaska and education or career goals is deeply important. This might mean students should start with

online training (e.g., through the University of Alaska's eCampus) or short-duration programs. One of the best bridges for rural students is Alaska's community college system. Many are part of the University of Alaska system; Alaska also has an independent community and Tribal college, Iḷisaġvik College in Utqiaġvik. Local campuses often tailor offerings to the cultures, languages, and needs of rural Alaska students and employers.

5. *Hire the right teachers.* Many CTE programs in rural Alaska run CTE courses as add-ons to the responsibilities of teachers certified in other areas. This is a disservice. Although the challenges of finding qualified teachers are real, your district can hire teachers who don't have bachelor's degrees but do have vocational or technical experience (via Type M Limited certificates). Although hiring is usually up to district offices, you can help your district understand site needs, and you may be able to influence job postings. You can also help current teachers by providing professional development that expands their CTE knowledge and skills. Any of your teachers can grow in a CTE field; don't forget that CTE is much broader than "shop class." CTE includes graphic design, natural resources, technology, arts, finance, and a range of fields that your teachers may already be familiar with or interested in. The Alaska Association for Career and Technical Education operates an annual conference and provides ongoing remote-delivery professional development for teachers, and the Alaska Department of Education & Early Development has a program administrator and resources that can support all schools.

Don't despair if your school or district has limited CTE offerings at the moment. Over the last two decades, a broad array of creative, accessible CTE programs has developed across Alaska. Although the constraints on offerings in rural schools are real (you may never have a welding shop), your students are likely to have access to excellent CTE programs at little to no cost. Your best approach is to reach out to colleagues on a regular basis and to regularly share program information with your students and staff.

Below is a brief history of the development of today's CTE programs in Alaska from former Alaska commissioner of education Jerry Covey, who also taught in Katyaaq (Kiana) and Laugviik (Kobuk) and served as superintendent in Qikiqtaġruk (Kotzebue):

When the rural school districts were created in 1976, we had students who were coming from all these residential programs that the state and the Bureau of Indian Affairs had. And there was a big flurry of building schools. And in Kiana, where I first spent two years, that high school was built with a shop in it, as were most all of them at that time. These schools, they might have been able to have a small woodshop, and we had all kinds of things . . . but there were plywood floors! You couldn't have everything you'd want. For example, we had to have welding outside.

Districts learned over the course of years that it's really hard in these small schools to provide quality programs. They don't have specialized teachers for art and vocational education. We were trying to hire Voc-Ed (*Ed.*: CTE) teachers and we just couldn't staff up. And if we did hire them, there wasn't really enough for them to do. They wound up teaching other subject areas that they weren't prepared for. We either had a Voc-Ed teacher that wound up teaching the general curriculum, or we had a general curriculum teacher that wound up teaching Voc-Ed. And we weren't getting anywhere—we weren't preparing students to enter the workforce.

Then, in the early 1990s, we had the Galena Air Force base close down. The school district (Galena City School District) had a very entrepreneurial superintendent at the time; one of the things he did was [he] made plans with the Air Force to take over that facility and start a vocational high school. So Galena opened as a residential program and began attracting students. At that time, superintendents didn't like it much at all, because they were losing students and losing money every time their students went there. But it kind of opened the door. And following that, Nenana and Nome successfully wrangled enough money to build small residential facilities to house rural students. Nome set up a program with Bering Strait School District [and] the Northwest Alaska Career and Technical Education Center, which started offering short-term, two-, and three-week long programs. Students could come multiple times. And Chugach School District bought a house in Anchorage, and started bringing in students, not so much for CTE, but just for additional academic and life-skill experiences: how to succeed in the city, and so on. What we saw over a period of about 15 years was several rural districts establishing a variety of CTE programs. And then we started seeing the short-term programs, like NACTEC [Northwest Alaska Career and Technical Center] and Kotzebue and Chugach, making their programs available to other school districts, and sharing students back and forth. If you were interested in certain things and you were a Chugach student, you could go to Kotzebue for three weeks and live in their dorm. And there was reciprocity. The school districts didn't charge each other. So that expanded opportunities. And then you had Lower Yukon School District, who built this connection with Anchorage School District with its own twist. Students are in for a semester, and they go to King Career Center (in the Anchorage School District).

What we have now in Alaska is a network of long- and short-term programs, residential programs. And if you look at Galena, Nenana, LKSD [Lower Kuskokwim School District], Bering Strait, Northwest Arctic, Kuspuk, Chugach, Lower Yukon . . . this is all driven by need. It's not a top-down thing, it's a bottom-up thing. And I think it's viable because you have these centers that you can't duplicate. No school district can afford to put these in every village. No school district can hire experts for every village.

I remember talking to a couple of students in Kotzebue who took a two-week program in culinary arts. They were about 15 years old, these boys. They were so fired up about culinary arts! They just couldn't wait to graduate and come back to the tech center and get the training and go to work on the Slope. I mean, it was exciting!

If you really want to prepare your students for further education or jobs or careers, you have to take them to the program. And some of these programs are really sophisticated programs. I mean, they're not just going through the motions, they're really doing the job. Students are leaving with marketable skills. And CTE educators become very adept at helping these students transition from a small village for the first time into a residential setting and developing skills to succeed. They're very adept at knowing who's struggling, who is not, and providing the resources internally to support them. They're doing a really good thing. I think it's become a very critical part of our public education system. And it's available to anyone. Our job is to educate students. And part of educating students is providing them with CTE skills, but it's also providing them with life skills.

CTE CAREER CLUSTERS AND SUBSISTENCE

Some of the most popular and useful CTE programs in rural Alaska emphasize skills relevant for subsistence activities, from emergency medicine or navigation to small engine repair or marine science. Unfortunately, there is not yet a single subsistence career pathway in Alaska. Part of the reason is bureaucratic. CTE programs in Alaska typically rely on federal Carl D. Perkins funding, and as a result, they must comply with expenditure and reporting requirements. The US Department of Education describes 16 CTE "career clusters" for students, all of which are geared toward the market economy. For example, although fishing appears in the Agriculture, Food, and Natural Resources Systems cluster, the standards are clearly focused on wage labor; for example, essential skills standard ESS02.11 (exhibit public relations skills to increase internal and external customer/client satisfaction) and standard ESS09.04 (maintain a career portfolio). Does subsistence fishing involve "public relations skills" or a "career portfolio"? No.

So how can schools include subsistence activities in a recognized career cluster that meets requirements? The A-CHILL program is one example of how to do this. The program focuses on veterinary science and meets Alaska and federal requirements (career cluster: Agriculture, Food, and Natural Resources) by having academic standards, a four-year plan of study, multiple entry and exit points for students, and recognized postsecondary credentials (college credit-bearing courses in veterinary technology and science). Throughout the A-CHILL program subsistence skills and traditional knowledge are interwoven explicitly, including via credit-bearing coursework for middle and high school students focusing on local history, time spent with Elders, and dog mushing and husbandry in Alaska.

Your district will need to gain approval from the Alaska Department of Education & Early Development (DEED) to offer such a tailored program, and DEED has forms for such things. Tackling the paperwork to do so may seem daunting, but the chance to link subsistence with academic, cultural, and employability standards through engaging courses and activities is too important to ignore. You will need to identify a "recognized postsecondary credential" toward which a subsistence-focused career pathway would aim. Many are viable; you can review skills assessments DEED recognizes here: https://education.alaska.gov/tls/cte/perkins/Public/TsaList. And you can review the credentials most in demand in Alaska here: https://credentialsmatter.org. A subsistence career pathway leading to an EMT/paramedic license (no. 9 credential earned among CTE concentrators in Alaska in 2021), for example, could be broadly useful in rural Alaska *and* for the labor market.

You will need to be efficient in staffing CTE courses; DEED recommends rural districts consider stacking CTE courses (i.e., offer a single instructional period containing students of different skill levels who may be working on different courses). For curricula, the district may be able to help, or dual enrollment (especially through Alaska's community colleges) may support students in the upper grades.

Whatever you do, *do something*. If only 30% of Alaska's workforce has a bachelor's degree, that means the vast majority of Alaskans are working, living, and paying bills without a four-year degree. CTE programs are one of the most powerful means schools have of preparing students for family, community, and subsistence living *and* for pursuit of postsecondary opportunities.

CTE AND SUBSISTENCE: 10 THINGS YOU CAN DO FOR FREE AND/OR CHEAP

1. *Learn about subsistence practices* with Elders or tribal officials. Ask, What are the most valued skills and knowledge among adults in the community? And how can we recognize and credit the academic skills involved?
2. *Invite local people to share* local history, traditions, or subsistence knowledge or skills throughout the year. Provide food/coffee and compensate community members who share time and knowledge. You will need job descriptions and a hiring process; grant funding can simplify payments.
3. *Contact the bilingual and/or cultural education leader* in your district. Ask, What's one way the school can more regularly teach and reinforce cultural knowledge and skills?

4. *Identify industries, Native corporations, and employers* in your school's region. Invite representatives to visit your school or discuss needed skills or qualifications. Ask corporations and foundations about post-secondary training and scholarships for your students.
5. *Contact the district CTE leader* to identify opportunities for students. Ask, Which of the 16 career clusters do we offer (https://careertech.org/career-clusters), and how can we adapt these clusters to this region? How can students apply to CTE programs in or beyond this region? Advertise and encourage student applications regularly.
6. *Explore opportunities to partner* with other programs in Alaska. A good starting point could be exploring opportunities for students to do short-term (two- to three-week) residencies or exploring distance-delivered opportunities. See programs list in this chapter.
7. *Offer at least one dual-enrollment course* annually. There are small fees for credits, which are absolutely worth it. You will need to work with your district to make this happen, whether via distance delivery to school or by using existing credentialed staff at school.
8. *Consider expanding CTE options* by doing paperwork. Identify a CTE cluster aligned with local subsistence priorities, and start the DEED-approval process with your district. You need standards, curriculum, and an earned credential (https://education.alaska.gov/cte/curriculum). Many clusters require little additional overhead (i.e., clusters in education and training, government and public administration, and information technology).
9. *Hire student workers.* Most common are office/administrative interns or tutors for younger students. A class or club might open a before- or after-school store or run concessions at games, or teachers can put students to work on a web page about local people that is linked to an Alaska history class. Do the process: hire, train, give responsibility, and pay. As with compensating local people, you'll need a job description, hiring process, and oversight.
10. *Ensure students complete the following:*
    ◦ AKCIS career plan (starting in fifth grade): https://acpe.alaska.gov/PLANNING/AKCIS
    ◦ WorkKeys assessment (junior/senior year): https://workkeyscurriculum.act.org
    ◦ Free Application for Federal Student Aid (fall of senior year): https://acpe.alaska.gov/FINANCIAL-AID/The-FAFSA
    ◦ Alaska Student Aid Portal application (senior year): https://acpe.alaska.gov/FINANCIAL-AID
    ◦ Alaska Native Corporation/Foundation support application(s) (senior year)

ALASKA NATIVE SCIENCE AND ENGINEERING PROGRAM

ANSEP began in 1995 as a scholarship program for University of Alaska students. The goal of the program was not necessarily CTE or subsistence education, but rather "to effect systemic change in the hiring patterns of Alaska Natives in science and engineering by placing our students on a career path to leadership."

Since 1995, ANSEP has grown substantially. It now includes partnerships with multiple school districts and a range of summer and school-year opportunities for students in grades K–12. ANSEP supports Indigenous students in earning college credits, navigating the university system, developing student skills, and adjusting to life away from home, while promoting engaging, hands-on science, technology, engineering, and mathematics (STEM) projects and coursework.

I mention ANSEP here not as a one-stop solution for a lack of CTE or subsistence programming in rural Alaska schools but because their programming has consistently highlighted applied fields for Indigenous students for many years. Their track record is strong; ANSEP graduates from rural Alaska have gone on to leadership roles in Alaska's oil and gas industries, as well as in natural resource management, construction, health care, government, and education. One appealing aspect of ANSEP is that it explicitly prepares students for independent living in university and urban environments, which for many rural Alaska students will be entirely new experiences. Former commissioner of education Jerry Covey commented on the role ANSEP has played for rural Alaska students over the years:

> I remember talking to one young guy, he was a high school senior, and he was just finishing up. And he said—he was from the Lower Kuskokwim School District, "My high school had two rooms in it. And there were six of us . . . I'd been there for two years, and I just had to say to myself, What do I want for my future?" He'd been going to ANSEP summer programs, and he said, "I'll never get out of here if I don't do something." So he *did* something. And, you know, here's this student, years later, he's on his way to becoming an engineer. The world opened up because of that. When people create that kind of opportunity, I think it has to be appreciated and recognized.
>
> I was talking to some [ANSEP] folks once, and they said, "Our students don't have homework on weekends. On Fridays we review what was taught during the week and make sure all students understand it. If any students did not get some of the content, we work with them to make sure they understand it before they leave for the weekend."

Well, just think what's it teaching students. It's teaching them that content matters, that it matters to get your work done. It matters to be knowledgeable. It matters to help other people. It matters to not leave anyone behind. All of those things. What a model! When you think of that, it's pretty impressive.

LAST THOUGHTS

How can school leaders in rural Alaska start improving CTE programs in the next week, month, or year? A last word from Jerry Covey:

> I think the starting point is to make strong connections with programs. If you look at Northwest Arctic, all those students can access these two-week programs in Kotzebue. Every secondary student in the district knows that they can go into Kotzebue for two weeks and stay in this dorm with other students from their village, and they can access a whole number of things. And then they can do a two-week dip into IT, if that's their thing. And they can go back multiple times and explore different career fields. This type of exploration creates the mindset that it's good to explore. And support that! That's the time to try things out! And so, I think for school leaders, I'd build strong connections with district programs that have CTE opportunities.
>
> You'll see these programs trade students back and forth too. Chugach will send students up to Kotzebue [who] have never been in the Arctic before. They'll go up there for a couple of weeks, they get to dip into their programs, and Northwest will send students down [to Chugach]. And all of a sudden, you've got students camping, shee fishing in the spring, catching giant fish through the ice . . . I mean, all these opportunities, and [these students have] never been north of Fairbanks, probably, in their lives. And so, you create all of these things where students get these connections. It just lights them up! And why shouldn't it? Why wouldn't it?

TAKEAWAYS

- Schools should integrate subsistence knowledge and skills into the general academic program for all students.
- Schools should provide CTE opportunities to all students.
- Schools should provide dual-credit coursework to secondary students.
- Alaska has a broad network of vibrant CTE programs for students available at no or modest cost to districts.
- Schools should ensure students complete career plans and apply for post-secondary training and financial aid.

RESOURCES (GENERAL)

- Alaska Commission on Postsecondary Education (including AKCIS [Alaska Career Information System]): https://acpe.alaska.gov/planning
- Alaska Department of Labor (AVTECH, performance Scholarship, apprenticeships): https://labor.alaska.gov
- University of Alaska (contacts, career pathways, and overview of dual enrollment): www.alaska.edu/research/wd/de.php

MIDDLE AND HIGH SCHOOL PROGRAMS

- Alaska EXCEL (Consortium of Iditarod, Kashunamiut, Kuspuk, Lower Kuskokwim, North Slope, Yukon Koyukuk, and Yupiit School Districts): https://alaskaexcel.org
- Alaska Gateway School District (Aurora Schedule—students from outlying schools travel to Tok for two-week elective / CTE programming): www.agsd.us
- Alaska Technical Center (Northwest Arctic Borough School District): www.nwarctic.org/atc
- Bristol Bay Regional Career and Technical Education (BBRCTE) Program (Consortium of Bristol Bay Borough, Lake and Peninsula, Southwest Region, and Dillingham City School Districts): https://bbrcte.org
- Galena Interior Learning Academy (Galena City School District): www.galenaalaska.org/gila
- Kusilvak Career Academy (Lower Yukon School District and Anchorage School District): https://lysd.org/kusilvak-academy
- Nenana Student Living Center (Nenana City School District): www.nenanalynx.org/page/living-center
- Northwestern Alaska Career and Technical Center (Nome City School District and Bering Strait School District): www.nacteconline.org
- University of Alaska (Dual-enrollment/college-credit programs for high school students): www.alaska.edu/research/wd/de.php
- Voyage to Excellence (Chugach School District): vte.chugachschools.com

POSTSECONDARY PROGRAMS

- Alaska Apprenticeship Training Coordinators Association (clearinghouse of union-sponsored trade apprenticeships, many available to high school students): https://aatca.org/
- Alaska Technical Center (Northwest Arctic Borough School District): www.nwarctic.org/atc

- Amundsen Educational Center (faith-based vocational center in Soldotna with a focus on construction; financial aid and housing available): www.aecak.org
- AVTECH (state-sponsored vocational training school in Seward, offers short- and long-term programs across a variety of trades; financial aid and housing available): https://avtec.edu/
- Iḷisaġvik College (Tribal college in Utqiaġvik, offers broad array of CTE programs, financial aid, and housing): www.ilisagvik.edu
- Northwestern Alaska Career and Technical Center (Nome City School District and Bering Strait School District): http://www.nacteconline.org/
- Partners for Progress in Delta (state-sponsored workforce development center in Delta Junction): www.partnersforprogressindelta.org
- Southwest Alaska Vocational and Education Center (state-sponsored workforce development center in King Salmon): www.savec.org
- Yuut Elitnaurviat (nonprofit in the Yukon-Kuskokwim region, offers culturally relevant vocational training programs for recent high school graduates): https://yuut.org

Chapter 6

Teaching Through Culture

Abby Qirvan Augustine

Skip and Barbara Winslow, a recently married young and adventurous couple, arrived in Imangaq (Emmonak) in the 1970s to stay for a week during the summer as part of their teacher preparation. They had been in Fairbanks for six weeks through the Rural School Project, taking courses in anthropology and English as a second language, and they'd been listening to experienced teachers who had taught in rural Alaska.

On that first summer day in Imangaq, an Elder, Maacuar (Mary Trader), delivered to the Winslows a wheelbarrow full of salmon. The couple was touched! Elder Maacuar ran home to get her *uluaq* (traditional woman's knife) to show them how to cut the fish to store in the freezer. They observed. They listened. They learned.

Once settled, determined to connect with the community, Skip and Barbara participated in local Yup'ik dancing with support from good friends. This meant practicing nightly, especially when it came closer to the weekend of the annual winter potlatch. Skip and Barbara can be seen dancing in an award-winning ethnographic documentary, *Uksuum Cauyai: The Drums of Winter* (https://vimeo.com/ondemand/drumsofwinter). It was directed by Leonard Kamerling and Sarah Elder and filmed when young new dancers were presented to dance in public, a traditional practice among the Yup'ik.

The respected Imangaq dance leader at the time, the late Cakicenaq Stanley Waska, had given Barbara his own deceased daughter's Yup'ik name, Tatung'aq. In her loving memory, he also carved an *ipuun* (wooden ladle) for Barbara. In appreciation, Barbara recalls making *akutaq* (Eskimo ice cream) for him. Barbara also learned how to sew skins, like her *atkuk* (parka), *qaspeqs* (cloth covering for parkas), and *piluguk* (mukluks), which she found challenging. Knitting gloves and socks and crocheting were also crafty ways to pass time while Skip was out hunting. The newlyweds continued to observe, listen, and learn. They were respectful. They built lifelong relationships with community members.

Skip recalled once traveling during the winter in minus-52-degree temperatures. He was happy to be learning critical survival skills taught by local experts. During one outing on the flat tundra near Qip'ngayak (Black River), he learned how observant hunters had to be, which included knowing the direction the grass would fall during the first storm. Joe Cikigaq Gregory, another local resident and Skip's hunting partner, said that if Skip ever got disoriented, he should dig in the snow and feel the direction of the fallen grass for better directional guidance.

After a long day, men took fire baths. Skip recalled how he was invited for the traditional fire bath in a *qasgiq* (men's communal house). Skip's wife said he would come home dirtier because of the soot from the walls! Skip added that he'd learned so much during these times and felt like he learned more than he taught.

Thankfully, much has been learned from the days of boarding schools, where the background of the students and their cultures were not considered for instruction. The Winslows, on the other hand, excelled in teaching through culture, without (perhaps) even realizing that's what they were doing. They simply were respectful, and they listened, observed, learned, and grew.

In the boarding school days, students were treated quite differently, without regard for their backgrounds, cultures, traditions, and rituals. Students were removed from their villages, communities, and families without regard for their emotional well-being, then sent to schools far from home, often outside Alaska. Students were strangers to the land, the community, and each other. These students did not have the support systems necessary to guide them and lend them assistance when confusion arose, loneliness set in, or challenges presented themselves. Instead, these students had to figure it out on their own; many failed. Many returned home. Few moved on to higher education.

Boarding school experiences for students from rural Alaska (these lasted through the 1970s) were mostly an indoctrination, an attempt at assimilating students into Western worldviews, ways of learning, and lifestyles. Boarding schools emphasized the teacher-driven methodology of stand and deliver rather than observe, listen, and learn, showing little regard for the students' learning styles and backgrounds. The curriculum contained content based upon a worldview very different from that of Indigenous peoples, and very little content was connected to the students. Basically, they relied on Western methods of teaching, which were in stark contrast to natural, Indigenous ways of learning.

Boarding schools did not just fail students, they also left many of those same students scarred for life (see the first chapter for a brief overview). Beyond the physical abuse, which was rampant, the schools were never designed to meet the needs of young people from rural Alaska. No culturally responsive teaching strategies were used, no Indigenous worldviews were considered, and certainly no Indigenous ways of knowing were discussed. Students never heard nor were allowed to use their home languages. It was a miserable time for learners in these culturally barren environments.

Luckily for students in Imangaq, the boarding school era in Alaska ended in the late 1970s, following the 1976 *Tobeluk v. Lind* consent decree, often called the Molly Hootch decree. Molly Hootch was a 16-year-old student from Imangaq who sued the state of Alaska for its failure to provide local high schools in rural Alaska.

Under the tutelage of the Winslows, who used a natural approach based on knowing their students, the community, and the place in which they lived, students in Imangaq thrived and loved learning and being active in sports. Respect and reciprocity go a long way in instruction, as does honoring both the value systems and beliefs of the local people.

The Winslows gave back. In line with their reciprocity and respectful approach to belonging within the community (one which honors the beliefs and value systems of the local people), Skip and Barb encouraged new teachers to get out and not be afraid to welcome new experiences, like trying traditional foods. Skip, an avid outdoorsman, found time to hunt seals, game, and fish when invited. Cakicenaq's son, Raymond Iraluq Waska, loaned Skip a used *nuqaq* (throwing board to propel a dart). Skip was left-handed and wasn't comfortable with it, so Iraluq carved him one designed for left-hand use. Teaching through culture starts with listening, learning, and building relationships.

Skip and Barbara were genuinely interested in being involved and building relationships with their Yup'ik community. They became part of the village and participated in community events in addition to making learning challenging and fun for students like me. Barbara was my fourth-grade teacher, and Skip was my sixth- and seventh-grade teacher. One memory I have is when I was wondering what souvenir to send to my pen pal, and Skip suggested I send a seal whisker. I thought that was very clever, and I appreciated that he was accepting of my culture.

Another is when I was in sixth grade, Skip shared with me that he had confidence I could make it through college, something I hadn't thought of before. His encouragement really sparked an interest. I graduated from college, receiving both my undergraduate and graduate degrees in education, and taught for 27 years! His believing in me and sharing that belief in me was powerful. Having high expectations for all students is key for them to

Figure 6.1. Yup'ik values, Togiak School, Tuyuryaq (Togiak), Alaska. *Courtesy of Emily Hendricks.*

grow, learn, and succeed. It begins with knowing your students. Building on the relationships he had made in the community, Skip saw our individual potential, believed in each of us, and encouraged us in life. Skip cared about our futures, and we knew that. We cared about him.

While in Imangaq, the Winslows helped organize what was then called the Eskimo Olympics. This event involved academic and sports competitions, including wrestling and cheerleading, with nearby schools. When Skip and Barbara moved to Kuiggluk (Kwethluk), Barbara organized a music band, and Skip supported wrestlers who would travel to competitions and stay with host families in California, Washington, and Oregon. The Winslows were reciprocal in their learning and teaching, exposing our Yup'ik students to other ways of living while, at the same time, embracing and respecting Yup'ik lifestyles. Reciprocity is essential for showing respect for communities in rural Alaska. There are many ways to give back; you simply need to decide how to make that happen.

One year the Winslows and a handful of other teachers and administrators in the Yukon-Kuskokwim Delta organized and managed a student leadership camp that ran for three weeks during the summer, Camp Nu-Na-Hak, on a lake in Wasilla, Alaska. This experience allowed students from rural Alaska to experience urban Alaska, where they learned the ways of the city, such as ordering food from a restaurant and going to movie theaters on trips to Dgheyaytnu (Anchorage). Students from within the Yukon-Kuskokwim Delta became lifelong friends, and some would become leaders later in life. Part of the aim of Camp Nu-Na-Hak was to support students in engaging with and adjusting to urban Alaska. These experiences were important for students from villages in order to lessen their culture shock and increase their comfort when traveling from their rural homes into cities.

Long before "teaching through culture" became the popular educational phrase it is today, there were respectful non-Indigenous teachers building relationships, learning about the place they lived, and using that newly gained knowledge to respectfully teach in rural Alaska. Skip and Barbara Winslow were such a couple. Today "teaching through culture" and "culturally responsive teaching" have their own pedagogical frameworks, along with many publications. Teachers and leaders new to the profession and new to rural Alaska are learning how to connect lessons to students and places. For Barbara and Skip in the 1970s, teaching through culture was listening first, building relationships with the community, respecting all people they met and lifestyles they experienced, and getting involved by doing. Then they gave back by authentically teaching through culture before it was ever labeled as a powerful approach to pedagogy.

Skip and Barbara Winslow left the Yukon-Kuskokwim Delta nearly 50 years ago. Yet whenever people who knew them mention their names today, they speak of them with high regard. Skip and Barbara certainly stir very happy memories of younger schooling years for many former students, including me. Thankfully, through social media, this couple has been able to reconnect with many of us Yupiit, including the children and grandchildren of those who are not here anymore. What a difference thoughtful, caring teachers can make!

PLACE-BASED TEACHING STRATEGIES

One culturally responsive teaching strategy is labeled "place-based" for obvious reasons. The curriculum is designed to connect to the place where it is being delivered. Teachers must spend time learning about the place where they live and teach and then create lessons connected to that place so students can better comprehend the lessons being taught. Place-based teaching is all about connecting teaching and content to students and place.

In "A Formula for Success," Eva Rivera Lebrón (2021) shares how teaching using a place-based approach builds on our students' cultural knowledge and personal backgrounds. Place-based teaching can be valuable for students' academic, social, and emotional development. The Alaska Rural Systemic Initiative (AKRSI)—a decade-long partnership (1995–2005) between the Alaska Federation of Natives, the University of Alaska, and the Alaska Department of Education & Early Development—sought to do just that in rural Alaska schools. An article about AKRSI by Dr. Emeka Emekauwa

Figure 6.2. Post office and community building, Qalirneq (Koliganek). *Courtesy of Emily Hendricks.*

praised "a new type of education that was place-based, culturally responsive, academically rigorous and capable of propelling the achievement of Native children" (2004). AKRSI codirectors Frank Hill, Angayuqaq Oscar Kawagley, and Ray Barnhardt concluded the following in their final project report:

> The educational reform strategy we have chosen—to foster connectivity and complementarity between the formal education system and the Indigenous knowledge systems in communities being served in rural Alaska—continues to produce an increase in student achievement scores, a decrease in the dropout rate, an increase in the number of rural students attending college, and an increase in the number of Native students choosing to pursue studies in fields of science, math and engineering. (2006, p. 5)

PLACE-BASED TEACHING IN IQUGMIUT (RUSSIAN MISSION)

Mae Pitka, a pre-K and kindergarten teacher in the Lower Yukon School District (LYSD) and a resident of Iqugmiut, shared that she included place-based education in her master's degree program. She credited LYSD's instructional leaders, including Mike Hull and Jason Moen, for this success. She wholeheartedly agreed that place-based education works with the support and involvement of the administration and community. The key is collaboration at many levels between school personnel and community members. This collaboration must be mutually respectful and genuine.

In her place-based lessons, Mae had students pick berries, go *manaq* (ice hooking for fish), and attend a local carnival. Photos were taken, and her students enjoyed writing about their experiences. Older students could attend both fall and winter camps. One history project the students enjoyed involved reading about their area, writing about it, and finding out what was available online about their Yup'ik culture. Mae and her students noted that online information can be limited because knowledge in Yup'ik culture is mostly shared verbally. Many Indigenous peoples have limited research resources available online due to their oral traditions, so it is important for educators in rural Alaska to recognize, acknowledge, and learn from the newness of the written history of people.

One of the aims of place-based learning in Iqugmiut was to engage students based on their backgrounds, as well as to help get them excited about academics. Teachers used a wide variety of materials, including ones for reading, writing, mathematics, science, Yup'ik, and social studies, in their lesson plans. Mae discovered that having Elders, the tribal council, the city, the church, parents, community members, and students meet together to create these place-based lessons was a great success! Having the whole community involved right from the beginning and seeing how their children were doing academically helped the entire community become educational stakeholders. It was a sight to witness! In a monthly newsletter article, principal Mike Hull (2002) shared:

> It is gratifying to see young people excited about what they are doing. It is even more special to see young people excited about who they are. Perhaps the community of Russian Mission has come to acknowledge the value of school because the school has come to acknowledge the value of the local heritage.

Place-based teaching builds on many existing philosophies, from Dewey's experiential learning to Montessori's "meet them where they are" beliefs and Freire's critical thinking. In addition to what these proven methods do, place-based teaching engages students by connecting learning to place and students. Place-based teaching, which can be uniquely powerful in rural Alaskan contexts, connects lessons to local geography, the region, the village, and the people, including their history and cultures. These connections engage students, enrich their learning, and make new content much more understandable. One approach for place-based teaching that has worked in a variety of rural Alaska schools is the development of a subsistence calendar that plans academic instruction around seasonal subsistence activities.

SUBSISTENCE AND ORTHODOX-ADAPTED CALENDARS (BY NITA YURRLIQ PRINCE REARDEN)

Each of the 54 school districts throughout Alaska develops a school calendar that includes a certain number of count days for student contact time as well as in-service days. In some cases, schools that involve students in subsistence activities with their educators count those days as learning or educational opportunity times as well. However, school calendars in Alaska have long been based on Western perspectives, which includes required student attendance during the fall, winter, and spring, along with a long summer break.

In rural Alaska, subsistence lifestyles demand work throughout the year that depends upon the food being gathered. Communities (including students) have often been forced to choose between subsistence activities and school, an unfair dilemma. Why not develop a school calendar more responsive to subsistence? After all, people in rural Alaska villages are learning year-round, every minute of every day; learning is not compartmentalized into a tidy group of academic months built around Western schedules.

One example can be found in the Lake and Peninsula School District, which adopted a 160-day subsistence calendar in 2017 (Hamilton, 2017). The calendar, which includes extended school days from early September through early May, is organized around the subsistence activities of the local people. It allows students to learn with their family members in the fall while fishing, hunting, and gathering berries. The calendar saves money for the district on expenses, promotes student engagement and learning, and respects local ways of living.

Many Indigenous peoples live a subsistence life throughout the year. Such a life includes gathering food, edible and nonedible medicinal plants, wood, and water for drinking and other uses. School calendars should be shared in the local Indigenous languages and become part of community life. Each region is different as to what takes place: salmon arrive at different times, berries ripen at different times, and hunting seasons vary, though readers should understand that some subsistence activities like moose hunting are not always based on local-resource availability. Hunting and fishing are regulated by the state of Alaska and federal agencies, not by Tribes, and they are not necessarily in line with subsistence-living lifestyles.

In some regions, school calendars allow families to go camping and hunting in September, a week before or after Labor Day—in line with many subsistence lifestyles. Districts could schedule that time for teacher in-service or other professional work while students are out with their families (although this may present conflicts for employees who practice subsistence). Alternately, designated subsistence days could be an opportune time for teachers to go camping with their students while learning about the region. Note, though, that teachers new to Alaska or the region should only observe and should not assist with the hunting. There are rules to follow. Traditions. Teachers and school leaders can learn about their students who are out in the wilderness as well as about how local people do what they do.

Leaders can authentically engage communities in discussions about creating a subsistence calendar to guide academic decision making and all yearly events at the school. First, teachers need to observe in order to learn. Doing so is respectful and honors Indigenous ways of knowing.

> There are many villages where the Orthodox Church's Christmas, or Slaaviq, is celebrated. Because the Orthodox calendar includes Christmas Day on or near January 7, schools in these communities usually opt to resume their holiday breaks when Slaaviq is over. When building the yearly calendar, it makes sense to also determine whether or not the Orthodox Church Christmas is a part of the local community and should be given consideration.

Schools should include fall and spring subsistence activities as part of learning or "seat" time for both educators and students. What a great way to start the year in getting to know one another! Educators can integrate all content areas with cultural knowledge through the use of subsistence calendars. Teachers can plan lessons and refer to cultural events throughout the year. The yearly plan for instruction can only be strengthened if coordinated with a subsistence calendar.

CULTURAL STANDARDS

The Alaska Department of Education & Early Development has required that the Alaska Standards for Culturally Responsive Schools be included in teacher evaluations since 2015. School leaders in rural Alaska can support teachers (and learn themselves!) by arranging professional development on how to be culturally responsive in their classrooms. The most effective professional development will be in partnership with local people, who can help teachers understand how to respectfully help students meet cultural standards in each classroom. Teachers should learn how to engage students by connecting content to local culture, history, and regional values and belief systems. The cultural standards present great opportunities for teachers and administrators to learn about local cultures if they are done with respect, care, openness, and listening to Elders and other culture bearers.

It's also important to remember that rural Alaska villages need people with a wide range of different skills. Some of those skills are cooking; small-engine repair; electrical, carpentry, and construction work; record keeping; natural resources management; wildland fire prevention and response; technology; and aviation, to name a few. Career, technical, and subsistence education are discussed at length in a separate chapter; keep in mind that teaching through culture also means schools should offer courses and training in skills needed in rural Alaska. In smaller secondary schools sprinkled across rural Alaska, opportunities to learn and gain vocational training can be very limited. Steps you take to ensure that students have access to vibrant career, technical, and subsistence education opportunities can also support the broader goal of ensuring your school becomes more truly culturally responsive.

A HISTORY OF INDIGENOUS LANGUAGES AND ENGLISH

There have been varying degrees of language loss within different Indigenous groups in Alaska, and there are many reasons for this language loss, which is in part due to assimilation efforts during colonization. The Alaska Native Language Center at the University of Alaska Fairbanks has published a color-coded map, *Indigenous Peoples and Languages of Alaska* (www.uaf.edu/anla/collections/map); go order one if you don't have it on your wall already. The map depicts Alaska's diverse Indigenous language groups, showing their distributions in differing colors and shades. As beautiful as the map is, unfortunately, all of Alaska's Indigenous languages are now endangered (Alaska Native Language Preservation & Advisory Council [ANLPAC], 2022). This next section addresses some of the stories dealing with language loss, attempts at revitalizing Indigenous languages, and proposed next steps for addressing this most important issue.

A STORY ABOUT LANGUAGE LOSS

A personal story comes to mind whenever I speak of language loss. One winter during my Christmas holiday break from my Yup'ik language-immersion teaching position at Ayaprun Elitnaurvik in Mamterilleq (Bethel), I decided to take a public sauna in my home village of Imangaq, on the Yukon Delta. I recall one elderly lady and a couple of her young granddaughters were taking a sauna when she voluntarily began sharing her reason for never speaking in Yup'ik to her grandchildren.

She had gone to Akulurak (a Catholic mission school and orphanage), where she had experienced trauma by the Ursuline Sisters whenever she spoke her Native tongue, Yup'ik. Her mental anguish was so strong that she vowed to herself that she would never speak Yup'ik to her grandchildren so that they wouldn't experience the same negative effects. I respected this Elder, and I just listened with horror at what she wanted to express. I respected her and so did not want to add to her grief by questioning her decision. She was determined with her decision. Later I wished I'd had a chance to visit with her more and ask about her experiences.

On social media one of my friends shared that she wished to learn to speak her Yup'ik language, Nunivak Cup'ig. Many of her social media friends chimed in with a few suggestions. Among the comments there was one response that sounded familiar to the elderly lady's experience shared during our sauna. One young lady expressed her hatred of the trauma that kept her from learning her language from her grandmother. That sentence struck me because I thought she'd be angry with her grandmother for not teaching her their language. Instead, she was angry at the trauma her grandmother had experienced.

During the first decades of contact between Indigenous peoples and non-Indigenous newcomers, the federal government contracted with religious groups to be in charge of schools. Missionary schools had the explicit aim of promoting Christianity and their ideas of "civilization" among Indigenous populations. For many rural communities in Alaska, this was their first exposure to formal schooling and sustained attempts by missionaries to replace Indigenous beliefs and value systems.

The trauma experienced by Indigenous peoples in Alaska as a result of boarding schools, colonization, assimilation attempts, Western educational pedagogy, and teachers lacking the knowledge to be culturally responsive is real, ongoing, and requires that specific steps be taken to stop the cycle. Leaders must make sure they and their staff all understand this trauma and that they secure the necessary professional development so schools can become knowledgeable and improve. Invite appropriate guest speakers, and have ongoing, open discussions about historical influences on Indigenous learners. It is essential that if we are to help students learn and grow, then the instructors must learn and grow first.

Language loss was real and significant; the number of speakers declined over the years as missionaries and government officials banned the speaking of Indigenous languages. Many Indigenous languages were lost completely, and the threats to Indigenous languages are not gone. As the 2022 ANLPAC report summarized, "every Indigenous language in Alaska faces threats from colonial English-only policies and practices, and all of them are endangered" (ANLPAC, 2022, p. 11).

In the early to mid-1970s, many Indigenous communities began to incorporate bilingual education into their schools, thinking that bilingual/bicultural programs could help preserve or revitalize Indigenous languages and cultural knowledge. However, there was little consistency among programs—and long-standing assimilationist cultures in schools remained. Whatever the stated goals of these bilingual programs were, students were often largely taught, assessed in, and rewarded for English and Western cultural proficiency. As a survey of Alaska's bilingual programs in 1975 noted, "many programs, particularly those in communities (with few language users), necessarily stretch most formal definitions of bilingual education to include native languages as subject matter rather than as mediums of instruction" (Orvik, 1975).

Whether advocates of these bilingual programs carried good or bad intentions, the outcomes were often indistinguishable from the age-old assimilation goals of English-only schools. This is a great example of miscommunication about education—one where community members advocated for programs they thought would revitalize Indigenous languages and cultures in schools—and where school officials have often failed to deliver.

LANGUAGE PROGRAMS FOR REVITALIZATION

Many areas of Alaska have seen the development of language preservation or revitalization programs, including language immersion programs. One of the longest-standing programs, in the Lower Kuskokwim School District, is Ayaprun Elitnaurvik, a K–6 Yup'ik immersion school in Mamterilleq (Bethel). Ayaprun Elitnaurvik was built on parent and community advocacy. In the early 1970s, when LKSD's "bilingual" program was just a half-day kindergarten program, parents on the Bethel Advisory School Board formed a committee that formally requested improved Yup'ik language programs, increased hours per week in Yup'ik, and that Yup'ik instruction be required for students in grades K–6. Over a period of 20 years, the sustained efforts of parents, teachers, and school leaders led to the opening of a K–6 Yup'ik immersion school in 1995: Ayaprun Elitnaurvik. The school shifted to charter school status in 1999, and it has since been operating as a K–6 Yup'ik immersion charter school. Students in the early grades were initially taught by teachers exclusively using Yup'ik; English was gradually added as an additional language as students progressed to the sixth grade. However, despite the district's best efforts, students were still leaving school in the late 1990s and early 2000s without being fully proficient in Yup'ik and English (Lower Kuskokwim School District, 2022).

A new approach was needed. Using a survey to consult with families, Gayle Miller, the previous director of academic programs, learned that most people wanted their children to be proficient in both languages, Yup'ik *and* English. This would require students to be dual language learners (DLL). After researching different DLL teaching models, Miller found a successful method from Texas had been discovered and was being used primarily with Spanish-speaking communities: the Gómez and Gómez dual language enrichment model. This scientifically based model was chosen by LKSD to promote effective learning using sheltered instruction observational protocols (SIOP); the program noted the following:

> The route to "academic English" and long-term achievement for DLLs is through a strong education in their native language and well-balanced and sequenced English instruction. Although instruction in [Indigenous languages] appears counter-intuitive to English language acquisition, it is the best route because it is focused on academic learning that involves cognitive and linguistic development and on-grade-level learning. (Gómez & Gómez, 2022)

Miller also mentioned that the schools that were excited about the model were doing better—namely, they had school and staff engagement. Many schools and programs in Alaska are at various stages along the way to immersion or dual language status (see www.alaskanativelanguages.org). It would seem there is much room for growth in the preservation and revitalization of Indigenous languages in rural Alaska and that this journey is still in its infancy.

School leaders in rural Alaska would be wise to work with communities to determine multiple ways for celebrating Indigenous speakers, sharing Indigenous language vocabulary within the school building, honoring all who learn and speak the local Indigenous languages, respecting the part Indigenous languages play in culturally responsive teaching, and bringing to the staff and community strategies for Indigenous language use.

COMMUNITY ENGAGEMENT/WELCOMING ELDERS AND OTHERS INTO SCHOOLS

Many teachers are not familiar with establishing a classroom environment that extends into the community. Welcoming climates and friendly school environments are key for successful teaching in rural Alaska, and leaders may need to facilitate this step for their staff. Such welcoming environments could be created in a variety of places, including classrooms and other spaces in school. Ask yourself: Are there places for guests? A designated "Elder's Corner" or rocking chair? Places of honor? There are many other ideas and questions to ask. How do you and your teachers keep your community advised of your school's events and classroom activities? How do you become involved in the community?

Ideas for creating welcoming environments include having professional photographs of locals posted in the school's hallways or offices, items labeled in local language(s) sprinkled throughout the school, and weekly, monthly, or special yearly events planned into the school calendar for celebrating villagers, especially Elders, perhaps on their birthdays. Can your school host a celebration for an Elder each month, involving all staff? It's an excellent idea to have free coffee and breakfast for any parents or Elders when they drop off kids in the morning. Feed everyone when you do parent conferences. And do the Pledge of Allegiance in the local language.

It is very important to learn the history of the village where you reside and to celebrate its accomplishments, local events, and history. Is there a place of recognition of the village located somewhere in your building? Do your staff know the history of where they are? How can you help facilitate their gaining such knowledge? What are the morning and afternoon routines at the school, and do they include using the language of the village?

The wise school leader will embed local ways of knowing into the daily routines of the school and make good use of every opportunity to use the local language. Welcome your community into your school, your daily routines, your planning, and your life, especially as a leader of their future generations. It is essential that your community members feel validated and welcomed, as well as a part of their children's education.

INTEGRATING NEW TEACHERS INTO COMMUNITIES

Reciprocity is often key in many Indigenous worldviews; as you create a welcoming climate and friendly environment for the community, they do the same for you. Many villages welcome their new teachers by hosting community potlucks where teachers can experience parts of the culture through tasting new foods or watching Yup'ik dance. Some new foods to experience for the newcomers may include smoke-dried salmon, seal oil, *akutaq* (Eskimo "ice cream" using local berries), herring eggs, half-dried/half-smoked salmon, whale, fried bread, moose, and caribou, to name a few.

During dances, community members gather in the community hall or the school gymnasium to warmly welcome the teachers and other staff. Attend these welcoming ceremonies and events; participate as the new leader for the school, there to educate the children. Model for your teachers exactly how important it is to be seen in the community and to participate in the reciprocal welcoming events, then help guide your teachers into hosting their own welcoming events within their classrooms. Reciprocity is a key ingredient to building relationships that matter. Show through your actions that the community and its people matter to the education of the children. Show through your actions that you care about them all.

CULTURE CAMPS

Some districts offer cultural immersion camps to familiarize new teachers with rural Alaska ways of life and values. One example is a project by the Alaska Humanities Forum that collaborates with three rural regions: North Slope, Northwest Arctic, and Southwest (www.akhf.org/ecci). It is important to note each of these regions is very different from one another. There is no such thing as a typical Indigenous person in Alaska, just as there is no such thing as a typical European or American. Diversity exists throughout and within each region of Alaska. It's important to learn the characteristics, history, and attributes of the region in which you lead and the village in which you live.

Calista Education and Culture has been hosting a successful culture camp for years now in Umkumiut, a traditional village near Nunakauyaq (Toksook Bay) in the Lower Kuskokwim School District (www.calistaeducation.org). The purpose of the camp has been to connect Indigenous youth to their cultures (both traditional and modern) and to connect them to their environment with subsistence hunting, fishing, and harvesting. New teachers are recruited to participate in these culture camps so the teachers can become immersed with the local traditional ways and gain better understandings of village life. Central to the camps are the Elders. Mark John, such an Elder, summed it up best when he said, "Our grandparents were our teachers. Whenever you give Elders the opportunity to step into their traditional role as teachers, they will take the role as they did centuries ago."

As the leader of a school, you should get to know your Elders, as they are the leaders of the community. Then together, Elder and school leader, build bridges between village and school. Discover the local protocols, embrace them, and, whenever possible, embed similar protocols within the school's routines. Honor and respect the local ways of knowing and learning, and help your teachers to do the same.

CEREMONIES AND TRADITIONS

By knowing local traditions and ceremonies, you can do a better job of teaching through culture and connecting state-mandated objectives to student backgrounds. Cultural connections engage students in ways that motivate

Figure 6.3. Teachers and paraprofessionals at culture camp near Uŋalaqłiit (Unalakleet).
Courtesy of the University of Alaska Fairbanks, K–12 Outreach.

them to learn. Lessons and content will make more sense if connected to student backgrounds, so it is essential to take the time to understand local ceremonies and traditions.

Some communities continue to observe annual celebrations such as Curukaq (potlatch), Yup'ik dance gatherings, and/or Slaaviq, the Orthodox Church's Christmas. Unfortunately, Yup'ik dance was suppressed in many communities over the years by different religions that aimed to eradicate Indigenous traditions. Moravian missions were established on Kusquqvak (the Kuskokwim River) in 1885, and the Catholic Church came a few years later, on Kuigpak (the Yukon River). These religions considered dance and the making of masks to be connected to shamanistic practices and forbid dancing altogether. Thankfully, starting in the late 1960s, Delta residents began to regain appreciation for traditional practices, including dance. Yup'ik dance came back from the brink of extinction, according to James H. Barker, a documentary photographer (Barker, 1993). Knowing this background will inform school leaders and teachers, and if incorporated into lessons, it will go a long way toward validating and affirming the history and past of the people. Such connections are respectful, informative, and key to building trust between the community and school.

Ceremonies and traditions can take up much of local people's time and will influence the life of the child and events at school. It is best to coordinate school events with community events so there are no conflicts for time, assignments, and participation. In villages that maintain annual potlatches, many community members participate, and neighboring villages are specially invited guests. First, Yup'ik dances are celebrated, which is a very special occasion for families, as they are presenting a new dancer to the community in a formal, traditional way. Usually, a new dancer is a child wearing new dance regalia that may include a *nasqurrun* (headdress), *piluguk* (mukluks), *tegumiak* (dance fan), *qaspeq*, a dance belt, arm fur bands made out of wolverine and wolf, and a seal skin to dance on, as well as, at times, a new parka. During potlatches or dance gatherings, dancers may begin Friday evenings and conclude on Sunday nights. Knowing the time involved in the gatherings, for some schools, teacher in-services could be planned the following Monday, after potlatches, so that students (as well as adults) have extra time to recuperate from a long, exciting weekend.

There are some teachers who also participate in and enjoy Yup'ik dancing, just as the Winslows did when they came to Imangaq so many years ago. Leaders can help affirm these celebrations by not scheduling conflicting testing, school events, or other requirements during these celebrations and traditional events. Teachers can embed activities that affirm and reinforce whatever is being celebrated. Collaboration among all stakeholders—community, parents, leaders, teachers, and students—in the planning and carrying out of these events is respectful and helpful, and it builds strong relationships between community and school. Everyone wins.

SUMMARY

This chapter on teaching through culture is designed to help rural Alaska school leaders better understand the importance culture and language play in the education of children in rural Alaska. Several Indigenous values have informed this chapter: respect, relationships, reciprocity, connections, listening, observing, and learning. Perhaps most important is the realization that Indigenous peoples have been successfully educating young people for thousands of years, and what matters most is that their children grow up to be happy, productive citizens of the world. As leaders in rural Alaska, we need to ask ourselves if we are doing everything possible to make sure that our actions support that goal.

TAKEAWAYS

- The history of education in rural Alaska must be learned by all teachers and leaders.
- Relationship building is at the heart of teaching through culture.
- Teaching and learning requires reciprocal relationships.
- Bilingual education can be a significant opportunity for schools in rural Alaska.
- Elders need to feel validated, welcomed, and recognized as contributing members of the school community.

Chapter 7

Academic Success

Leadership That Drives Change

Robert S. Thompson

Martha loved coming to school. She loved seeing her friends there. She loved her teachers and the other friendly adults. She liked getting to eat lunch with her friends. And she liked to work hard at lessons that teachers had carefully prepared for her. She was in the first grade at a school with 150 students in a remote part of northern Alaska. The school staff liked Martha too. She was a happy person, very polite and cooperative, and eager to try hard to do the work asked of her. Martha was pleasant and fun, and she had a supportive family that loved her.

At times, Martha had difficulty keeping up with her peers in learning to read, to understand numeracy, and to remember from day to day what she had been taught. School was fun, but the learning was difficult. With parental support and following many meetings with teachers, specialists, and administrators, Martha was referred for special education services. She was tested and qualified in reading and math for additional services. The school had an excellent, caring special education teacher, and the teacher and Martha got along extremely well. The learning was still hard, even when working one-on-one with the special education teacher.

Some of the other teachers at the school made private comments about Martha, such as "She has trouble remembering," "Martha probably suffers from fetal alcohol effects" (although there was no evidence for this), and "Kids like Martha need to be on a vocational track where they can be taught manual skills that will be useful to them."

As her school years progressed, Martha continued to work hard, with assistance. After thirteen years at the school, she proudly walked across the stage on graduation day and received her high school diploma. Parents, friends, community members, and teachers clapped and cheered for her.

Some educators in the audience, however, may have been thinking, "Martha will make a good housewife. She is such a pleasant person."

Well, Martha had other ideas. Within a couple of years of graduating, Martha decided to move to the larger community of Utqiaġvik. She moved in with friends and began taking classes online and in person at Iḷisaġvik College, just east of town. She was dedicated to her schoolwork and made steady progress. The years of persistence and assistance were paying off. Within a few years, Martha had earned a technical degree as a medical assistant.

Martha now works as a medical assistant in Utqiaġvik. She still lives with her friends and has not, in fact, become a housewife. She is happy and successful. She enjoys time with her family when she can and participates in many subsistence and cultural activities. Martha is an academic success.

ACADEMIC SUCCESS

So what is academic success? It is hard to measure, but, boy, do we try. There are hundreds of metrics attempting to show how successful a school might be. State and federal governments have laws requiring testing and complicated algorithms for ranking school success. These sources of data should never be overlooked. They can provide valuable information if you take the time to understand what they tell you and, sometimes even more importantly, what they don't tell you. However, no data can show the whole picture. There is much, much more to academic success than getting a proficient score on a state test.

Unfortunately, we tend to focus on what is easy to measure. Reading is the most vital skill taught in schools, and there are multiple ways to measure successful reading instruction. Academic goals for schools are often focused around improving reading scores for students. Enormous resources are poured into this effort annually. As they should be.

The numbers don't lie, but what do they tell you, and what do they not tell you? Can functional reading skills be enough for a successful life after school, or do all students need "grade level" reading skills? Functional reading skills can be defined as reading skills that enable each student to function well in life (as Martha did) and to be successful. You will not find a metric for that type of learning, but isn't the goal of empowering students to be successful in life something we should all strive to achieve? Students who leave school and have successful lives are true academic successes.

LIFE BEYOND SCHOOL

Success in life usually begins after a person leaves school. You go to school to be able to do something else. If that something else is driving a bulldozer, the skills required are specific and complicated. If that something else is working in a hospital lab, the skills required are enormously different yet still specific and complicated. In mostly Indigenous rural Alaska schools, there are also subsistence skills, traditional knowledge, and local languages to be learned. Is it your job as an instructional leader to prepare every student to be able to do all of these things? A more practical approach would be to prepare each student to be successful in their individual pursuits with an eye on their futures, as well as to let the community assist with those skills with which you are not familiar.

The teachers at Martha's school were good teachers. They cared about students and worked hard to enable them to be successful. They teamed up and always tried to do what was best for students. However, life beyond school is not predictable. Understanding why Martha was successful, although she was not "proficient" on grade-level assessments, can be a useful lesson.

The reasons for student success, such as Martha's, are complex and involve many interrelated elements. Teachers and administrators who never give up on a student and constantly strive to get each student to reach their potential are key. Instilling attributes such as perseverance and attention to detail in students can be just as important as pedagogy. Celebrating success at each stage of learning can create motivated and confident learners. Involving local people, especially in a rural Indigenous community, can contribute greatly to the overall effort. Maybe most important is creating opportunities for a student to be successful every step of the way, with a coherent progression of learning. Schools do not need to set predetermined levels of academic "proficiency," but they should support all students in reaching the highest levels possible.

Rick Luthi, an administrator with Lake and Peninsula School District, says that if we truly want to know if a school is successful at educating its students, we need to know what happens to those students after they leave the school. It's not easy to know. After graduation, students disappear to places unforeseen, whether it's next door or halfway around the world. What if you had information on lives beyond the school? How would that change your priorities? Given good data on the postgraduation lives of students—training or education, jobs, volunteer or other community service, or marriage and family lives—what would you do differently? Such data would definitely better inform you about the success of the school's academic programs than test scores alone. You might find that some students with proficient scores struggle more than you thought they would at navigating life after school. Or that some students with less-than-proficient scores (like Martha) are able to build happy, successful lives.

Does having knowledge about your students' success in life matter? Do you just continue pushing for proficient test scores and good grades and hope for the best, or do you look for ways to better ensure that life beyond school is a success?

There are many rhetorical questions asked here to provoke thought and discussion with your staff and peers. This chapter tries to look at some ways to think about student success and to help you discover aspects of teaching and learning that can help you and your school or district staff make your students academically successful.

USING DATA

Test scores matter. Understanding assessment and how to use data to improve decision making is a key skill for all school leaders.

Assessments offer insights into specific things. For example, you can set a goal that all students will read a grade level passage fluently with 97% accuracy. That's a high expectation for any school. Commonly administered fluency assessments can tell you certain things, such as reading rate or accuracy, given an assigned passage. Does a high score on a fluency test lead to academic success? Not necessarily. Fluency tests tell you nothing about comprehension. Although fluency and accuracy are important reading skills, they're only part of the story. We must test for comprehension if that is the skill we wish to measure. Too often, we use data from a particular test—because we have it, or because it's easy to administer—to make determinations that the test was not designed to support. That is a mistake.

Multiple assessments, including formative and summative, are needed to truly understand a student's abilities and potential. This means that you must understand what each assessment tells you; it also means that you must not interpret or use the data in ways that were never intended.

PARENTS WANT THEIR CHILDREN TO SUCCEED

Carlton Kuhns, an educator and school leader with more than 40 years of experience in rural Alaska, including in the Lower Kuskokwim School District, noted the following:

> There is not a parent out there that says "I don't want my child to do well in school." People are super motivated within their context to see their children

succeed, and they know what is important. What we as educators need to understand is that our definition of success may not align entirely with that of the parents we serve.

To find out what these parents care about and what they know to be important requires you as a leader to engage with them. It can be pretty much guaranteed that not one of them will ask for a higher reading rate on a test. That does not make reading rate unimportant; it only emphasizes the point that academic success has many components and meanings to different stakeholders.

How often have you heard from parents that they just want their child to be happy? Does that mean having a high-pressure job from Intel, designing microchips? Maybe. Does that mean becoming a whaling captain and a community role model for young people in a village? It could. The rest of this chapter looks at what you need to do in order to meet the goal of students being academically successful.

ARE RURAL STUDENTS AT A DISADVANTAGE?

Carlton Kuhns adamantly shared that rural students should perform as well as their counterparts elsewhere:

> It is not okay to accept underperformance. Achievement has to do with having options in life and having doors that open or doors that close. There have to be high expectations for academic achievement. A child's Yup'ik background is not a deficit, it is an added benefit.

Suzzuk Mary Huntington, coordinator of cultural programs for the Bering Strait School District, said simply:

> Village schools are the ideal place for Indigenous kids to learn. They're small, they're in the middle of the community and enmeshed in family and strong social ties, [and] they often have people intimate with language, subsistence, local employment, and living goals. You could not imagine a better setup to do well with these kids.

High expectations can come in different places. Take, for example, the senior class trip at Alak School in Ulġuniq (Wainwright). Historically, students had taken senior trips to Disneyland or Seattle. One teacher at the school saw an opportunity to do something really special. The teacher instead proposed that seniors go to Costa Rica and participate in a research program run by the University of Florida. They would study the flora and fauna of a

Figure 7.1. Students performing a Yup'ik dance in Tuyuryaq (Togiak). *Courtesy of Emily Hendricks.*

place completely new to them. Taking all of the seniors was the goal, which would not have been possible in a large, urban school. The students could raise money by running the school store during the year.

It worked. The students raised the money and ended up counting butterflies in the jungle, looking for green sea turtle nests on the beach at night, and counting birds in a sanctuary.

There was also an unanticipated benefit to the trip. The research project attracted a couple hundred high school students from across the country. All of the students stayed at a lodge in the national park. Of course, socializing was a big draw. In the evenings after dinner, the students would gather in the lobby to talk and play games. It just so happened that one of the seniors from Alak School was a state record holder in an event for the Native Youth Olympics and another senior was a champion in a different event.

It didn't take long for the seniors from Ulġuniq to hang a ball from a stair railing at the lodge in Costa Rica and to demonstrate the Alaskan high kick, the one-hand reach, and the one-foot high kick. Soon everyone had to try. It became a nightly event. Other students became curious and impressed by their new friends from Alaska. Alak School students realized that they were not just disadvantaged kids from the North Slope. All of the other high school kids were thrilled to be able to meet true Inuit people. The students from Ulġuniq and their Inupiaq culture were indeed famous. This experience helped the students to understand that their culture was recognized and valued by students from all over the United States. It was a game changer for them. They knew they could hold their own against peers who lived far different lives than their own. It is important that you, as a school leader, support opportunities that enable students from rural Alaska to see their cultures and peoples held in high esteem.

CONTINUOUS IMPROVEMENT

There are few examples of so-called school turnarounds in American schools, despite decades of efforts in underperforming schools. The Center for School Turnaround and Improvement at WestEd in San Francisco is a leading national group that uses research and looks at best practices that can lead to a school turnaround (https://csti.wested.org). Just remember that a center's work and researchers are not going to change your school and help your students. You and your staff have to do that.

Schools are only rarely able to replicate the successes of other schools or districts. For example, the Chugach School District was recognized in the 1980s for making substantial achievement gains among students. The state of Alaska, to great fanfare, launched the Quality Schools Initiative in 1996, seeking to replicate the Chugach model across the state (Holloway, n.d.). Schools in Alaska have now mostly abandoned these efforts that were so popular in the 1990s. Why? The problem was that the efforts of the Chugach School District were organic. Teachers and administrators in the Chugach School District spent five years developing the program, including detailed performance assessments in all subject areas. When others tried to replicate the Chugach model, they did not have the buy-in nor the understanding of purpose and depth of knowledge achieved by the developers.

The answer that speaks to how school turnaround works is that it must come from within. It takes a leader with a vision for how to improve and one who can motivate others to take part, including parents, staff members, and community members. We tend to think of things like turning around a school as some kind of rocket science. It is not. It takes knowledge. It takes effort. It takes perseverance. It takes a team effort.

The problem that many school- and district-level leaders have is that the day-to-day management and operation of school systems can overshadow long-term school improvement efforts. On any given day, having food to serve at lunch takes on a higher priority than improving reading scores. One way to deal with that is to take baby steps with school improvement.

The idea of rapid school turnaround needs to be put in the trash heap. What you want is continuous school improvement. A 10% improvement should be celebrated. It shouldn't end there! Keep going. Perseverance will get better results than a one-time shot in the arm.

EFFECTIVE ACTION PLANS FOR SCHOOL IMPROVEMENT

School improvement plans have become a regular part of the school-year cycle. Far too often, they are useless exercises merely fulfilling requirements. The plans are formulated early in the fall, and maybe a few actions take place, but for the most part, operation of the school takes over. For a principal, day-to-day issues, constant interruptions, continual problem solving, paperwork, and pressing issues consume time and energy. May comes around, and maybe a meeting takes place. *Did we meet the plan goals?* Not sure; the state test results are not out yet. Okay, let's get back to work and finish out this school year. . . .

You should think about the above ineffective action plan—or a very similar one—and truthfully acknowledge how many times you have seen something like this take place in schools wherever you have been. It is no wonder that it is hard to turn around or improve a school. This process rarely works, yet we keep doing it again and again. Stop it! Instead, consider the practical suggestions below for an alternative way to implement continuous school improvement.

PRACTICAL SUGGESTIONS FOR CONTINUOUS SCHOOL IMPROVEMENT

- Create a process that will be followed over a period of years to
  - set goals,
  - set timelines,
  - assign roles,
  - measure progress,
  - amend the goals, and
  - make new goals.
- Have staff, with community input, set goals that are simple and doable.
- Make goals time-bound with short timelines. Twelve weeks is long enough; two weeks can work for some goals.
- Consider nonacademic goals, student-behavior goals, parent-involvement goals, or social-emotional-learning goals. If effective, these will lead to academic improvement.
- Stay student centered.
- Delegate tasks. Assign clear action steps for individuals. The best people to implement a goal are the people that created it!
- Multiple goals can be worked on at the same time as long as different people are working on actions to implement and measure the goals.

- Set aside a small amount of time, no less than weekly, to review goals, measure or estimate progress, and determine next steps. These meetings do not have to be more than 20 minutes.
- Report goal progress to everyone in the school after each weekly meeting, either in person or electronically.
- Continually adapt and improve on goals.
- Your school improvement plan does not need yearlong goals, only incremental steps.
- A vision for school improvement can be a guiding statement for developing incremental goals, but do not fall into the trap of making the vision the goal.
- Celebrate every time an incremental step is accomplished.

You plan, monitor, and then adapt continually. When you look at building a school-improvement plan, ask yourself questions such as the following: If we wanted to improve reading abilities among our students to "grade level," what would have to happen? What would be the first incremental step? It may not happen this year or the next, but what progress can we make, and how do we do that? Here is an example.

INCREMENTAL K–3 READING GOALS FOR DECODING IMPROVEMENT

- Goal 1: Have a small group review materials for grades K–3 for explicit help with decoding, including teacher materials, books for students to read, and stories to be read to students.
  - Your timeline is two weeks.
  - For communication, present to all K–3 staff.
  - At the end of two weeks, be done. Celebrate. Move on.
- Goal 2: Implement a new school schedule within a week of collecting or purchasing decoding materials for grades K–3.
  - Your timeline is one week after all materials are available.
  - For professional development, ensure all K–3 staff know how to properly use the materials in instruction. (This will take more than a one-time training. Take whatever time is needed to ensure proper use of materials.)
  - For communication, let the community know about changes being made.
  - At the end of the week, be done. Celebrate the new schedule. Move on. Devise the next steps.
- Goal 3: Put students in groups of six or less for 30 minutes daily, where all school employees and maybe some community volunteers will implement a three-tiered plan for decoding improvement that has students in each group rotating through a workshop-like system.

- For 10 minutes, students are to read on their own, monitored by a community member or another person.
- For 10 minutes, students are to be read to by a community member or another person.
- For 10 minutes, one or two students at a time are given explicit reading instruction in phonemic awareness and decoding by a certified staff member.
  - Your timeline is that this is ongoing for 6 to 12 weeks.
  - For monitoring, check progress, and make changes when needed.
  - For communication, inform other staff, community members, and students of progress.
- Goal 4: Measure decoding skills. (This is in conjunction with Goal 3.)
  - Set a baseline using a common assessment.
  - Measure progress once every two weeks by giving an assessment for decoding, such as assessing nonsense words.
    - Your timeline is that this is ongoing for 6 to 12 weeks.
    - For monitoring, review progress every two weeks. Adjust as needed.
    - For communication, post anonymous results for all to see.
    - Celebrate success.

Make sure students are aware of what you are doing, and celebrate successes with them!

Making improvements in decoding is a process. It is also a set of incremental steps for a very specific goal. A similar process could be devised for reading comprehension, improving attendance, or integrating cultural knowledge into the curriculum. It just needs to be explicit, easy to implement, monitor, and adapt as needed. Take it step by step. Martha's teachers had a plan for her. The goal was not that Martha would be reading at grade level at the end of a given school year. The goal was one of continuous improvement and incremental progress.

The concept behind an incremental approach is one of "success breeds success." The simple accomplishment of each step is a success. It is a sign of progress that you can celebrate. Progress breeds motivation. You need to demonstrate to your staff, community, and students that you are making progress, no matter how small.

WAYS TO CELEBRATE

- Thank-you cards and staff appreciation banner posted in the school foyer.
- "Good job, everyone. Have some cookies, grapes, or bananas."

- "Good job, everyone. Let's play some games with students in the gym for the last hour of the school day on Friday."
- Review assessment results at weekly meetings, and share with the whole staff. They need to know about the hard work you are doing. ("Let's have some cheering!")
- There are 1,001 ways to celebrate. Do them all.

WHEN IS THE TIME TO DO THIS?

Good question. No one ever truthfully said this was going to be easy. However, there are efficient systems for school improvement that take a lot less time than you think. Get a lot of people involved. Delegate. Form groups that work on specific small items that do not take hours and hours of work every week. As a school leader, you have the job of overseeing what the groups do, not running the group meetings. As a district leader, you have the job of letting the school devise a school schedule where they can have 30 to 45 minutes each week to meet that will not be compromised by staff trainings and meetings as well as an additional 30 minutes each week for staff meetings where information can be shared with everyone.

Very small schools with only two or three teachers often disregard the need for these sharing sessions. It is assumed that these will take place in informal meetings. Yet setting aside time each week is important in small schools, too; that way it does not get overlooked.

Structure matters. Organization matters. Empowering others matters. Your job as a leader is to make sure that school improvement is an organized, structured system that is as much a part of the school as curriculum is. It is not a one-year plan, and it is not a five-year plan; it is an every-year plan. If this type of plan is not already in place, it is your job to create it.

Below we outline a school-improvement system that was used in a school in western Alaska. This is not necessarily a model to be adopted; it is a model to consider and adapt to your needs if you believe it fits your community, school, and/or district. One important element of the example is how it involves many staff members at the school and some community leaders. The other aspect to notice is how the system communicates progress. This communication serves as a means of accountability for progress as well as stakeholder involvement. Notice that the model is based upon the concept of incremental change. Long-term goals should be broken down into component parts. Keeping efforts small and manageable allows for work to continue with only 30 minutes a week devoted to school improvement. It is not a plan. It is a system.

A MODEL FOR A SCHOOL-IMPROVEMENT SYSTEM

- Spend time in the beginning identifying priorities for school improvement, involving everyone. Make it a series of community meetings.
- Take all the input from these meetings, and devise up to four priorities.
- Have a school leadership team make committee assignments for each priority. Involve as many people as possible, but keep committees to a manageable size of six or fewer people. Committees must have a cross section of stakeholders.
- Instructions to committees are as follows: create a plan, devise a measurement for progress, create a baseline, monitor progress and share at weekly meetings, and adapt as needed to meet a goal within twelve weeks or less.
- Create a schedule for the committees to meet and also to communicate progress. The following is an example:
  - Committees meet for 30 minutes each week.
  - Once a month, on a rotating schedule, committee members present plans, progress, and adaptations to the whole school for discussion. Suggest using 15 minutes at a weekly staff meeting, rotating through the four committees each month.
  - Once a month hold a community meeting to present plans, progress, and adaptations to the community for discussion.
  - Always share progress with students.
- As a leader, delegate responsibilities, monitor activity, empower others, and celebrate success.

The school in Western Alaska using this system made considerable progress on their goals of reading comprehension improvement, increased community involvement, and better attendance. The school reestablished the same small committees the following year with new targets and higher aspirations. The process of plan, monitor, and adapt became a regular function of the school.

PERSONALIZING SCHOOL

A wonderful advantage of the small- and medium-sized schools that you will find in much of rural Alaska is the ability to personalize education. Many schools do a fairly good job of personalizing in elementary grades using Response to Intervention (RTI) or Multi-Tiered System of Supports (MTSS) models (when implemented well). Similar opportunities exist in secondary grades as well.

Imagine two students in your school: one wants to learn to operate heavy machinery, and the other wants a professional career working in a laboratory.

Every high school in America faces the challenge of preparing students for highly variable life and work aspirations following school. The answer many schools and school leaders have come up with is to set a high bar in terms of core standards, which we assume will prepare students for all possible futures.

A one-size-fits-all approach does not work for all students. Personalizing education and adapting curricula to meet the needs of individual students is possible in most rural Alaska schools. Recognizing that there is a broad definition of academic success requires including but moving beyond proficiency measures.

Let's look back at Martha. All indicators were that Martha was not going to work in a field that required a high level of math and reading skills, as she never performed at "grade level." However, Martha put other factors to work in her favor: a good work ethic, a can-do attitude, a level of independence, support from friends, and professional support from teachers. And, importantly, she'd believed she was accruing the skills needed to succeed.

Our egalitarian approach is that one size fits all. In reality, students demonstrate a wide range of educational strengths and needs, and schools need to embrace a broad understanding of academic success. Terri Walker Aviññaq, superintendent of the Northwest Arctic Borough School District, suggested that academic success may best be understood *after* the school years, not before or during:

> When I think about measuring success, I think about the end result. . . . By the time a student graduates from high school, it's the beginning of their adult years. We want them to have the knowledge and skills to be independent, and independent learners, so they can be anything that they want to be. It's really important that people enjoy and are happy with what they are doing. I think everybody deserves happiness! So, they should be happy with what it is that they want to do. And it's our job to provide them with the necessary skills that they need to be successful.

Martha was successful because of her own initiative; however, it was her teachers and community who gave her confidence and motivation and who helped her build a strong work ethic. What ways can be devised to measure some of these more intangible successes? Try using questionnaires for students, teachers, and parents. Use personal interviews. Devise tasks that demonstrate specific skills. Consider finding ways to measure traits not measured by tests. Here are just a few suggestions:

- Initiative
- Confidence

- Work ethic
- Motivation
- Curiosity
- Interpersonal communication
- Organizational skills
- Traditional knowledge
- Home and community support

It should be mentioned that career and technical education is one area that needs more attention. Some regions have greatly expanded opportunities for students, but in rural Alaska, the costs are often prohibitive. Take a look at this book's chapter on career, technical, and subsistence education for a more in-depth look. There is an opportunity in smaller schools in rural Alaska to really personalize education to meet the diverse requirements of every student, whether that is through CTE or adapted academic programs. Do not resist being innovative or bold.

CRITICAL THINKING

There is at least one area where the heavy equipment operator, the lab technician, and Martha overlap. That is the ability to solve problems, to see fact from fiction, to be rational and make inferences. There is no more important method of instruction in today's classrooms than teaching students how to think critically. Yes, it is even more important than teaching quadratic equations (not that there's anything wrong with a good quadratic equation).

Advances in technology in the last two decades have brought us a world where content knowledge is at the fingertips of anyone carrying a phone. When was Napoleon defeated at Waterloo? What's the state capitol of Louisiana? How do I convert Celsius to Fahrenheit? Google it. All of it. Most any piece of information you want or need to know is available in seconds. That is not to say that teaching content is not needed. Background knowledge in science, history, and math is still very important. It is also true that knowing what to *do* with knowledge is more important than knowing isolated facts. The question is how people make knowledge useful in today's world.

Critical thinking is the ability to think clearly and rationally. It is understanding the logical connections between ideas. It helps us decide what to believe. In an information-flooded world, critical thinking has become a life skill needed in every walk of life, including jobs, communities, friends, and ourselves. Some schools and districts, recognizing the value of critical thinking, have promoted an integrated approach to teaching and learning. They shift the emphasis in all subjects from disconnected facts to tasks that require the application of knowledge and skills to complex problems. Students are encouraged to recognize their unique personal strengths, as well as their potential for growth in all areas.

The potential for such approaches should be readily apparent for rural Alaska students. Creating an environment that enables students to see the relationships between subjects taught in school and life outside the school is place-based education. A focus on critical thinking makes instruction culturally relevant. It can bridge the gap between Western ideas and Indigenous ways of being. Angayuqaq Oscar Kawagley put it this way:

> The modern schools . . . are giving a lot of information to the students without also showing them how they can transfer the information into useful knowledge for making a living . . . [to] see how the usable knowledge could be transformed into wisdom to make a life. (Kawagley, 1993, p. 196)

If the goal is empowerment of Indigenous peoples, learning to think critically is a vital aspect. All students, including Indigenous students, must learn to navigate the world. Skills needed for critical thinking are varied. They include observation, analysis, interpretation, reflection, evaluation, inference, problem solving, and decision making. We use these skills in everyday life. When preparing to shoot a caribou or put out a setnet, one finds every one of these skills comes into play at some level. The goal for you as an educator is to enhance and refine these skills. Students should progress from a merely intuitive reaction to an intentional, skilled, and thoughtful process that is put into play in multiple ways and in multiple situations.

Thinking critically improves the quality of information you process and share. You, as well as your teachers and students, ask deeper and better questions and are able to make better decisions. Have you ever tried to explain yourself and not been understood? Or had a hard time understanding another person's position? Have you ever been unable to argue convincingly for a claim that you believed? Or been in a situation where your values were misunderstood? What does it mean to be part of society, to be part of a community, to be connected to a culture? All of these questions require critical thinking—not just once but continuously over time.

Interdisciplinary project-based lessons can provide the opportunity to develop critical thinking skills. Instructional techniques using discussions and open-ended questioning provide opportunities for students to exercise critical thinking skills. Including these elements in everyday teaching can provide motivation and engagement, especially when integrating local culture(s).

Your job as a school or district leader is to ensure that critical thinking skills are embedded in instruction. When teachers design lessons, we want students to regularly practice and demonstrate critical thinking skills in a variety of ways.

WAYS FOR STUDENTS TO DEMONSTRATE CRITICAL THINKING SKILLS

Ask students to do the following:

- Think about topics or issues in an objective and critical way.
- Identify as many different arguments in relation to a particular issue as possible.
- Argue for positions that you (the student) may not personally hold.
  o Why might a person say what they are saying?
  o What are valid reasons for the position?
  o What flaws exist in an argument?
- Constantly evaluate the strength or validity of other people's positions.
- Constantly focus on explanations for your own positions.
- Answer the question, "Why?" Always provide the rationale and evidence.
- Apply common flaws, or fallacies, to reasoning in evaluating arguments, such as
  o *ad hominem,*
  o *ad populum,*
  o red herring, and
  o straw man.
- Explain the links between information, knowledge, and local ways of knowing and being.

WHAT ARE YOUR STUDENTS CAPABLE OF?

Academic success creates conditions for students to be successful in life, no matter what productive path they choose. A school that is academically successful is one that creates a lot of Marthas. It is one where nurturing and caring adults help students develop confidence and the ability to be what they want to be. Gguitka Sperry Ash, a Sugpiaq elementary school teacher who is from Nanwalek and works in Kodiak, said,

> The way I see it ... there is a lot of potential, a lot of strength, a lot of power, beautiful power, you know, such great [power in our students], and I just feel... that if we can find it ... that is a pretty cool thing. Believe in the people, in the students, [and] in the parents and the community. I think that's a good place to start.

Part of academic success is helping students take advantage of being from rural Alaska. The students from Alak School learned that they were not just people at the end of the road, forgotten and unimportant. They learned that they were a unique part of the human race and they had things to offer that others did not. They had a place in this world.

Effective school leaders can establish a high-performing learning environment and climate by ensuring that both adults and students put learning at the center of daily activities, both inside and outside the school. Responsiveness to student needs and having a sense of collective responsibility can create pride in all stakeholders and allow collaboration toward a greater good (Wallace Foundation, 2013). Ruthie Sampson, a champion of the Inupiaq language, talked about empowered communities:

> An empowered community . . . in Alaska means a community where children are well taken care of. . . . An empowered community is where the children graduate from high school and go on for more training or school and still feel comfortable to come back to the village and work in jobs that pay well. (Sampson, 2002)

Michael Heidelberger, biochemist at the Rockefeller Institute for Medical Research, said of Rufus Cole, the first director of the Institute's hospital:

> He would sit there and listen to whatever was going on, and then he'd ask a question. Sometimes the question seemed almost naïve for a person who was supposed to know as much as he did, but the result always was to bring out things that hadn't been brought out before and to get much deeper down into the problem than one had before. (As cited in Barry, 2004, p. 81)

In order to be that leader that creates a high-performing and empowered community, you must believe in your students and be the one with a vision developed by listening and asking the right questions.

TAKEAWAYS

- Academic success should be defined broadly and include skills needed for a fulfilling and productive life.
- Multiple measures are needed to understand academic success, including life beyond school.
- A system for school improvement should emphasize continuous improvement through incremental steps.
- Critical thinking skills are essential and can provide engaging, place-based teaching opportunities in rural Alaska.

Chapter 8

Small K–12 Schools

Evelyn Willburn, Deidre Jenson, and Benjamin Glover

SMALL SCHOOL CHALLENGES
Evelyn Willburn

As a new leader of a very small school, you will likely first notice the sheer number and variety of the hats you are expected to wear. Some of the sections in this chapter, such as "Multigrade Classrooms" and "Other Duties as Assigned," will help illustrate this point. For starters, though, here's an anecdote:

I'm not a science teacher. However, as the secondary teacher and lead teacher of a three-teacher school (two classrooms, one special education), I had no choice regarding middle school science. For this group (six kids ranging from fifth to eighth grade), I had to wing it. I knew that nobody would judge me too harshly if I just assigned readings and end-of-section questions from the textbook, but that got wearisome, even for me. So one day I said, "Let's do science projects!" I told the kids to choose something related to physical science that was reasonably safe and easy to do. Young Jimmy said he wanted to make a lamp out of a pickle. I read up on the topic and saw that it had been done many times without electrical fires or loss of teaching credentials, so I agreed.

Setting up the project was terrifying—at least it was to a person who has to fight the notion that electricity is actually some form of voodoo. First, we had to cut the cord off an old lamp. Then we took the cut end of the cord and peeled off all the plastic insulation, leaving the bare copper wires. These we twisted into two separate strands, each of which we stuck firmly into either end of the pickle. Then (oh, my heart!) we cautiously plugged the cord into an outlet in the classroom. The pickle began to glow in a most satisfactory manner. We turned the lights off for greater effect.

Jimmy was pleased with his results and cheerfully wrote about the experience in his science journal. But then he murmured, "I wonder if it would work with a potato?"

Emboldened by our success with the pickle, I agreed to try it. We removed the wires from the pickle and attached them to Jimmy's potato. (Apparently, he had brought a big box of assorted vegetables in the hope that he might make many kinds of lamps.) Anyway, the wise little monkey who sits on my shoulder tried unsuccessfully to get my attention as we carefully plugged the cord back into the wall.

For a split second, nothing happened, and then there was a huge bang, and the lights went out all over the building. I screamed "Sh—!" thereby raising my career total of swearing in front of the class to two. I pulled the cord out of the wall as quickly as possible, but the breaker was well and truly thrown. I shakily called the district office, trying to skate around what had actually happened. It was about three hours before someone arrived to reset the breaker. In retrospect I could probably have done it myself with a bit of coaching. But for the moment, I just wasn't in the mood.

So you see, trying to be all things to all kids can take you in some unexpected directions.

MULTIGRADE AND MULTISUBJECT CLASSROOMS
Benjamin Glover

Many teachers assume that the single-room school is a relic from works of fiction like *Little House on the Prairie*. However, when you move to rural Alaska, this belief will soon be extinguished. More than 40 of the 54 districts in Alaska have at least one multigrade classroom. This does not mean that the majority of classrooms are multigrade (they are not), but it does mean that they are common. In fact, as of this writing, there is an entire district (Pelican City School District) that is one multigrade classroom.

To be clear, when talking about a multigrade classroom, we are talking about a class that is intentionally multigrade and where you teach numerous, if not all, subjects. Usually, this is because the school is too small for each grade to have its own class. Tetlin School in the Alaska Gateway School District, for example, has 36 students one year when I served as principal/teacher, with the largest single grade having only five students. A district cannot afford to give five students their own teacher, and it would not necessarily be educationally advantageous anyway. Small schools are the main—but not only—reason for multigrade classrooms. In Indigenous communities there are efforts to strengthen local Indigenous languages by offering language-immersion programs in a multigrade format, where all subjects are taught in languages such as Yup'ik, Inupiaq, or Xaad Kil.

There is little research on multigrade, multisubject classrooms (see Thalheimer, 2010, for a good overview). As Evelyn's experience with science projects demonstrates, teaching in a multigrade, multisubject classroom has many challenges. There are, however, best practices that those who work in those classrooms have found to be useful.

CHALLENGES OF MULTIGRADE, MULTISUBJECT CLASSROOMS

- Wide range of ability levels and wide range of skill levels
- Less reliance on direct instruction of students
- Requires more self-discipline by students who often work independently
- Requires significant preparation time
- Needs a teacher who understands the developmental characteristics of learners across age levels
- Requires more time for organization and record keeping
- Requires teacher creativity and innovation

You should carefully consider your classroom aides. With proper support, they can be invaluable in multiage classrooms. Aides can give instruction using scripted programs in reading, math, or even science as long as a certified staff member is the teacher of record and guides

Figure 8.1. Teacher aides in Uŋalaqliit (Unalakleet). *Courtesy of the University of Alaska Fairbanks, K–12 Outreach.*

instruction and evaluation. You can provide training yourself or through workshops such as those developed by the Alaska Statewide Mentor Project. As aides gain experience with the curriculum and teaching methods, they become important assets to multiage classrooms. Often, the more responsibility given to a person, the more they value the job and take pride in their work.

Most of the time, classroom aides will be individuals who have lived in the village for decades, if not their entire lives. These paraprofessionals and classified staff often provide the stability that holds the school together and connects it to the community. These employees provide continuity that can be hard to maintain when hiring people from outside the community, the region, and even the state.

Unless you are from the community where you lead, local staff are also much more plugged into the values and family dynamics in the community than you. Remember that these people not only know the children, but they are likely to be parents, grandparents, aunts, or uncles of some of the children. Learning how to work within these relationships can be very valuable. I often memorize the telephone numbers of the parents of the children in my class and then start reciting them if the students begin to act up. Having their aunt there is twice as valuable.

> Jessica Angalkuruk Mark, a paraprofessional in the village of Ingricuar (Twin Hills), said that paraprofessionals, who are almost always locals, are the glue that holds the school together: "When students in my classroom promote to high school, they come to me, telling me they'll miss being in my classroom when they get to high school next year. This keeps me going, to keep up the relationships I've built, and to build relationships with new students that come into my classroom."

TEACHING TIPS FOR A MULTIAGE CLASSROOM
Benjamin Glover

First, you must combine lessons and instruction where possible. In multiage classrooms with multiple subjects, you could face the impossible task of planning 24 separate lessons each day, every day. It cannot be done! You can probably teach one social studies lesson and one science lesson to the whole group and then group at least two grade levels for your reading and writing lessons. Teachers can still differentiate in terms of the assignments and expectations for students; planning 8 lessons a day is much easier than planning 24.

Second, when grouping, do so by ability level, not grade level, whenever possible. It is important that all students receive instruction in grade-level curriculum and content; however, ability grouping allows for combining lessons. Time constraints just do not allow for individual instruction at grade level all of the time for all students. In some groups a particular student may be slightly ahead of the others, and in another group, that same student may be slightly behind the others. There may be certain lessons and subjects where you must evaluate differently by grade level, but do not allow that to guide all of your instruction.

Third, be open to blended instruction (that combines in-person and remote/online instruction) and playlists. In a multigrade classroom, especially in subjects like math and ELA, you are likely to be teaching more than one lesson at a given time. All students need clear tasks at all times, including while you are teaching other students. Blended instruction and playlists provide opportunities for students who are not being directly taught to work online and independently. Just keep in mind that a seventh grader is likely to work much quicker than a fourth grader and may be capable of more in-depth independent work. You can tailor playlists and online instruction for each student in a way that's hard to do with larger groups or whole classes. The concept of a playlist is that students are given a list on Monday of everything that is expected of them for the week. Therefore, they have clear tasks outlined for them to do during class until the entire list is completed. Additionally, this is a great way to differentiate instruction since there is no rule that all playlists must be the same.

Figure 8.2. Students in Qalirneq (Koliganek), Alaska. *Courtesy of Emily Hendricks.*

BLENDED INSTRUCTION IN MULTIGRADE CLASSROOMS

- Blended learning combines face-to-face classroom learning with online learning in which students can work independently and have more control over the pace of their learning.
- Blended learning in rural Alaska schools requires work to be done in school rather than at home, as many students do not have online access outside of school.
- Blended learning, with its mix of technology and traditional face-to-face instruction, is a great approach for extending learning time without direct instruction from the teacher.

Finally, sight lines in your multigrade classroom are even more important than they are in a traditional classroom. There will always be classroom management challenges, but in a multigrade classroom, you have now added the dimension that some students are much larger and older than others, and they are more savvy about misbehavior or bullying. It is imperative that you can see and hear what is going on in your classroom. You will need to think through your groupings carefully.

There are also advantages to having a range of ages in a classroom. Older students can be role models. They can also tutor or read to younger students. These types of activities promote cohesiveness in the school and can mitigate some problems before they occur.

ADVANTAGES OF MULTIGRADE, MULTISUBJECT CLASSROOMS

- Students learn to be more independent and self-directed.
- Cooperative learning can become a common/everyday feature of class.
- Interaction with people of different ages and skill levels matches life beyond school.
- Students can assume roles as leaders or supporters in a variety of contexts.
- Connecting curriculum across content areas and levels can enhance understanding.
- There are many opportunities for project-based learning and activities.

RECRUITING AND KEEPING QUALITY EDUCATORS
Deidre Jenson

We have mentioned that classified staff in a small school can provide needed stability and cohesiveness. Hiring quality certified staff is critical. Keeping quality educators in rural Alaska can be a challenge.

Reality shows like *Alaska Bush People*, *Life Below Zero*, and *Alaska: The Last Frontier* have become increasingly popular—despite their many inaccurate depictions of life in rural Alaska. It's true that Alaska offers a variety of environments, cultures, and outdoor activities. It's less true that life and teaching in rural Alaska revolves around drama and quality camera work. Given Alaska's ongoing need to recruit and retain teachers and leaders, broad interest is welcome . . . but recruiters (including you as a school leader) must have honest conversations with prospective employees about the challenges of working and living in rural Alaska. Openness and honesty about these things is fair and can help with retention. One of the worst things you can do during recruitment is set people up for unwelcome surprises.

From kayaking to fishing, hiking to caving, hammocking in the Southeast rainforest to winter camping in the tundra, outdoor Alaska activities are often eagerly anticipated by those coming from Outside. Less obvious to many is that at least as much reward comes from integrating into the community and region. An excellent goal for rural Alaska school leaders is to help new employees connect with people, perhaps by joining locals in berry picking, fishing, bingo or other games, sewing, carving, or participating in community activities and celebrations where they may be welcome. Cross-cultural learning can certainly be mutual between communities and the teachers and leaders that serve them.

If new hires are not from rural Alaska, the culture(s) and activities in the community may be very different from where they have grown up. It is important for new staff to observe and listen, participate when invited, and be open to different ways of doing things. You should be ready to help them learn about Indigenous ways of learning and living. Doing so will make their transition into the community easier.

Being in the middle of a new environment can provide new hires the opportunity to reflect on where they have come from and where they have arrived. Being in an unfamiliar place can isolate people from family, friends, and other resources and activities they've been used to. Grocery stores and health care facilities in rural Alaska are often different than in urban places, and they may need to transition from movie theaters, bowling alleys, bars, and libraries to new entertainments in rural Alaska. You may need to help new staff replace prior habits or expectations (e.g., going to a restaurant on a Friday night) with new ones (going to a Friday night potluck with teacher friends) available in the community. Doing so can make a big difference.

New staff need to be encouraged to maintain connections with family and friends while also building new relationships with colleagues and community members. Once new relationships are established, they may gain what many refer to as a second family within Alaska; educational teams in rural Alaska schools are often very close. After relying on each other for their basic and emotional needs and spending so much time together (including holidays), many educators stay in touch years after their teaching assignments end. As a school leader, you must find and create opportunities for school staff to interact socially apart from the professional setting of the school. Pickup basketball or volleyball games after school are great for camaraderie and exercise. Activity nights that invite in the community are fun and great for building social relationships. Crafts, games, and food are always best sellers.

For newcomers, living in rural Alaska can be a magnificent, life-changing experience. It is important to inform prospects of the challenges as well as the opportunities and joys. Tell them about Evelyn and the pickle-lamp science project. But also, do not hide the experience with the potato. Being honest and open is always the best approach.

It is equally important for those doing the hiring to learn as much as possible about their prospect's attitudes and capacity for resilience. Finding the right fit for your school community (rather than the perfect person on paper) helps to retain hires and increase job satisfaction. Hiring and supporting the people who work in a school is the most important job for school leaders both at the school level and the district level. Getting it right will pay dividends for a very long time. Equally important is providing for self-care and improving self-efficacy through professional development and mentorship; both are discussed below.

PROFESSIONAL DEVELOPMENT AND COLLABORATION
Deidre Jenson

Obviously, Evelyn could have benefited from some training in teaching science. However, as she mentioned, it is not possible to be all things to all students, especially when you are new. At the very least, school leaders have the responsibility to pursue as much training relevant to the job as possible. Professional learning and growth opportunities in rural Alaska can be extensive, at least in part because of high teacher turnover rates. Virtually all districts in Alaska must provide regular professional development because they have new staff coming in each year. Professional learning opportunities can vary widely by districts; opportunities may be in person, online, or at professional conferences. Many rural districts have Title I, or school-improvement, funds available to support a variety of opportunities based on school needs. In-house professional development that each district provides can be particularly valuable for new staff. Districts may have itinerant employees who rotate from site to site, offering ongoing training. Often collaboration time is built into the school calendar. This collaboration time can be driven by teachers' needs and requests. Consultants, mentors, and coaches can sometimes be brought in to work directly with teachers in their classrooms. Don't forget that paraprofessionals need professional support as well; they are often responsible for a large amount of direct work with students in small schools. As a rule, plan for professional learning opportunities that meet the needs of the entire staff—not just the teachers.

> Jessica Angalkuruk Mark of Ingricuar mentioned the importance of providing quality professional development for paraprofessionals. She recalled joining two colleagues at a conference on trauma-informed education. "It's great," said Jessica, "especially if it's a PD that you can get passionate about!"

Many districts provide access to a variety of mentors, including teacher mentors within the school who can answer general questions about travel, rural living, or district protocols. There is also the long-standing Alaska Statewide Mentor Program that provides an experienced mentor for first- and second-year teachers in rural Alaska (www.alaska.edu/asmp). These mentors may observe teachers and offer instructional suggestions as well as support for the challenges new teachers may face. The Alaska Statewide Mentor Project provides this mentor with the goal of improving quality of instruction and teacher retention in Alaska.

It is also possible that your school qualifies for support from the Alaska Department of Education & Early Development. If so, you may have the services of a school-improvement coach who may assist with data analysis, goal setting, instructional coaching, and general school-improvement support. In the past, some districts have even paid for their own coaches, and many have staff acting in similar roles. It is worthwhile to see what your district has to offer along the lines of professional support for you and for the rest of the school staff.

Teachers often say the most valuable professional development they receive is about the communities in which they are teaching. While a general overview of Alaska history and Indigenous peoples (knowing both is required for teacher certification) provides valuable knowledge, knowing the specific history of the community can help staff understand why things happen the way they do. Teachers who learn the role of Tribes, Alaska Native corporations, regional corporations, and regional nonprofits can find ways to bring those organizations into their unit-planning process and may be able to welcome important visitors to the school. A community mentor may help you and your teachers learn about local cultures and ways of life. One example of a community asset that provides robust educator support is the regional corporation for

Southeast Alaska, Sealaska (www.sealaska.com); many others provide trainings and ongoing learning resources for educators across Alaska.

ALASKA PROFESSIONAL DEVELOPMENT AND SUPPORT ORGANIZATIONS

- Alaska Professional Learning Network (AkPLN): www.asdn.org/akpln
- Alaska Rural Innovation and Student Engagement Network (AKRISE): www.alaskaruralteachernetwork.org
- Alaska School Leadership Academy (ASLA): https://education.alaska.gov/information-exchange-blog/the-alaska-school-leadership-academy
- Alaska Staff Development Network (ASDN): www.asdn.org
- Tribal Law and Policy Institute (TPLI): www.home.tlpi.org

A collaborating, close-knit community of educators is an important part of the puzzle for small schools in rural Alaska. Another huge piece is community engagement—that is, bringing in local talent.

ENGAGING LOCAL TALENT
Evelyn Willburn

The first thing you will likely notice in your new community is that it is truly bursting with talent. Depending on the region and peoples, you might find individuals who can sew traditional garments, gather and preserve subsistence food, or create a beautiful sculpture using a chainsaw. You will probably be tempted to start lining people up to volunteer at the school right away. But hold on just a second: these folks don't know you. Take some time to get to know the people and to learn about the community. Go to local events and participate in local activities. Show appreciation for local talent and local knowledge. After that maybe you will be ready to start scheduling some community volunteers.

However, you must understand that your schedule is just that: *your* schedule. If you have had a typical Western education, you have learned to love schedules, and your duties as an educator in a Western system only reinforce that affinity. Teachers often have their days planned down to minutiae. As a school leader, you may have a bit more scheduling flexibility, but you also have to allow time for teachers to plan ahead. So how do you create partnerships with people that are respectful of both local cultures and school routines?

It may be tempting for you to call up the local artisan everyone has been talking about and say, "How about Thursday at 2:00 p.m.?" That person might say some variation of "Fine," then not show up. They may call to cancel, or they may not. When this happens, it will probably irritate you.

How are you to bridge that gap? Some artisans have embraced programs like Artists in Schools (https://arts.alaska.gov/arts-in-education) and will contract with you to provide lessons during a certain period of time, cheerfully following the schedule that you love so much. Others, however, will be happy to come and share a story or a lesson in beading, but you must understand that if the day is right for seal hunting, berry picking, or a trip to town, your planned event will be off. It is much better to extend an open invitation, continue business as usual, and be prepared to flex your own schedule should the opportunity for a special lesson arise. It is important that you, as the school leader, inform teachers of this as well.

Ken Yates is a volunteer who has worked for some years with local schools in K'aaws Tlaay (Craig) to produce Alaska Native theater and to celebrate Elizabeth Peratrovich Day (Elizabeth Peratrovich [Ḵaaxgal.aat] was Tlingit of the Raven Moiety of the Lukaax̱.ádi clan; she was a civil rights activist who advocated for the passage of Alaska's Anti-discrimination Act of 1945, the first antidiscrimination law in the United States). While Ken and I were talking one day, we reminisced about a year when we'd collaborated on a theater production. This production had been part of a community event imagined and realized by Ken's niece Julie Yates-Fulton, a teacher at Craig Elementary School, and Debbie Head, a Tlingit language and arts teacher at Craig High School. This event included an original play cast with Craig fifth graders and community members, a community dinner, and an exchange of gifts made by Debbie's students in the Southeast Alaska Living (SEALS) class. Ken said that this event allowed Indigenous and non-Indigenous peoples to work together in the school and community to weave a "beautiful tapestry" of inclusion, diversity, and celebration of heritage for all groups. He also suggested that if new school leaders want to encourage partnerships with teachers and community members, they must be "real." To Ken, this means that school leaders must be humble, teachable, and not avoid challenging conversations and situations.

Karla Edenshaw of Higdáa Gándlaay (Hydaburg) said that parents and the community need to be involved in the schools. She recalled walking into school one time right before Christmas, and she was shocked to see no sign of decorations. She volunteered on the spot and got the kids to make ornaments and help decorate the halls. Last spring Karla taught home economics at the school as part of a community engagement grant. Karla said that teachers deserve a huge pat on the back and that schools and communities need to work together and support each other.

Now imagine you have everybody working closely together: students, parents, certified staff, paraprofessionals, Elders, community leaders . . . there are bound to be some misunderstandings. Conflict in a small school is different than in larger schools. How should you handle these conflicts?

CONFLICT AND CLIMATE IN SMALL SCHOOLS
Deidre Jenson

Small communities provide a unique dynamic. Just as small places can be intimate and interconnected, so too can family ties and histories bring conflicts that can be difficult for school leaders to navigate. Such conflicts may become all too real when you are supervising staff in small schools. Aunties, uncles, grandparents, and other relatives of students often work in the school as teachers, paraprofessionals, cooks, secretaries, custodians, and so on. Teachers may teach their own children, raising questions of favoritism (founded or not) among staff or students. If you lead a small school, you will need to successfully navigate the politics of hiring, supervision, and classroom issues while trying to nurture a positive school climate. Past experiences, positive or negative, can impact how well teams work together in a school.

Small schools also provide unique opportunities and challenges for students. When there are only two or three students within the same grade, relationships can be deep and enduring. Yet conflicts can have notably high stakes, as there are few other same-age peers for attention, support, or friendships. With small numbers, students eat, learn, collaborate, travel, and play together. They become like siblings, and siblings can fight more than friends. Supporting students in small-school classrooms requires purposeful educators who pay attention to the social-emotional context. You and your teachers can't just approach class the same way you would with twenty or more students. You may need to approach class in ways that more closely resemble teaching family—not least because many students *will* be family.

You will need to pay attention to the social-emotional learning needs of students in small schools, and you'll ideally be informed by knowledge of the community. If you or your teachers are unfamiliar with the community, with families, or with the relational network in which you serve, reach out. Others in the school will have history and knowledge of the families and place. Find out as much as you can about your families. Find out who community leaders are, how families provide for themselves, and what they hope the school provides. There are many organizations in Alaska that can provide support for efforts to provide positive learning environments in small schools. A good start can be found in the Alaska Department of Education & Early Development's School Climate and Connectedness resources (https://

education.alaska.gov/schoolcounselbhlth/scc). A small school is, we think, the perfect stage for implementing student- and family-centered supports. Always include the community in these efforts. Collaboratively, you will succeed; alone, you will struggle.

All that said, small communities stick together like glue when it comes to hardships. They are there for each other through thick and thin. We need to look for these positives and build on them. Take the opportunity to encourage helpful attitudes and create opportunities for families to have fun together as well as to work together to overcome obstacles.

Julie Vasquez and Lisa Cates, who comprise the full certified staff of Hollis School, stressed the importance of relationships between teachers and students. The school has approximately 25 students. Lisa has taught in Hollis for seven years and Julie, a few years longer than that. Lisa shared, "We don't call the principal; we don't send kids home or do [in-school suspension]. We practice restorative justice."

Julie said that adverse childhood experiences training (http://www.beyondconsequences.com) and Phlight Club (www.brightwayslearning.org/phlight-club) have been invaluable to their students. Julie also said that she believes kids should come first and that small-school teachers must have the autonomy to create lessons and curricula that will meet their kids' needs.

Lisa cheerfully mentioned their "bus plan": "If Julie and I both get hit by the same bus, we have a plan for the school and community to continue right on with the way we do things. You can't let your initiatives be solely dependent on the teachers."

CURRICULAR, COCURRICULAR, AND EXTRACURRICULAR OPPORTUNITIES
Evelyn Willburn

If you look on the Alaska Teacher Placement website (www.alaskateacher.org) under, say, the Anchorage School District, you might see postings like "Chinese Immersion Teacher" and "Boys' Middle School Soccer Assistant Coach." Now take a quick look at one of the rural district sites. You might see that many of these schools are looking for a "Secondary Generalist" or maybe even a "K–12 Generalist."

My science-via-exploding-potato lesson highlights one challenge teachers face when they are trained in one area and asked to teach in others. We don't always know what we're doing and have few economies of scale. You might be the school leader, but you might also have full-time teaching duties. You might find that all of the K–5 students are in one room, and your only secondary teacher is a math/science person. Who is going to teach secondary

ELA? Who is going to coach the basketball team? Maybe there are exactly three high school students who want to play basketball. What can be done?

In small schools, many paraprofessionals take on what are essentially teaching duties, with the certified folks acting as teachers of record. This might worry you because it's not strictly by the book. Please don't fret. Plan on as much oversight and communication with paraprofessionals as possible, and show your support and appreciation for their willingness to take on substantial responsibilities. Let paraprofessionals help however they can, but don't hide from your obligation to provide good plans, to evaluate student work, and to assign grades. Maintain regular communication, and work to stay ahead of potential problems.

Also, consider some creative ways small schools in rural Alaska are providing opportunities for their students. Distance delivery of secondary courses (and even, in some cases, of elementary core instruction) is becoming increasingly common. Some districts, for example, offer high school courses (both core and elective) over video. Classes may be offered by teachers working elsewhere in the district (or, with agreements in place, through another district or via dual enrollment in Alaska colleges) and can include students from any number of sites. If you have students participating in these programs, they will need a consistent on-site person to supervise and assist. If you have only one student in a course, you may not need somebody watching them every minute; that depends on the student.

Keep in mind that internet connections in rural areas are often inconsistent. Jessica Angalkuruk Mark said that, even when offering meaningful internet-based activities (such as including students from other sites in a class), rural communities often struggle with bandwidth. You and your teachers will always need a back-up plan for the days when the internet is down.

ONLINE LEARNING MUST ALSO INVOLVE STANDARDS-BASED LEARNING TO BE OF VALUE

Karla Edenshaw of Higdáa Gándlaay (Hydaburg) offered a caveat about using technology to supplement education in small schools. She related an anecdote from a friend who had taken over a career and technical education (CTE) classroom. This friend noticed a variety of certificates posted on the classroom wall by the previous teacher. One of the certificates stated that a current student had mastered the art of changing brake pads. The teacher asked this student to take a small group and show them how to do it. The student stared blankly and said, "I don't know how to do that." The teacher pointed to the certificate. The student waved it off and said, "Oh, that. I just took an online tutorial."

Another solution for limits on small-school course offerings is offered by many rural Alaska school districts under slightly different names and formats. Southwest Region School District calls it exploration week (E-week for short). One week per quarter is devoted to think-outside-the-box course offerings. These courses are often designed and implemented by the teachers, drawing on their own interests and skills. In addition, secondary students can travel to a larger community for CTE courses, such as welding and health care. Students taking these courses can earn high school credit and be better equipped to transition from high school to the workforce. Southeast Island School District started a similar program years ago and now offers students opportunities at various sites, including a restaurant, a greenhouse, and animal husbandry. Northwest Arctic Borough School District sends students to Qikiqtaġruk (Kotzebue) for two weeks each year for CTE and Inupiaq cultural studies. Alaska Gateway School District has offered an Aurora schedule that brings students from smaller sites into Tok for electives and CTE offerings. Don't see your district listed here? This practice is spreading, so it's worth finding out what your district is doing or thinking about doing.

And what about those three students who want to play basketball? Many rural districts have composite teams; your students might be able to practice at home and travel to meet their team members for games. There are several examples of students traveling to nearby communities for practices via four-wheeler, snowmachine, or skiff. Some rural school districts live on a mini road system, and students can travel by private or school vehicle for such purposes. In general, the answer to challenges in small schools is creativity: If your school doesn't have something, who does? How can you help create access? Keep in mind that creating new things involves some trial, some error, and an understanding that new things might not look the same as others. Is a two-week welding class the same as one that lasts all semester? No. But it's much better than a zero-week welding class.

Local talent is a great way to involve the community in extracurricular activities for your students. Don't get stuck thinking basketball is the only activity worth supporting. Native Youth Olympics is a statewide program operated by the Cook Inlet Tribal Council, and all kinds of assistance are offered from individuals dedicated to the program. There are also academic events, such as Science Olympiad, Poetry Out Loud, and Academic Decathlon. Anything you can do to carve out time and space for students to expand opportunities—including cultural and subsistence activities that local people may be willing to lead—is worth the effort.

There are many opportunities in small schools to provide engaging activities for students. All it takes is a few dedicated individuals and a school leader who supports involvement. It comes under the heading of "other duties as assigned."

OTHER DUTIES AS ASSIGNED
Evelyn Willburn

If you are juggling all of the duties and responsibilities that we have laid out for you, you are busy indeed. But wait, there might be more! Has there ever been an education contract without "other duties as assigned" at the end of the list of responsibilities? This is nowhere more relevant than in a small rural Alaska school.

Custodian, cook, or coach; hauler, health aide, or heavy equipment operator; chauffeur or chaperone. Whether you are a paraprofessional, teacher, or administrator, you may be asked to do any or all of these things. You may have to help rid a house of bedbugs, haul food from the airport, or step in as a substitute teacher (meaning teaching your class as well as another). Resources are limited in small sites, and the school needs all team members to step up and help out where needed. Be willing to help. Many hands make the work light as well as more fun.

You may be given the title of principal or lead teacher (lead teacher is a fancy term for a principal who teaches all day). Regardless of your title, you will find yourself pulled in many directions in small schools. First, there will be your teaching duties, as those cannot wait. Second will come your administrative duties: routine paperwork and reports, hiring and supervision, setting daily schedules, and working with the local advisory board, to name just a few. That might seem like plenty, but there are a million and one things that keep a school running: cleaning and repair work, meal preparation, after-school activities, bear safety (this *is* Alaska), transportation to and from school, travel for students, travel for staff, testing, curriculum, and unpredictable technology and bandwidth. Pair the above with unpredictable weather, delays on grocery and supply orders, unfilled classified (or certified) positions, late-night text messages . . . we're making it seem awful.

Don't despair. Please remember that while you will indeed be wearing many hats (and swapping them out with amazing speed and agility), delegation *is* possible. Experienced certified staff and district office personnel can turn out to be amazing resources, as can paraprofessionals and others with long experience in the school and community.

As a general rule, do not wait for people to offer help. Make it your business to find out what people's areas of strength and interest are and to offer them leadership roles in these areas. Does one of your paraprofessionals love to bake or sew or carve? If so, have them teach some electives. What happens when your cook or custodian doesn't make it to work? You do not need to pick up the slack all by yourself. Try having a contingency plan where staff members can take turns filling in and helping out. Some people truly don't want to step outside of their narrowly defined roles, but most of those people do not live in rural Alaska. Overwhelmingly, people will contribute as team members as long as you let them know what's needed and you treat them as respected colleagues. Remember the section on hiring and being open and honest with people?

Finally, don't be afraid to exercise the power of saying no. This is, of course, a fine line to walk. You don't want to be the "that's not my job" type, but neither do you have to say yes to every opportunity that comes along. The textbook selection committee, for example, can probably wait until next year. You have to have time for you, for your own health and well-being. Speaking of which . . .

SELF-CARE
Evelyn Willburn

Self-care is not an afterthought, is not a selfish behavior, and is not impossible. There are three areas to keep in mind: healthy diet, cardiovascular exercise, and mental health care.

Diet

Many rural communities in Alaska lack fully stocked grocery stores. Unless you are experienced and comfortable with an entirely subsistence-based diet, you will need to purchase food. These days you can order everything you need online and set up subscriptions to items that you will use regularly. Fresh foods can be tricky—you may have to give up on bananas in January— but many types of produce will keep if properly stored. Avoid stress eating. You must plan ahead and have good, healthy food available at all times. And drink lots of water. Some communities have delicious water; for others, you may want to use a filter of some kind.

Exercise

Try to build it into your day. Sometimes, the weather is quite fierce and you would be foolish to take a walk. Are there stairs in your building? Are there tasks in your building or in your house that would give you some exercise? Does the school gym have equipment you can use or evening recreation you could join? The internet has yoga and all manner of other workout videos; maybe you can invite staff and parents to exercise with you. Just keep moving.

Mental Health

School leaders are almost by definition kind and empathetic people. If this is not you, maybe work on that. If it is, you are likely to absorb the pain that others feel. This can quickly translate into burnout and depression. How are you to combat this? Well, diet and exercise can help, but what about somebody to talk to? As a school leader, you definitely don't want to confide your innermost feelings to the people you work with or to parents and community members. These people are your allies; what you need is a confidant (Heifetz & Linsky, 2002).

A confidant is a person you know you can trust, who will listen without judgment or agenda, and who will help you process your feelings so that you can choose the best course of action. If you have come with your spouse or significant other, this person will want to support you but may not always be able to listen and respond in the way that would be most helpful. A peer coach, someone with experience leading in rural Alaska, can be a huge support. If your district doesn't provide one, you can find good networks through the Alaska Council of School Administrators (www.alaskaacsa.org). You might also consider signing up for counseling. In a perfect world, educators would have automatic access to counseling through their districts. Until that time, however, you may need to set it up on your own. There are many agencies around the state that will deliver services remotely. If you're not sure where to start, you can contact the Alaska Department of Health and Social Services to learn about resources in or beyond your region (https://dhss.alaska.gov).

Taking a Break

You do need to leave town occasionally. Some districts provide a stipend for one trip out of the village per year, and if yours offers one, take it. Go to the nearest hub city, go shopping, get a haircut, buy some fresh fruit, and talk to people who you don't see all day every day.

Sometimes, you just need a helping hand. Logistical questions will come up, so who can you ask? There may be a teacher or a paraprofessional who has worked in the school for several years or someone in the district office who knows your community. You may find yourself feeling foolish when you ask, "So how do I make sure I have enough paper towels?" or "When the air carrier agent says, 'I'll call you,' how long do I wait before I check again?" It is important to find someone to be your go-to person. So be your own best friend, and ask someone. Remember that you are your most important resource, and you must make every effort to safeguard every aspect of your own well-being.

WHO TO CALL

What about when things are really tough? You've had an awful day, and you just need someone to help you sort it out. At times like this, you can consider calling the Alaska Crisis Services "warm" line. The "warm" part means that you don't have to be truly in crisis; they will be happy to talk to you even if you just need a listening ear. The number is 877-266-4357, and you can call from anywhere in Alaska: https://carelinealaska.com.

Leading a small school in rural Alaska is obviously a tough job. So why do we do it? Here are just a few of the reasons:

- The personal nature of a small school and community is a strength. A small community will more easily band together to solve problems or address issues. Community support is often strong and consistent.
- Looping (working with the same students over multiple years) is built in. This also saves time in getting to know students' skills every year. As soon as school starts in the fall, a teacher knows the students' strengths and weaknesses and can pick up where they left off with only the small consideration of the summer slide.
- Small schools lend themselves to cooperative learning opportunities and project-based learning.
- Community and parent relationships are easier because everybody is right there. Many parents and other relatives of students work in the schools. You can have a barbecue for the whole community and know everybody by name.
- Establishing a positive learning environment can be easier in a small school with the help of community members and community organizations.
- "It takes a village to raise a child" becomes very real. Small communities become like families, with support and interconnectedness that benefits everyone. Sometimes, the entire staff and students in a school will work together on a single project, with each individual contributing as they are able.
- Multiage classrooms, while they take a special art to navigate, can provide mentoring of younger students by older students. Older students learn to assist younger students and understand to a greater extent what it means to be a role model. This can provide unique learning opportunities for both mentees and mentors.
- If you come from outside of the community, you can learn about ways of life and people unlike your own. Rural Alaska is a magnificent, diverse place, and people who get to experience it are fortunate indeed.

What memories the writing of this chapter has brought up! The three of us, Deidre, Ben and Evelyn, have collectively spent many, many years working in small rural Alaska schools, and we wouldn't have it any other way. If your takeaway is that *small schools are a challenge, but they are worth it*, then you understand this chapter's message. Small schools are personal and caring institutions dedicated to learning. Isn't that what all schools should be about?

We will leave you with one anecdote (among many) that keenly illustrates the "still water runs deep" quality that we encounter in so many rural Alaska students. Evelyn shared,

> I was sitting in the lunchroom in a small school with my elbows on the table. A kindergarten student sat across from me, quietly eating his lunch and examining my freckle-enhanced forearms out of the corner of one eye. "Miss Evelyn," he said after a moment, "you got a lotta beauty marks on you."

TAKEAWAYS

- Small schools often have multiage, multisubject classrooms that require planning.
- Collaboration, interpersonal relationships, and targeted professional development are all elements of successful small schools.
- Small schools present many opportunities, including strong relationships and interdependence.
- Paying attention to self-care and the care of others is important.

Chapter 9

School Climate, Safety, and Learning
Lesa Meath and Janice DeVore Littlebear

Susan Hubbard, longtime rural Alaska educator—teacher, lead teacher, principal, and statewide mentor—shared a story to illustrate the importance of being present:

> Years ago I was a mentor in a small [Southwest] Alaska community. After school on a beautiful fall afternoon, I did a "walk and talk" on the boardwalk around town with an early career teacher I was mentoring. The teacher was sharing her struggles as a first-year teacher and her heartfelt feelings of floundering to adapt to a new culture. As we were walking, we came upon an Elder who was heading in the opposite direction. I smiled and nodded to the Elder as we passed. The Elder did the same back with me, but my teacher, naïve about the importance of this chance encounter, never stopped talking to me nor acknowledged the Elder. I knew she had missed a valuable opportunity to connect to her new home and community.
>
> As soon as we were out of earshot of the Elder, I did a quiet little time-out to draw her attention to what I had just observed. I suggested, "Let's redo this." We circled back around in order to encounter that very same Elder again. This time we stopped. We said hello. We had important conversations about children and the weather, and everybody walked away with smiles on their faces. Most importantly, this first-year teacher walked away with a crucial connection to her new home.
>
> You have to take advantage of those opportunities. If there is a funeral, you have to go. I don't care if you stand in the back and you never speak to anybody, your presence will be appreciated. If there's a community potluck, take something if you cook. If you don't cook, go to the village store and buy a bag of chips or something. Take something! And again, just stand in the back of the room, if need be, until you get your bearings and you know what the protocol is. Again, speak to anybody [who] will look at you and speak to you. Never miss an opportunity. Your presence will be noted. And more importantly, if you are

not there, your absence will be noted. Maybe you will be judged by your presence or your absence.

All relationships, especially those outside the school, are important for the health of the school, village, and community. The positive environment a site leader seeks to create within a school can be found within these relationships. Community members will return the respect you model by simply getting to know them. Your natural curiosity and caring for the community and its members in respectful ways will be returned tenfold. The person at the top sets the tone for the building. A school lead's demeanor is felt by everyone: staff, students, parents, and community.

SCHOOL ENVIRONMENTS

Villages in Alaska have learning environments that are ready-made for education, so pay attention. Our first advice for leadership is to learn about the village, its people, and the local ways of living. This chapter discusses school environments and how they can support rural Alaska student success. We will discuss school environments by sharing stories from three areas: climate, safety, and quality places for learning. We begin with climate.

CREATING A WELCOMING ENVIRONMENT THROUGH CLIMATE

When Jim (a pseudonym) served as a principal in the Bering Strait region, he walked the grounds each morning with the custodian Dan (also a pseudonym). Together they carried bags to pick up trash and carefully examined the paths and play areas for harmful debris and litter. Their morning routine sent the clear message to all community members that the grounds should be presentable prior to the students' arrival and that teaming with staff is the norm. Attention to the building and surrounding area contributed to a shared sense of pride.

You should ensure that everyone who enters the school receives a warm welcome. Ask your staff, "What do students and families see, hear, and feel when they walk into the school?" Can they say, "This is a welcoming, caring place for me?" Offering greetings in person to families, staff, and guests sends a strong message of respect and welcoming. There should be comfortable seating available both inside and outside the building. Elders should be welcome to join students for breakfast or lunch, and school leaders should ensure that Elders are provided meals at no charge. Schools should display cultural values prominently throughout learning spaces, as well as display common phrases and vocabulary in the local language(s). Caring, thoughtful,

School Climate, Safety, and Learning 163

respectful routines, whether based in the school or in the classroom, are the building blocks of a welcoming environment and establish a climate designed for student success.

CREATING WELCOMING SCHOOL ENVIRONMENTS

- School leaders set the tone for buildings. Is your school a happy and welcoming place?
- Do you routinely include community members and Elders in your school, as well as celebrate the local culture(s)?
- Climate includes cleanliness, organization, visual appeal, noise levels, disruptions (announcements), camaraderie, unity, and so much more. How is your school doing?
- Climate also includes communication among teachers and families, teachers and students, and school leaders with . . . everyone. How clear and regular are home-to-school and within-school communication?
- How is the school using professional development to improve school climate or to make school climate more culturally responsive?

KNOW THE VILLAGE AND PLACE WHERE YOU LIVE

Being present—whether at the grocery store, out on the trails, or at the bingo hall—means finding ways to get out in the village and be seen. Encourage

Figure 9.1. School entrance, Qalirneq (Koliganek), Alaska. *Courtesy of Emily Hendricks.*

teachers not to fall into the "triangle trap," limiting themselves to the home-to-school-to-store paths. More than being seen, your interactions should be about truly getting to know the place where you lead. Making efforts to get out and greet individuals shows a commitment to learning about your new community. What better way to learn about the area than to be present in it? Knowing the place where you live and work is a first step for creating a culturally responsive and welcoming climate.

SCHOOLS AS HOSTS

The school can serve as a hub for nonschool events that are important to the community—for example, hosting celebrations, basketball tournaments, dances, holiday events, spay and neuter clinics, and even outside visitors. Principals in rural Alaska need to be aware of visiting groups, programs, and events that can impact school schedules. Schools in rural Alaska often have modern facilities—including reliable internet, running hot water, and space for events—that can support community events, so school leaders should find ways that they can partner to support the goals and interests of communities. Of course, you can count on the unexpected, including bad weather, changing flight schedules, and impromptu visitors. The school building is often the only available "hotel" for visitors, and you won't regret keeping a stash of extra bedding (air mattresses, sleeping bags, and pillows) handy. Stay flexible while always keeping what is best for students at the forefront.

ADVISORY SCHOOL BOARDS

Rural schools in Alaska typically have an advisory school board (ASB). These are required under Alaska statute for communities with at least fifty residents. ASBs are intended to give communities a voice in school operations. One of your first jobs as a school leader should be to meet with each ASB member, find out why they are serving, and identify goals they may have for the school. You will need to account for those goals (provide data, a plan, etc.) whenever you meet, otherwise the ASB may become frustrated with you, and their role will be less than it could be. "I am here to learn" is the mantra one successful principal reminds herself as she greets members before every ASB meeting. She sets the agenda, inviting input from all while fully recognizing that conversations may drift. Often the greatest amount of learning comes from the birdwalking (unexpected stories) shared among members. As long as snacks are available, chairs are comfortable, and the door is open, the stage will be set for important talk and shared decision making. A successful site leader does not presume their view to be the only one. For some, it can be a challenge to stop looking at the clock in order to allow whatever time is needed for conversations and decisions.

PROFESSIONAL DEVELOPMENT: HONORING PLACE, COMMUNITY, AND HISTORY

Professional development and staff meetings are venues in which school leaders and staff can come to understand how schools in rural Alaska have shaped and been shaped by the histories of communities. This knowledge should then be used to create a more welcoming climate. A veteran teacher in Bering Strait, Evan (a pseudonym), told of how his early teaching practices were transformed by developing a relationship with a local Elder:

> In my first year living in the village, I got to know Elder Peter, who was known for befriending the new teachers. He and his wife shared stories of the history of the area and provided tips for keeping the frigid cold out around the windows. They were generous with seal and fish. They had several grandchildren and great grandchildren enrolled in the school. It was Peter who enlightened me about the damage and trauma inflicted upon Indigenous peoples through colonization. My intern experience 3,000 miles away in the Minnesota suburbs ill-prepared me for a tiny Alaskan village of 350.
>
> In my third year, the principal notified me that in addition to English Language Arts, I would start teaching social studies. As I read over the purchased curriculum, it was clear that the materials offered were incomplete and highly inaccurate. Even the Alaska history section didn't begin to portray the legacy of oppression. Missing were examples of celebrations, accomplishments, [and] the strength and beauty of the cultures of Alaska. At the encouragement of my principal and under the guidance of Peter and other Elders, I decided to construct a semester-long unit. I wanted to empower my students to see their traditions, language, and spirituality as integral to their whole selves. These same Elders, who as young students saw their culture adversely affected, became [recognized as] gifted experts. [N]o matter how much I read and try to learn, it will never equal the lived experience of an Elder.

Welcoming climates within the school contribute to a caring educational environment where students can succeed. Let's move on to safety.

SAFETY CONTRIBUTES TO A WELCOMING ENVIRONMENT

As you read this section on safety, you might be expecting a check-off list covering fire and earthquake drills and how to handle physical altercations on the playground. Fortunately, there are handbooks, school board policies, and statutes to provide some guidance on those. Such guides are certainly a solid starting point. However, safety is more than the physical building and check-off lists; safety includes all sorts of serious issues and a variety of local events that may arise in rural Alaska:

- *Suicide prevention*: Some villages have suicide-prevention protocols. Does yours? If not, how do you create them? Suicide warning signs and ready responses to keep kids safe and well are an essential safety protocol in most villages. Be on top of the process.
- *Child abuse/neglect/sexual abuse*: Reporting is handled by the Office of Children's Services (https://dhss.alaska.gov/ocs/pages/default.aspx) and, in some cases, by Tribal authorities. Do you know the steps required by your district and the Tribe and how those steps fit with the norms of your village?
- *Health clinics and public safety*: Your community may have a health clinic, regional health association, village public safety officer, village police officer, or the Alaska State Troopers. What do each of these entities do? How do they fit within your school? When and whom are you to call?
- *School safety*: Many basic issues are covered by school district training or through the Alaska Department of Education & Early Development (see resources below, including Alaska's safety-related eLearning modules). Everyone is worried about liability, so it is key to become familiar with your district handbook (if you are lucky enough to have one). Keep it handy as a resource. Share with staff the pieces they need to understand and follow. Regularly revisit to make sure all are in the know.
- *School safety plans/crisis management*: Learn (and regularly share) the basics, such as the handling of keys, chain of command, communication, fire safety, weather, and travel. Do all staff understand these protocols?
- *Risk management:* Basic supervision of minors is important, especially with a high volume of visitors and travel. How does your school generally host visitors or supervise student/staff travel? How will students and staff be supervised and protected at all times?
- *Counseling and social work*: Resources vary by village; rural schools are often without counselors or social workers on site. How will you handle ongoing needs for supports in your school? Do you have a plan?
- *Ethics*: Alaska has a professional code of ethics your teachers need to understand and follow (https://education.alaska.gov/teachercertification/20aac10). Do you understand the steps required to make sure the guidelines are known and followed?
- *Local supports*: These may include Boys & Girls Clubs, churches, the Tribe, and others. Are you familiar with the many supports available to you, and do you have the referral names/numbers at your fingertips?

Figure 9.2. Students in the wind, Qaaktuġvik (Kaktovik), Alaska. *Courtesy of Seth Adams.*

Practicality is an important aspect in a rural Alaska school. Learn what the local habits and village protocols are that govern adult-to-child interactions. For example, in many villages, calling the Office of Children's Services is frowned upon. Get out in front of this issue. Let everyone know that you will follow the law, yet you do not want state interference in situations that are better handled locally. Sometimes, there is a tension between what you might think is right and what others may think. *How can you navigate?* Ask yourself, How can we follow the law and still respect the community's ability to handle personal or family issues?

With safety, policy is the best medicine. Make sure policies are in place, explicit in nature, taught to others, and followed. Follow up routinely, such as on the no-smoking rules. You can say, "I can't let you smoke here; can you move away from the school to smoke?" or "Do you think we should build a smoking shelter just off school grounds for people who want to smoke when coming to basketball games?" Be creative, collaborative, and part of a team when establishing all of these safety protocols, and then make sure your staff knows what to do given any circumstance.

DISTRICT HANDBOOKS

If one is available, start with your district handbook. Pay particular attention to safety protocols, and make sure routines are understood and practiced by all. Fire drills, communication methods, building access, and security of hazardous tools and materials all need explicit expectations. Keep detailed records showing you are following the appropriate protocols. In a village school, the kitchen may be used for a funeral potlatch or wrestling teams traveling for a tournament. The responsibility to supervise always remains with the site administrator or designee to ensure safety. Circumstances not covered in a handbook may need to be determined at the site level, such as access to showers and sleeping accommodations. Maintaining the school grounds' cleanliness, cafeteria rules, and the rules for hosting overnight school visitors requires knowing the safety protocols. Where are these guidelines kept? Can staff readily access if needed?

Safety doesn't always require heavy lifting. Susan Hubbard, an experienced rural Alaska educator-teacher-principal, shares that her favorite superintendent helped pick up the trash and empty the wastebaskets. Remember that you set the tone for the school. What you do matters. Yearly (at a minimum) share safety guidelines with all staff, both certified and noncertified. Check in with paraprofessionals about what has and has not been effective in the past. Don't be afraid to ask questions. Truly, safety is a 24/7 responsibility. Be prepared. Safe schools require more than handbooks.

TRAUMA-INFORMED INSTRUCTION

The power of establishing a safe, consistent, and caring school environment is not in debate. School systems that prioritize trauma-informed practices achieve positive outcomes. Dr. Laura Bruner, a pediatrician in Fairbanks, said the following during a presentation on the Fairbanks radio station KUAC: "With the support of good parenting by either a parent or another significant adult, a child's cognitive and social development can proceed positively, even with a lot of adversity." Trauma-informed care can and should include the experiences young people have at school.

Consider a student who comes to class tired and surly because he was up all night playing video games. Or worse. Do teachers insist that he sit up straight, answer questions, and behave like a model student for the entire period? Or is there some small logic in allowing a quick cat nap, with his head down on a desk?

We're not suggesting that letting surly kids nap is an always-right answer, yet it's also probably true that teachers can try to fight biology, get hostile responses, and end up kicking kids out of class. Whose interests are served? We suggest that teachers and leaders must usually choose how to respond to students (and their behaviors) based on individual student knowledge and relationships. So while a "no heads on desks" rule may be clean and easy to support in the abstract, does it work? A useful way to think about trauma-informed instruction is one that considers student outcomes. When students face stressors at home, in relationships, or emerging from family or community responsibilities, what are the odds that adding avoidable school stress will help students learn? Trauma-informed instruction is not a call for inaction or pity; it is instead a pragmatic way to ask, What do students need to help them learn?

Be the leader of a school that puts the focus on learning instead of controlling behavior. Rather than using the phrase *classroom management*, why not talk about *classroom environment*? What child wishes to be managed? The damaging results of managing students can be lifelong. Ronalda Cadiente Brown, Aantooxu.aat, an experienced school leader and the associate vice chancellor for Alaska Native Programs at the University of Alaska Southeast, shared her thoughts on a decision to be supportive when interacting with students during a conflict or crisis. She considered what her actions now might mean for the days and years to come:

> One day, that student is going to be an adult and encountering me in public. What kind of eye contact do I want? In other words, I'm not going to paint them in a corner. I'm not going to be unnecessarily harsh or judgmental. I want to see growth. And I want I them to learn from the experience.

Later, Ronalda's respectful interactions with students at school were rewarded when she encountered many of these same students, now grown. They picked up where they had left off; relationships were still strong. Leaders should practice this lifelong perspective, as well as encourage such a mindset among staff.

TRAUMA-INFORMED SOLUTIONS

One school outside of Mamterilleq (Bethel) identified attendance and engagement as a long-standing challenge and decided to pursue improved social-emotional learning as a means to overall school improvement. Rather than placing blame for behaviors on students, staff examined what they could do to create a learning environment that was positive and connected lessons with students. The school provided professional development from the Alaska Department of Education & Early Development and in partnership with Tribal health care experts in the region. One secondary teacher described her learning:

> I knew my students faced challenges, but I never considered what I might be doing that was causing harm. I now see steps I can take to provide a safer environment. I haven't been doing enough to validate and acknowledge my students

for the great job they are doing. My goal is to name and notice accomplishments and call them out in a good way.

A school leader who values *working with* instead of *doing to* students is a colearner with staff as they develop techniques for positive communication and trauma-informed solutions. Such work is integral to transforming our rural schools into welcoming learning spaces that respect human diversity and dignity.

ELIMINATE LABELS AND BIAS

In rural Alaska schools, when students are labeled by teachers or other staff (as "good" or "bad"), those labels can be long-lasting. Veteran educator Gguitka Sperry Ash explained that favoritism can cause real harm:

> I think we should recognize [that] not only does it disrupt the potential of a child in the classroom, [but it also] extends out to the families and communities. And that's where what happens in school really weeds us out. Favoritism just melts the rug right under them. It happens. It happens a lot.

Schools can unknowingly set the stage for identifying families as "better" or "worse," and harmful narratives can spread. You may hear stories or gossip about students and their families. Be very aware of bias, and avoid categorizing students. Sometimes, it is best to just be direct and say, "I don't want to hear anyone talking negatively about a family or a child." Such negative talk is damaging and has no place in schools or among staff.

HISTORICAL TRAUMA AMONG INDIGENOUS PEOPLES IS REAL

While a reckoning with historical traumas among Indigenous peoples in the Americas is still emerging, the evidence of harm is well established. Genocide, epidemic-related deaths, land theft, and disruptions of culture and language during the assimilation/boarding-school era resonate today and shape the context of your work in rural Alaska (Dunbar-Ortiz, 2015; Pember, 2021; Treuer, 2019). It is essential that school leaders help all staff be able to understand and value communities and their histories. It is also essential that the school find pathways to culturally responsive teaching and to the kinds of supports that students and families need. Be part of the solution by leading the school in ways that demonstrate respect and that honor the futures communities most value for their young people.

SUICIDE

Suicide is perhaps the most urgent safety issue in rural Alaska schools today. We each have power to help. There are resources for you and for communities. See the Alaska Native Tribal Health Consortium for good supports across rural Alaska: www.anthc.org/what-we-do/behavioral-health/suicide-prevention. For immediate crises, call Alaska Careline at 1-877-266-4357 or visit www.carelinealaska.com. All teachers and leaders in Alaska must complete suicide-prevention training; details and free modules are available at the Alaska Department of Education & Early Development: https://education.alaska.gov/tls/suicide.

Here is a story from Cetuyaraq (New Stuyahok) that may be useful. When a just-graduated student died by his own hands, the village was traumatized. Action was taken by local people. The village, Bristol Bay Health Services, and the Tribal government got together and crafted a plan. The school principal was given a list of 30 people to call whenever there was evidence that a student may be at risk of self-harm. The principal would call these people, who would quickly put together a group of five or six people (mostly women). They would go to the home of the student to talk. There was always follow-up.

This is how prevention can work in rural Alaska—collaboratively and from the ground up. We need everyone able to recognize depression, recognize and respond to abuse or neglect, and understand their role when young people tell us they need help.

CULTURALLY RESPONSIVE SCHOOLS CREATE CARING EDUCATIONAL ENVIRONMENTS

An essential element for student success is creating learning places that are culturally responsive. Gguitka Sperry Ash commented: "If students walk into a classroom and nothing is reflective of them[,] they think, 'Wow, I am not a part of this. This [school] is not a place for me.'" He went on to say that a common response from educators not from rural Alaska is to say, "Well, I want to expose them to everything *else*." The problem, then, is that everything else often becomes *all* that rural students are exposed to, leaving little room for the lived experiences of the students. Becoming a culturally responsive place for learning ensures that rural students' experiences and narratives are an essential piece of school.

Figure 9.3. Student in Curyung (Dillingham). *Courtesy of Emily Hendricks.*

CONSIDERATIONS FOR CREATING QUALITY, CULTURALLY RESPONSIVE LEARNING ENVIRONMENTS

- Use input from the staff and community to identify elements of culturally responsive learning environments for all students.
- Explore how district and school behavior plans can fit with the existing cultures, norms, beliefs, and value systems in the village. Adapt wherever needed.
- Learn, implement, and monitor the use of the Alaska Standards for Culturally Responsive Schools (https://education.alaska.gov/standards/cultural).
- Use and make sure all staff understand place-based teaching strategies.

HIGH EXPECTATIONS

One Elder and paraprofessional from Western Alaska lamented, "Our kids have the same lessons every year. Third grade, fourth grade, all the way to seventh grade, the same stuff. These teachers don't think our kids are smart."

Sadly, a common narrative about schools in rural Alaska is their lack of rigor. Instructional leaders need to ensure teachers are addressing appropriate academic standards and using effective instructional methods. Students vary in interests and skills, yet teachers must believe each student capable and teach in ways that promote academic success. High expectations for learning should be the norm, not the exception.

High expectations are demonstrated when teachers connect content to learners, develop lessons based on knowledge of the students, incorporate local history and culture, and invite families to contribute to educational decisions. This overall goal has been described succinctly by the Alaska Standards for Culturally Responsive Schools in Standard E: "Culturally-responsive educators recognize the full educational potential of each student and provide the challenges necessary for them to achieve that potential" (Alaska Native Knowledge Network, 1998).

School leaders are required to provide evidence that teachers are meeting the Alaska cultural standards during evaluations. You should help staff regularly self-assess their performance in this area—you will be glad you did, and you will be setting your students up for success. One approach you can take is to partner successful, experienced teachers and paraprofessionals, who can model quality place-based instruction, with early career teachers.

The first step for everyone is knowing students and their individual needs. Next is creating or adapting curricula to meet student needs by connecting lessons to students and their background knowledge. During a Sealaska Heritage Institute lecture series aimed at bringing the community into culturally responsive education, Tlingit educator Shgen George stated, "Culture is a lens that we access the standards through. Presenting this way [through culture] gives our kids the opportunity to live in both worlds and have those worlds come together" (Sealaska Heritage, 2020).

PLACE-BASED LEARNING

One August, a principal in a Lower Yukon village learned that his two newlywed teachers were unable to fly in as scheduled. The plane was grounded in a neighboring village because of smoky conditions caused by burning grass. The principal knew there were people from his village attending a funeral where the teachers were grounded, so he made a few calls. He connected the people attending the funeral with the new teachers and arranged for them to travel by boat up the Kuigpak (Yukon River) in place of the unavailable flight. Those two teachers were blessed with an immediate immersion into the local culture, which included stopping along the way to pick blueberries and listening to stories as they navigated the winding river to their new home. By the time all reached the school site hours later, the teachers had made new friends, parents had connected with the teachers, and relationship building had begun.

Site leaders can be travel agents as well as administrators of their schools—a skillset probably omitted by required coursework for becoming a principal. Two assets for all school leaders in rural Alaska are the place and the people. You may or may not be able to scare up a boat for stuck teachers, but you can certainly find ways to help staff develop relationships and for the educational experiences of students to be grounded in where they are.

Culture camps can be a great investment for connecting educators and place in rural Alaska. Learning to fish, gather berries, forage, and dance are life-changing experiences for teachers who participate—and what better way to become more literate in the strengths and needs of students? Each region, each community, is distinct. It is essential that everyone at school learns where they are and how to shape experiences in ways that are meaningful for young people.

INDIGENOUS LANGUAGES IN SCHOOLS

Schools with healthy Indigenous language programs and bilingual/bicultural programs have better climates and better academic outcomes than those without (Alaska Department of Education & Early Development, 2020a; Hillman, 2016; Kim, 2019). Indigenous languages are a foundational component of culture, knowledge systems, and identity. Languages shape how we think. School leaders must find ways to honor and respect local languages. You may not be an expert at languages yourself, but you can certainly invite language speakers to share how they think the school could support language preservation or revitalization. Elsewhere in this book, we discuss at length cross-cultural leadership and teaching through culture, including discussion of Indigenous language revitalization and immersion programs. If you are lucky enough to be in a school with a vibrant Indigenous language program, embrace it. You are in a good place. And if there's progress yet to be made at the school where you lead, consider how you can contribute. The work ahead will be valuable and rewarding, and it will likely have you learning right beside staff, students, and the community.

LOOKING AHEAD

Not one of these essential elements for creating a welcoming, friendly educational environment—climate, safety, or quality places for learning—is simple. There is no single answer. Rather, each element works in concert with the others to create a school where students can succeed. Rural Alaska is filled with generous, wise, and inquisitive individuals. Listen to them. It is amazing to learn from those who intimately know the cultures, histories, and land. As was mentioned early on in this chapter, you lead in a community and school context that is ideal in many ways for the learning and development of young people. The students are familiar with the land and the community. Their families are present for support, and their histories have been a part of their lives from birth. What better place is there for providing an education?

Be open to new ideas and perspectives in your leadership. Gguitka Sperry Ash described one way to think about our charge as leaders of rural Alaska schools: "If we meet halfway, versus always making them come to us on our terms and our clock, and on our curriculum . . . if we meet them halfway as a human, as humans, then we're working together."

TAKEAWAYS

- A welcoming environment requires collaboration.
- A positive school climate includes organization, cleanliness, and respect.
- School leaders must know plans, policy, and people to ensure schools are safe.
- Trauma-informed schools and staff are essential to help all students.
- Culturally responsive and place-based instruction create quality learning environments.

RESOURCES

- Alaska Department of Education & Early Development: Alaska Standards for Culturally Responsive Schools. https://education.alaska.gov/standards/cultural
- Alaska Department of Education & Early Development: school safety and emergency management (includes safety-related eLearning modules). https://education.alaska.gov/safeschools/safeandemerg
  - Child Abuse and Neglect
  - Domestic Violence and Sexual Assault
  - Equity Training for Educators
  - School Crisis Response Planning
  - Suicide
  - Trauma Sensitive Schools
- Alaska Department of Public Safety: https://dps.alaska.gov/AST/VPSO/Home

- Alaska Mental Health Trust: https://alaskamentalhealthtrust.org/
- Alaska Native Justice Center: https://anjc.org/services/
- Alaska Native Tribal Health Consortium: http://www.anthc.org/what-we-do/behavioral-health/suicide-prevention
- Alaska Careline: 1-877-266-4357. www.carelinealaska.com
- Alaska School Counselor Association: www.alaskaschoolcounselor.org
- Alaska State Troopers: https://dps.alaska.gov/AST/Home
- Indian Child Welfare Act: www.childwelfare.gov/topics/systemwide/diverse-populations/americanindian/icwa
- Suicide Prevention Resource Center: www.sprc.org
- Trauma Sensitive Schools: Helping Traumatized Children Learn. https://traumasensitiveschools.org
- Adverse Childhood Experience; US Centers for Disease Control and Prevention: http://www.cdc.gov/violenceprevention/aces
- Alaska Department of Education & Early Development; Trauma Engaged Schools: https://education.alaska.gov/apps/traumawebtoolkit/new-framework-page.html

Chapter 10

Supervision

Recruiting, Improving, and Keeping Good Teachers

Robert S. Thompson and Christian P. Wilkens

Samantha Johnson (a pseudonym), the principal at a nine-teacher K–12 school in Interior Alaska, hesitated before returning a call from human resources. It was mid-January, and the district needed to make decisions about teacher contracts for the following school year. Sam (as everyone called her) wasn't sure what to recommend concerning the school's special education teacher, Colleen Woods (also a pseudonym). Sam knew how hard it had been to recruit Colleen. There were no guarantees *anyone* would be out there to replace Colleen if she was not offered a contract to return.

The issue with Colleen, thought Sam, wasn't active student harm. Colleen was pleasant as a colleague and person; she didn't yell at the kids or miss work or complain. Students appeared to enjoy spending time with her and visited her room throughout the day (a point of contention with other teachers, whose classes were occasionally skipped). She had a couch, snacks, and laptops—and she showed little inclination to monitor what students did with them.

The issue, Sam thought, was that Colleen did almost entirely her own thing. For example, Collen refused to support or use the adopted math curriculum, claiming that her students needed something "more concrete." As far as Sam could tell, that meant copying lots of worksheets Colleen had brought from her time in other rural Alaska school districts. Nor did Colleen spend time in other classrooms to work with fellow teachers or students, as previous special education teachers had done. And, unlike her colleagues, Colleen consistently declined to supervise student activities, chaperone trips, or helping out during tournaments or other activities at school. Colleen's absence beyond regular hours was in notable contrast to the other teachers, many of whom regularly stayed after school, dashed home for dinner, and returned for evening activities.

Most recently, Colleen had returned from winter break with a dog, a large golden retriever. Having dogs in teacher housing was fine, but Colleen had started bringing the dog to school. She had set up a bed under her desk and declared at a staff meeting that the dog was a "therapy" dog. It was true that some students liked the dog, occasionally sneaking treats from breakfast or lunch to Colleen's room. It was just as true that district policy prohibited dogs at school and that some students were afraid of dogs. When Sam had brought up the no-dogs policy, Colleen had told her that it didn't apply to therapy animals—*and* she wanted to know who, precisely, had complained.

Sam was torn. Colleen was a certified teacher who seemed to connect with her students in an area hard to staff, yet she was imperfect in several known ways. Sam needed to call HR but didn't know what to recommend. Bring Colleen back? Move on? Something else entirely?

Everyone has a wish list. Maybe yours includes a new stove or boots that don't leak. (A pony?) High on the list of most school leaders is a collection of good and caring people for every position in the school. Notice we're not saying *perfect* people. There is no such group of humans. Instead, school leaders in rural Alaska need to recruit, supervise, and retain staff members with diverse strengths and weaknesses. Effective supervision isn't a single act (e.g., visiting classes and providing brilliant feedback). Effective supervision is a process that involves learning about each individual, recognizing how their work does (or doesn't) contribute to student success, and identifying ways to support professional growth. Colleen is one such individual who, like many in rural Alaska, isn't perfect. How you approach staff like Colleen shapes your success as a school leader and, ultimately, the success of the school.

Staffing challenges are near universal in rural Alaska. It can be hard to find good people, hard to help them grow professionally, and hard to keep them for more than a year or two. Rural Alaska schools have seen sustained high turnover ($\geq 35\%$ annually) for generations (Vazquez Cano et al., 2019). Vacancies and turnover harm students, drain resources, disrupt community relationships, and can demoralize even the best leaders. As Ty Mase, former superintendent of the Lake and Peninsula School District, commented,

> It's probably one of the most frustrating things about the job . . . the fact that you could build a dream team, you could give them the best professional development, you could have an incredible focus on, for example, early literacy . . . and two years down the road, close to half of those people are gone!

In rural Alaska, teacher retention and stability are among the best predictors of student achievement (Roehl, 2010). Fit with communities is another good predictor of positive impact (Tetpon et al., 2015; Amarok, 2014; Hirshberg, 2019). And nationwide, experienced teachers are generally more effective than rookies (Edge, 2017; Kini & Podolsky, 2016; Chingos & Peterson, 2011; Papay & Kraft, 2015). It's hard to know precisely who will fit in any context. In general, the goal is to find people who care about kids, become part of the community, and are eager to learn and collaborate with staff. The good news is that you're in a place that's an easy initial sell for many. As Rick Luthi, administrator for the Lake and Peninsula School District, put it:

> Alaska is still, all things considered, a wonderful place to be called a teacher. I think the opportunity to impact kids' lives is great up here. How we can get that message out there is our challenge, but I think it's still the best place to become a teacher that I know.

Fortunately, school leaders often have influence over recruitment, and your role in supervision and retention is extensive. Salary isn't the only factor that's decisive (though it matters). New teachers may decide to teach in their home communities to "give back," or they might come from Outside, lured by imagined adventures, but they'll stay only if they feel supported by leadership, enjoy their days at school, connect with communities, and feel like they're effective (Alaska Department of Education & Early Development, 2021). Below are some approaches to supervision, recruitment, and retention that have succeeded in rural Alaska. Some may be good fits for the school where you work; others, less so. No matter what else happens, investing time and resources in this area is worth it. Get staffing wrong, and there's almost nothing else you'll be able to do right.

SUPERVISE EFFECTIVELY

Supervising effectively sums up your job as a school leader. Yet before you supervise anyone, you need to attend to the basics. Here's how McQueen School principal Lyle Melkerson in Kivaliñiq (Kivalina) described his order of priorities as a school leader: "Making sure kids are warm, making sure the water comes in, making sure the lights are on, sewage goes out . . . making sure the kids are fed relatively on time. Safety is, of course, our priority."

While attending to those basic needs, you must also turn your attention to supervising instruction. To keep from getting bogged down with day-to-day operations, you need a detailed plan; you can't be everywhere all at once. Depending on your role, you're likely to supervise a variety of people: teachers, paraprofessionals, administrative assistants, and perhaps others. Knowledge is a key first step. You need to know who is doing their job well.

Supervising effectively is dependent on two key attributes: trust and respect. Both of these attributes take time. Trust is built through honest communication and by frequently demonstrating your intentions to do what is best for students and the community. Respect is built through showing your commitment to assist your staff in any way possible, along with demonstrating your understanding of good practices and vision for improving student success.

You will also need to prioritize the needs of your staff. Supervision is most effective when it is collaborative. You must take time to discuss the needs of the whole school with staff and community members. You should, as a group, develop incremental goals that promote continuous school improvements.

EFFECTIVE SUPERVISION IN RURAL ALASKA

1. Build trust; give and earn respect.
2. Keep an open-door policy.
3. Visit all classrooms regularly.
4. Collaborate with staff to make school improvements.
5. Develop systems to handle multiple problems simultaneously.
6. Avoid hearsay; learn for yourself.
7. Communicate effectively and frequently.
8. Be visible in all places in the school and community.
9. Praise in public; correct errors in private.
10. Support staff in parent meetings whenever possible.
11. Get contractual details right.
12. Have courage when making difficult decisions.

You'll need to become comfortable evaluating staff within frameworks established by the district. Many districts in Alaska use Danielson or Marzano; there are others as well. Learning to use these tools effectively and efficiently will make your job of supervision much easier. When someone is doing good work, you should be able to clearly show that by using district tools. When someone struggles, that, too, should be clear on records, not just according to your intuition. Your district's human resources office is the best resource for learning the ropes and will welcome discussions when you have questions or concerns about specific positions or people. As a rule, do not surprise human resources.

Teacher evaluations should be used as a staff-development process, not merely a means of praising or criticizing. This requires regular classroom visits and individual discussions about improved instruction. Rather than general "you're doing just fine" discussions, try to focus on specific actions—for example, how a teacher creates a positive learning environment, delivers lessons, or provides opportunities for hands-on learning. Your observations and the evaluation process can then become focused and developmental, hence useful.

STAFF EVALUATIONS

- Create a weekly/monthly schedule of classroom visits; do more than required.
- Observe carefully and share specifics; this builds respect.
- Be specific with feedback; saying "Good job" is not as effective as "Students became really engaged when you connected the math lesson to subsistence hunting."
- Send short handwritten notes after walk-through observations (purchase cards with envelopes to emphasize care in making comments).
- Only talk to your supervisors about employee issues.
- Evaluations should not be one-sided; they are about improving teacher performance through collaboration.
- Always conduct pre- and post-formal observation conferences; these can be short.
- Ask what a teacher's needs are; develop a plan for addressing those needs.
- Remember that evaluation is about improving practices, not asserting authority.

Good judgment is necessary for good supervision. If a staff member is doing something that causes a negative impact, it must be addressed. For example, a teacher putting a student in a corner, facing away from the classroom, is not acceptable. Sometimes you will need to be direct and be critical ("It is not acceptable to put a student in the corner, facing away from the classroom."). Always be explicit in explaining problems and in directing what needs to be done differently. In some cases, this may require a letter of reprimand. Ongoing issues may require a plan for improvement. Just keep reminding yourself that this is about improving practices, not asserting authority.

Importantly, effective supervision in rural Alaska schools happens *in rural Alaska*. Not some idealized place elsewhere. You may have to tinker with staff responsibilities to fit the strengths of the people you have rather than wishing staff members were somehow different or better. In thinking about Colleen—our opening story—one consideration might be the context of the school: How does the collection of people here complement Colleen's known strengths and weaknesses? In this context is she more help than harm?

Especially if you're new, getting insight from others can be valuable. Being a school leader can be a very lonely job. In many small schools, you're it. You're the one making leadership decisions. How can you avoid making difficult decisions entirely on your own? This may sound simple, but find ways to connect with other school leaders. Those in your district share some of the same context, and those outside your district can share some outside perspective. If you're not sure where to start, ask your district for an assigned mentor, and/or seek colleagues through professional networks such as the Alaska Council of School Administrators.

Frequent, clear, and informative communication is essential for effective supervision. Daily emails or texts sent to staff can keep a staff informed without holding lengthy staff meetings. Staff meetings are important, but don't waste time in meetings on issues affecting only some staff. Hold separate meetings for those issues with affected people, and release notes to staff who do not attend. Include your paraprofessionals in all communications. Sometimes, this means holding a separate staff meeting with paraprofessionals. They are important members of your staff and deserve your attention.

Do not talk about employees with other people. Praising staff is always acceptable, but public criticism is never okay. When talking with individuals about their own practices, provide authentic praise before criticism. Be as positive as you can. Be specific. Always maintain confidentiality. And support staff in meetings with parents as much as possible; correct mistakes they may have made in private.

How you supervise makes a big difference in the life of the school. Do staff feel noticed? Do they have a sense that you care about them and will support them when they struggle? Are your decisions predictable and fair? Experienced Bering Strait teacher and administrator Suzzuk Mary Huntington said that supervision often comes down to a balance of patience, cheerleading, and trust:

> When we were getting our administrator training and talking about how to effect change, [we learned] how to watch and observe before . . . making changes. I mean, if something downright wrong is going on—yes, that has to be addressed. But it's rare that something downright wrong and dangerous is going on. When I supervised, there were often a whole bunch of things that I didn't like, that I desperately wished I could change. But no, it's not guns blazing. It's knowing how to discern the immediate changes that will contribute to setting the positive atmosphere. You wait for the time to be right.
>
> It really comes down to building the trust. I never offer suggestions during a first or second, maybe not even a third observation, I only offer praise. So [if] we're doing walkthroughs, which means we're in there for five minutes,

the only thing I share is the thing that earns the gold star. There might be other stuff happening. Establish that trust and show them "I see that you're doing this really well." [They might think,] "I'm doing that really well? Yay!" [Laughs.] And then over time, it becomes "What can I do better?"

As always, listening is far more important than talking. To be effective, an administrator must hear what employees are saying and respond in ways that promote a collaborative atmosphere. The more you can ask open-ended questions that lead to introspection, problem-solving, and understanding, the more clearly staff will feel heard and supported—critical components in job satisfaction and retention.

RETAIN PEOPLE YOU ALREADY HAVE

In rural Alaska it may be more effective to work with the people you already have than to replace them. Why? For one, they've chosen work in *this* community, with *these* students. And they already have some experience. They may not be "perfect" (whatever that means), but they're there. It's difficult and expensive to recruit, hire, and onboard new people in rural Alaska (one estimate was > $20,000 per teacher; DeFeo et al., 2017). What else could you do with $20,000? Buy some gym equipment? Professional development? Fresh fruit for staff meetings?

Teachers and staff in rural Alaska schools need to feel valued. Being explicitly supportive can go a long way in creating a positive climate and

Figure 10.1. Teacher in Qalirneq (Koliganek), Alaska. *Courtesy of Emily Hendricks.*

in shaping how people make stay-or-leave decisions. Emma Melkerson, an experienced elementary teacher in Kivaliñiq (Kivalina), outlined what she needs from her principal:

> I need a school leader to let me do my job. I went to college. I know how to do things. I need them to back me up. And I need them to listen. Sometimes, I don't need a problem solved. I just need you to listen to my problem for a second. I also need them to be flexible and be able to ask questions of me. When you come in and see me doing weird things, don't assume . . . *"It's not in the curriculum! She's not doing what she's supposed to!"* Ask me to explain myself. You have to be everybody's principal.

We shared a story in an earlier chapter about a school superintendent who walked around the building each morning, inspecting the grounds and picking up litter. That made a difference. You might not be able to pick up litter each morning, but maybe you can write down the names of everyone's grandchildren so you can ask after them. Maybe you can bring staff some Cinnabons next time you fly out through Dgheyaytnu (Anchorage). Just keep doing the little things along with the big things. They add up.

We want to be clear that we're encouraging you to spend time promoting retention of good teachers who care about students. Not just warm bodies. Anyone can tolerate a warm body. Not taking action to improve or replace ineffective teachers is one of the ways you can truly damage your school. We owe students far better. If your supervisory visits identify a teacher who is doing harm—who cannot organize a classroom, who doesn't understand how to help young people learn, or who is consistently negative or toxic—then your first order of business is to clearly specify what you see and what needs to improve. If they show an inability or unwillingness to improve over time, they need to go. Be sure to follow district policies and procedures concerning observations, feedback, documentation, and due dates so that you and the district can take decisive action. You will also need to have courage. It's not ever easy to tell someone that they have not met expectations. In rural Alaska schools, which can be intimate places, it can be even harder. You may know staff beyond the school walls as friends and colleagues who spend a great deal of time together, yet you still need to do the job.

Staff facing negative evaluations will almost invariably be hurt. Many will want to explain themselves, instructionally ("You came on a bad day!") or personally ("Things are rough at home; I've been distracted . . ."). Some will deflect blame to others ("If the third-grade teacher actually did her job before me . . ."), to students ("These kids just don't know how to act!"), or to you ("You never told me you wanted to see hands-on lessons!"). You should listen. There's a chance they're telling you true things, or they may be identifying what they need to improve, or they're just trying to avoid consequences.

In any case, when discussing evaluations, your best approach is to stick with what you observed—the evidence of what happened—including patterns that you've seen over repeated observations. A first negative evaluation may catch someone by surprise. Over time, however, if you've been in classrooms regularly and have been honest about what you see and what the school needs, there shouldn't be any surprises on evaluations, plans of improvement, or decisions about retention.

Every spring you will need to make recommendations about who should stay or go. Outliers (good or bad) are easy. Much harder are staff with a mix of strengths and weaknesses, like most of humanity, and like Colleen in our opening story. Principal Lyle Melkerson in Kivaliñiq (Kivalina) discussed his thinking about whom he recommends to stay or leave:

> People who are negative toward other staff, negative toward students, negative toward parents, and cause nothing but complaints . . . I don't see the utility in keeping them. But when you get rid of people like that, you end up with . . . this year, we're missing 2 out of 13 teachers. You may have a vacancy you can't fill for years.

We can't tell you what to do with any individual staff member. Learn the technical aspects of supervision in your district, and do them well. Be honest and build respect for and with your staff. Prioritize what the school needs in any given year. It's natural that you will identify some priorities on your own, but it is also important that you let the staff decide priorities for the school that all of you will work on. And try to make decisions that make your school a place where people want to work, where they find community, and where they feel successful.

DEVELOP OR RECRUIT INDIGENOUS TEACHERS

Rural Alaska is Indigenous Alaska. Rural Alaska schools need Indigenous teachers. Suzzuk Mary Huntington, coordinator of cultural programs for the Bering Strait School District, pointed out the following:

> We are still living in our land. The guests that are here, the teachers that are here, are welcomed and treated as guests. Our relationships are still strong to where we're not generally jaded and expecting you to leave. But we also expect you to leave! [Laughs.] I just had a conversation with a teacher who had been here for two years. They were like, "I can't believe I'm leaving. This time here has been so meaningful." And they were feeling a little anticlimactic, because nobody else was honoring the fact that this was not a monumental thing. I mean, we were glad you were here. But two years is a drop in the bucket!

It's worth asking, Who is likely to value these communities, the languages, and the young people in the school? Who will connect to local cultures and be invested in long-term improvement?

Indigenous teachers and staff are not a panacea, and hiring is just a start. In order for Indigenous teachers to find success in the work, schools must adapt what they do. School leaders must ensure that Indigenous teachers are supported as teachers while recognizing that Indigenous teacher success may look different—probably *should* look different—than non-Indigenous teacher success. Suzzuk Mary Huntington noted that Indigenous teachers often face pressures to adapt themselves to Western-oriented systems they didn't create or to become people they are not in order to teach:

> We have to really want local people to be teachers. And our minds say we want it. But our hearts are not there yet. We are still creating barriers that say that local people aren't capable of being the teachers we want them to be. We are still asking that they change who they are, and what they think, in order to become those teachers. What we set as the bar for local people is way higher than the bar we're setting for our teacher prep programs.

A complicating factor Indigenous teachers face is that communities may place additional burdens on them (spoken or not) that non-Indigenous teachers do not face ("Make the school more culturally relevant!" or "Integrate Indigenous values and Western bureaucratic requirements without breaking a sweat!"). This is referred to as an *invisible tax*, the burden of serving as a go-to for all issues relating to the community, to language, or to rural Alaska or Indigenous identities (Will, 2016). It is hard enough to be a teacher anywhere, but the work may feel impossible, given the extra demands. You and your district should ensure that your school's measures of teacher success value the skills and impacts Indigenous teachers may provide. You're not going to find criteria like "Patience explaining local traditions and culture to Outsiders" or "Robust knowledge of families and community that turns out to be super helpful for pretty much everyone, including school leadership, on a daily basis" in the Danielson framework for teaching. But maybe they should be there.

In rural Alaska, where less than 5% of teachers identify as Indigenous (Barnes, 2018), there's a clear disconnect between who teaches and who learns. We've noted in earlier chapters the many problems with nonculturally responsive curriculum. We've said that some of the most important work teachers can do is to adapt curriculum to meet local needs, as well as to form positive relationships in the community. You need to recruit, hire, and keep *local* talent. This means finding small and large ways to respect and support Indigenous staff in accomplishing very difficult work. It may mean being creative about managing conflicts between Western bureaucratic expectations and local cultural needs (e.g., fixed school calendars vs. variable but critical subsistence-harvest seasons). And it may mean encouraging classified staff to think about teaching. Good models for this can be seen in the Lower Kuskokwim School District and the University of Alaska Southeast's Preparing Indigenous Teachers and Administrators for Alaska's Schools program. In the last chapter of the book, we outline a teacher pipeline developed by the Lower Kuskokwim School District that has proven its worth many times over in rural Alaska. LKSD's model took years to develop and sustained action by the school board, the district, schools, and communities. It will always need investment to continue. We hope that seeing this model can help you think through variations that could work in different contexts in rural Alaska.

RECRUIT OUTSIDE TEACHERS

We've suggested that you need to supervise effectively, keep good people, and hire Indigenous teachers. You will also, for the foreseeable future, need more people than you can find locally. This means that you or the district will need to recruit and hire Outside teachers. One caution is that on average, Outside teachers turn over frequently. You may wonder about their motivation: Are they coming for the kids? The money? Some vague sense of adventure? You'll never have perfect information about new recruits. But what you *can* do is recruit those who appear to be good fits, support them while they're with you, and seek to extend the time each teacher stays. Be advised: bringing new people to rural Alaska creates responsibilities that school leaders elsewhere may not carry. As principal Lyle Melkerson in Kivaliñiq (Kivalina) described:

> You are their everything. You're their landlord. You're their plumber. You're their counselor, you're their cheerleader. You're their boss. When they get hurt, you're the one that teaches them how to go to the clinic. You're the one that teaches them how to get on a plane, you're the one that teaches them how to buy supplies, you're the one that teaches them how not to upset the lady at the post office. You're the one that teaches them how to do everything.

Ty Mase, the former superintendent in the Lake and Peninsula School District, shared:

> You know, it's something we've never completely figured out. They come up, we take them shopping, we do an induction. Try to throw as much support at them as we can. And you look at them sitting there, and their eyes are glassed

over, and they're trying to think, "Did I buy enough chicken? Do I need an area rug? What's my apartment going to look like? Oh my god, I can't believe I'm doing this!" And we're trying to ask them to teach in a standards-based, performance-based system like they've never taught before. So it's never been perfect.

Whether you want the job or not, hiring Outside people creates—in *their* expectations, anyway—a situation where you will be responsible for them, often substantially beyond school. If you will find such work overwhelming, then think seriously about who else could help. Does the district, the Tribe, and/or the regional nonprofit run summer (culture) camps for new staff? Can the school put together some sort of intake or orientation packet that can help new teachers? Do you have experienced teachers willing to serve as mentors, formal or otherwise? You'll need to meet their immediate needs ("How can I ship things to school? Will my phone work in the village? Will anyone meet me at the airport?") while planning for regular classroom support as the months progress.

RECRUIT STUDENT TEACHERS

Another option for recruiting new teachers is to bring in student teachers. They typically student teach for a semester or a year, a much longer tryout

Figure 10.2. Teacher walks with students in Sitaisaq (Brevig Mission). *Courtesy of the University of Alaska Fairbanks, K–12 Outreach.*

period than you'd get in a ten-minute job-fair interview. Alaska-prepared teachers are more likely to stay, so it's a good idea to develop relationships with Alaska programs, including those in the University of Alaska system and Alaska Pacific University. If you're looking Outside, consider contacting your alma mater or those of your teachers. Recruitment is far easier with established connections, and your presence (or that of current teachers) communicates clearly that people from Outside can be successful in rural Alaska.

Many rural Alaska school districts have found ways to recruit and host student teachers with modest investments—typically covering transportation and housing costs and occasionally offering a stipend for food or other expenses. Housing is one of the biggest challenges for small sites, but it's one that can be managed creatively, as Ty Mase, former superintendent in the Lake and Peninsula School District, explained while discussing student teachers and paid tutors:

> [When we have an extra bedroom in teacher housing,] that's sometimes how we decide where to put them. And sometimes we'll double them up. Sometimes one of our teachers will have an extra bedroom to rent out, or just let a tutor stay in, and the district will cut them a break on rent. So there's different ways to do that. We actually had a tutor in Port Heiden [who] stayed in the janitor closet. We put a fresh coat of paint in there, and a lamp, and a bed, and kind of made it inviting. And they lived in the school! It just adds to the adventure. You know? They just love it. They don't care. [Laughs.]

ALLOCATE RESOURCES FOR STUDENT TEACHERS AND TUTORING

Districts and schools in rural Alaska don't have unlimited budgets for recruitment. Lake and Peninsula developed a tutoring program that brings in December graduates to tutor students each spring. These tutors often end up coming back to teach the following year. Lake and Peninsula School District (LPSD) has managed to cover the costs through a mixture of dedicated recruitment funds, instructional funds, and grant monies. Here's Ty Mase again:

> We've always embedded some of [the costs] into almost every grant that we write. And it's a hard sell in a grant because it's hard to describe to somebody sitting in Washington, DC, why we would spend six figures on tutors. But six figures are just about what 9 or 10 tutors cost us. It's about $100,000, and that's a teaching position with benefits. [But it allows us] to bring in 9 or 10 tutors for the spring semester, just kind of revitalize what we do, and reach those kids [who] are behind. We've come to the conclusion that that's all day long worth a teaching salary. So that's how we've kept it going and justified it. And honestly, it fits really nicely into the migrant program, it's a good expenditure of migrant funds.

PAY ATTENTION TO PLACEMENT

The most brilliant math teacher in the universe will struggle if asked to teach social studies or if they are in a setting where they're miserable. A critical component of recruitment is the fit between not only the candidate and the position but also between the candidate, the school, and broader community. Many cautionary tales exist in rural Alaska schools of hires made from desperation without regard to fit. Some thoughts from Ty Mase on placement:

> It is so important to get the right people in Port Alsworth, to get the right people in Chignik Lake. And it's not just matching with the village, it's matching with the personalities that are already there. I think we've learned that if it's not a good fit, it just doesn't work. We had our first June hire a couple years ago, and [our HR director] didn't like it. I didn't like it. We hired the [teacher anyway], and she didn't make it to Christmas. You know . . . if we can't find the right fit, we just have to keep looking. That's why the tutor program is so nice too. Because that's when you really get to tell.

One Alaska district leader commented, "To keep teachers, always make a good hire instead of a fast hire. If you go through a pool of candidates and nobody jumps out, you're better off taking a long-term sub" (Vazquez Cano et al., 2019, p. 72).

We'd be remiss if we didn't point out that getting long-term subs in rural Alaska may be next to impossible. The point is that good hires are the goal, not necessarily immediate ones. Keep fit in mind, and keep trying. Recruiting teachers from Outside involves substantial time and energy without certainties concerning fit or length of stay. At a practical level, you'll need Outside people, so recruit well. But don't *only* recruit from Outside. Rural Alaska schools serve Indigenous students and deserve Indigenous teachers. This means you need to meet short-term needs while developing long-term solutions. It's not simple. Yet we also hope it's clear that we are optimistic. Good leadership can, we firmly believe, attract and support good people, can develop pathways into teaching that serve Indigenous Alaska, and can leave schools in better stead for the future.

DEVELOP A LEADERSHIP PIPELINE

Here is one last note about the future. What you do—school leadership in rural Alaska—is not easy. Very few people even try to do your job. In the future we will need more experienced, caring leaders in our rural Alaska schools. And as we've suggested above concerning Indigenous teacher development, the right people to lead rural Alaska schools in the years ahead might already work there. One of the best things you can do to prepare your school for the years ahead is to develop ways to grow administrators from within.

School leaders in Alaska must be educators first; Type B/administrative credentials (for school principals) require at least three years of teaching experience. You're likely to work with some excellent teachers in rural Alaska schools. Those teachers, counselors, and others already working in rural Alaska are perhaps the best source of future leadership in rural Alaska. As Ty Mase explained, developing leadership can start informally:

> With [developing] leadership . . . it's just always looking within your ranks. You have to start identifying your group of thirty-somethings [who] are going to come up and have ten years with the district and be able to take [leadership on] curriculum, be able to be an itinerant principal. And it starts right now! One young gentleman from Montana that entered into our master's program, we've been talking about him. That we need to start pulling him aside in in-services and say, "Have you thought about a Type B?" I think that makes them feel valued. It makes them want to stay. It gives them direction.

If your school is big enough to have an assistant principal position, you might think about how to structure that position as an internship/leadership-development opportunity. Over the course of a year—or multiple years—you should find ways to give them responsibilities for leadership work while you are available as a support. Good places to start include observations, coaching cycles, scheduling, data analyses or other instructional improvement projects, curriculum or textbook adoption cycles, and/or some exposure to facilities and operations.

Teachers may or may not tell you that they are interested in school leadership. Some may be unsure or simply not thinking about it, but please feel free to encourage anyone who is good for the kids and the school. They've already demonstrated some of the most important attributes for leaders in rural Alaska schools. It may take years between planting the seed ("Hey, you're really organized. Thanks for leading us through this data meeting.") and any kind of action on their part, but that's the nature of long-term work.

Just as rural Alaska schools need Indigenous teachers, so too do they need Indigenous leadership. Your encouragement and support for Indigenous teachers should include encouragement to consider or explore school leadership. There are resources available specific to Indigenous teachers, such as the Preparing Indigenous Teachers and Administrators for Alaska Schools program, jointly operated by the University of Alaska Southeast and the Sealaska Heritage Institute (https://uas.alaska.edu/education/scholarships-and-grants/pitaas.html). There may be additional resources available from your district office, from Alaska Native corporations, or from nonprofits in the region.

You can help teachers by doing some homework and making options widely known. What are the available Type B programs in Alaska? Does the district provide scholarships or tuition reimbursement (e.g., as part of a negotiated agreement)? What other scholarships or assistance are available? How does teaching fit with coursework, internships, or other needed program components? How long does all of this take? The more clarity you can provide around how a teacher in your school could gain a leadership credential, the greater the odds are that they'll take you up on it—and the greater the odds are that the school's next generation of leaders will be ready when the time comes.

TAKEAWAYS

- School leaders must recruit good and caring people for every position in the school.
- Supervision matters and influences recruitment and retention.
- Rural Alaska schools need Indigenous teachers and leaders.
- School leaders should find ways to develop leadership pathways for current teachers.

RESOURCES

- Alaska Council of School Administrators: nonprofit leadership development, networking, and advocacy organization; provides extensive professional development. www.alaskaacsa.org
- Alaska Pacific University: teacher education program in Alaska. https://www.alaskapacific.edu/programs/teacher-education-k-8-certificate
- Alaska School Leadership Academy: two-year support program for new principals, supported by the Alaska Department of Education & Early Development. https://sites.google.com/view/asla2020/home
- *Culture in the Classroom: Standards, Indicators and Evidences for Evaluating Culturally Responsive Teaching*: book; excellent discussion of how teachers can show evidence of culturally responsive teaching. https://education.alaska.gov/standards/cultural
- Governor's Teacher Retention and Recruitment Working Group: project group in the Alaska Department of Education & Early Development, includes Alaska district survey results and action plan. https://education.alaska.gov/trr

- Lower Kuskokwim Career Ladder Program: one district's approach to grow their own associate teachers, teachers, and administrators. www.lksd.org/departments/personnel/l_k_s_d_career_ladder
- Preparing Indigenous Teachers and Administrators for Alaska's Schools: teacher and leadership programs for Indigenous candidates in Alaska. https://uas.alaska.edu/education/scholarships-and-grants/pitaas.html
- University of Alaska: multicampus teacher education and leadership programs in Alaska.
  - Anchorage: www.uaa.alaska.edu/academics/school-of-education
  - Juneau/Southeast: https://uas.alaska.edu/education/
  - Fairbanks: www.uaf.edu/soe

Chapter 11

New Directions

Learning From Others

Janice DeVore Littlebear, Robert S. Thompson, and Christian P. Wilkens

While nothing in this book serves as a prescription for how to do things, much can be learned from studying what others have done. In this final chapter, we present some actions, ideas, and programs that are innovative and have been successful in improving rural Alaska education. Do not try to copy what has been done. Learn from others, and devise your own actions or programs that fit your community. Our previous chapters all opened with a vignette illustrating issues in the chapter. For this chapter, we open with a conversation.

CULTURAL AND COMMUNITY CONNECTIONS

If there is one takeaway from this book, it should be that connecting with local cultures and local communities is the key to success in rural Alaska schools. Below, we discuss how that happened with one school leader, Roger Franklin, principal of Shungnak School (Northwest Arctic Borough School District), and one community, Isiŋnaq (Shungnak).

> *Bob:* Describe what the climate of the school was like when you first started as principal in Shungnak.
> *Roger:* Students weren't coming to school, and the community was in an uproar about the politics of the school versus the community. The school was consistently blamed. There was very low attendance. Students were using profanity toward the teachers [and] toward each other, going in the teacher's lounge, having coffee, checking the teachers' mail, [and] leaving the school any time of the day. When they wanted to go home, they just walked out. There wasn't

any discipline. It wasn't effective at all. The students ran the school their way. It was like the . . . Wild West, basically.

Bob: What happened to change that environment?

Roger: The community knew me some from being a counselor there for about a year and a half. The Elders and several parents called a meeting. They wanted to speak to me about the environment of the school versus the village.

We had that first meeting, and I promised them three things. The first was we will work on the—and I didn't say *school* climate—we will work on the *Shungnak* climate. Together! With whatever means necessary. The second was we will be holding a monthly potluck meeting with the village so we can get everybody involved to reshape the community climate. The third thing was to use their culture as a role model, wrapping it around Westernized education to make sure we were being effective.

My first meeting with the entire town was on September 24, 2012. Everybody came up. We had one of the biggest feasts Shungnak had seen to date. I picked up two basketballs. I walked in through the back door of the gym and kicked a ball out of the gym door. Then I pulled out my pocketknife, and I punctured the other basketball. Flattened it! Just to send the message to them that we are not just about basketball. We are about education. We are also about unifying this village together. People clapped, cheered, smiled, and cried through it all.

Bob: You ended up adopting a slogan. How did that come about?

Roger: Every Tuesday night, there were ten Elder women coming to the school for sewing night. I would wait on them, get them tea, coffee, cookies, fruits, vegetables, soda pop, and whatever. Snacks. I provided whatever they wanted. They would just sit there from seven o'clock to nine o'clock, making traditional attire and crafts, singing songs in their Native language, and telling stories about the old days and how things were in the early 1900s. They would just have all this story time to share.

They would also discuss how things are now and what they were going through with their siblings, family members, older children, and grandchildren. They would go deeper into the Inupiaq values of how it was so important to respect Elders. That was how they were raised and how their parents were raised before them. I would just observe and listen.

One evening one of the Elder women said, "We used to do things as a group in the older days, and families would make sure they all pitched in as a community. We would take our families on boat rides, and the men would go hunt for a day or so. We did so many things to keep the culture and pride going."

The school counselor, Andie Zink, and I talked about the conversations of the Elders. There was something missing in the community. Community members would always say, "You are doing it." And I would say, "No, *we* are doing it." Andie and I kept realizing that we were becoming the gatekeepers of trying to reunite the community into one where everyone worked together and took responsibility not only for their own actions but for the actions of everyone. This generated a mantra through which we would try to bring the community together. The mantra became "It's a 'WE'"™—now a registered trademark in the state of Alaska.

Bob: How did you promote "It's a 'WE'"™ and get others involved and committed?

Roger: I promised the Elders that I would do whatever it takes to integrate their dreams of changing the community around Inupiaq values and traditions.

"It's a 'WE'"™ stands out more than anything because we don't talk the talk; the school and community do the job. It is the mantra for bringing this community together. Everyone in this community is responsible for their children and the community welfare, no questions asked. We are always going back over the three initiatives we had established in our first meeting, back on September 24: work to change the Shungnak climate, involve the whole community, and use Inupiaq values as models.

At one village meeting, we asked each person there to write down something positive and something negative that they wanted to work on. I asked people, "What do you need? How can you help? Are you up for the task?" It was crazy what they wanted to work on. We ended up focusing on Inupiaq values as our foundation and making sure that things weren't about "I." "It's a 'WE.'"™

Bob: How did you spread this message and involve everybody?

Roger: I don't work inside the building. I work in their habitat. I went to their fish camp. I went to their winter camp. I went down to the beach and to their houses and listened to them share their needs and ideas. We shared coffee, tea, and different traditional meals in their homes and in the school café. We developed the illustrations that became the vision for everyone. It was a total effort from the entire community.

In 2014, we started the 90% Weekly Parent Attendance Program in the school. We started using a time clock to track parents' attendance in the school. As a result, the parents began to offer support in many areas. They would get on the VHF radio or on telephones, asking other parents to visit the school to help out. This program increased the community engagement and helped build trusting relationships throughout the village. We learned to fail together and to succeed together as a village. It was "we" in many superb moments.

A side benefit was this program also boosted the daily attendance of students. Many stories were written that were published in the *Arctic Sounder* newspaper, the *Anchorage Daily News*, and on social media platforms. That is still going on to this day. It gave the community satisfaction to read and share with other family members and friends near and far about what "we" were accomplishing as a village.

Bob: So how does all of this community work translate to the school?

Roger: We focused on our natural resources, the children. That is the best commodity you could ever have when doing the work that we are doing. Those are our messengers, those are our future parents and community leaders, [and] those are our future Elders.

We started with a group of eight boys [in seventh and eighth] grade. They were called the Boys of Winter. Those eight boys took it on themselves to demonstrate the purpose and passion of building a community-wide support system. The plans involved everyone in the village. Their work continued until they graduated, six years later.

Now it is continuing with other students of all ages following in their footsteps. We took many things that their parents and Elders had taught them about their culture. We did it through the lens of Inupiaq values and the Inupiaq language.

We have all students check on each other daily, weekly, and monthly. Checking on their families. Taking care of the Elders by hauling water, stove oil, and food items. We are what you call service providers, asking for nothing in return. We help dig graves to make sure our people rest in peace. Our students haul the post office mail, shovel snow, cut firewood, harvest wild game, and help build houses. We make sure that our village has the necessities to feed and house families in every season. We've been doing these things for more than eight years. All of our students are youth leaders in their own way.

Our students punch time clocks when they walk in the door to clock in and clock out of school each day. It's providing them with accountability. They can see their time cards and know when they have been late or absent. Teachers are training them for the real world of work. School is the students' job. They use their time cards to learn how to calculate their wages, take out taxes, set aside savings, and all of that. Our students and parents now know that "education comes first, and education is a job!" That is our daily saying as well.

Bob: After eight years you're still making some incredible progress. Last winter the school sent a team to the state 1A basketball tournament for the first time.

Roger: We had never really had a basketball team of our own. The goal wasn't winning basketball games, it was to use the sporting events as a community engagement opportunity. We lost many games for two years with those eight boys, yet they continued to learn and play hard. The character of those young men showed the community what it meant to be successful.

Bob: What happened?

Roger: We take time out during halftime of sporting games at the school and set up academic meetings on the gym floor for parents to review report cards with staff or discuss their child's academic progress. We review the different types of assessments during halftime because that's when we have more people in the building.

We used the students' activities and Inupiaq traditions to help increase our academic scores. It worked. We built a foundation. Our academic framework became more rigorous as the staff built relationships that enabled them to help students succeed in and outside the classroom. We crawled our way up, and we are still moving forward.

We have built up our local career fairs using community members to showcase what type of work is in the village and also outside the village. Monthly, we have parents and community members come into the school to have conversations with the students. Several students are doing job shadowing and job trainings at different agencies in the village. The community is connected to everything. By incorporating parents and community members into this foundation for learning, it gives the community a better understanding of what their children are learning and how they can help instruct their students at home.

We also talk about the social ills that are happening in the village. We work on these issues together to support everyone. Those are magical times, listening to the community speak truthfully about the matters at hand, respecting the Elders, and respecting Inupiaq values. Currently, speaking with the community about their children is not just about behavior or academic progress, it is also about making connections, building relationships, and respecting cultural beliefs.

Bob: Where are you getting support, and what are your next steps?

Roger: We want to make sure it is going to be sustainable. That's why we have embedded it into the local community traditions. It is not just the school. The school has become integrated with the local culture. When other people come and visit, the community makes it known to them that "It's a 'WE'"™ here in Shungnak. The community members love to tell their story because that is something of which they are so proud. They are basically the owners of it now. It is about their traditions and culture, and it has set them apart.

Bob: What is your advice for people wanting to work in a rural Alaska school and make a difference?

Roger: I always ask a couple of questions in an interview. The first is "What are you really out here for? Are you out here for the money and adventure?" Because if you're out here for those two things, you don't need to be out here. That's why I also ask, "Are you ready to trade your life for another life?" It's a whole ball of "It's a 'WE'"™—and that's really it.

What Is There to Do?

The first steps are to observe and listen. Then take what you can use from the efforts of people in Isiŋnaq, including Roger Franklin, to improve community relations that will ultimately improve educational opportunities for your students.

CULTURE, LANGUAGE, AND PLACE-BASED CURRICULA

Culture, language, and place-based curricula are three essential pieces for successful rural schools in Alaska. This final chapter is designed in part to

Figure 11.1. Knitting in Cetuyaraq (New Stuyahok), Alaska. *Courtesy of Emily Hendricks.*

help you recognize and bridge the cultural divides between worldviews by learning from educational strategies that work in rural Alaska. We must begin by observing and listening. Consider a few voices on this topic.

Nita Yurrliq Prince Rearden

(Experienced Yup'ik educator)

> There are two ways to measure success in rural Alaska. One is by the Yup'ik language and culture. How successful are they [students] in the foundation of their identity, their self-esteem, their self-worthiness, their knowledge about the environment and where they live; . . . in subsistence activities, skills in arts and knowing how to be responsible, and self-care in a modern society? That's one measurement.
>
> Another measurement is by being educated in their society, [which] can lead a person to a good job; responsibilities of being able to support self, family, and being on their own, making decisions. I find Indigenous people who are fluent in their language, who have the foundation in their culture and language, are more successful people in the other [Western] world—or when you say, the second world they are going into.

Ronalda Cadiente Brown, Aantooxu.aat

(Teikweidí, Brown Bear clan of the Tlingit and Ilocano; associate vice chancellor for Alaska Native programs, University of Alaska, Southeast)

What is your relationship with the parents of your students? Are you making space for parent connections? I grew up with my mother, an Alaska Native, who had the boarding school experience, and my father, an immigrant from the Philippines. Talk about two different worldviews on education! My father: "Education is the answer! America's the world of opportunity!" . . . My mother: "No one listens. Why bother with parent/teacher conferences? . . . They talk over you, never with you. . . . They don't want to hear, they don't care. . . I don't trust them." Yet she would attend the school events. My mother was part of that era of being punished if [she got] caught speaking Tlingit in school. Her approach was avoidance if at all possible. Yet my perseverance came from their messaging about the importance of an education and high expectations of me and my siblings.

Dr. Pearl Kiyawn Nageak Brower

(Senior advisor for Alaska Native success, institutional diversity, and student engagement, University of Alaska; former president, Iḷisaġvik College)

When I think of our rural schools, I think it would benefit leadership to think about how they can be intentional about how they welcome community members into the space, especially Elders and language bearers. The more people who come in to the educational space and are engaged, the more comfortable our students will be in that space. . . . If you want students to feel comfortable, want them to be successful, [and] want them to want to hang out, you need to make the space feel like a space they want to be in. Incorporate art, pictures of Elders, pictures of the community, [and] have people they know and trust in the space so they know they are still [in] a part of their community versus walking into something that's alien to them, unwelcoming, cold, harsh.

What Is There to Do?

Start by listening. Adapt curriculum, and connect to culture and language. Create a welcoming environment within the school space for the community, parents, and especially the Elders. That's a perfect place to start embedding culture, language, and adapting curriculum for the learners.

STUDENT SUCCESS

It is important to make sure all staff have a shared understanding of what it means to be culturally responsive. What better way to address culture and language in our schools than by defining what student success would look like? Dr. Brower shared her thinking about success: "The concept of student success really could value from being defined by the communities in which that success is being measured."

When it comes to deciding whether a school is successful in educating its students, involve the community in defining what success means to them. Does your school definition include the community's understanding of success?

What Is There to Do?

Work to ensure there is agreement on what student success is among the staff, community, parents, and all the stakeholders. Professional development, culture camps, using local value systems, and partnering with local community members—especially Elders—are all resources to support embedding these key pieces into the school's environment.

LANGUAGE

How can you honor Indigenous languages if the school is not actually teaching them? Do you have a committee making sure translations and language are visible within your school? Where do you start? How do you begin? Dr. Brower has several ideas for honoring the Indigenous language of your village, even if those in the school are, for the moment, unable to actually deliver the instruction in that language:

> Schools could change to support the culture and language in their communities. Schools could offer space for language classes and cultural classes and open up their doors to the community. And I see it as kind of a two-way street. We

Figure 11.2. **Students dissecting an owl pellet.** *Courtesy of the University of Alaska Fairbanks, K–12 Outreach.*

want our kids to be connected to culture and language. Well, in order to do that, we need to open up the opportunity for culture and language bearers to get into the school. Even if you are unable to teach the language, use resources to print materials that can be shared [or] put on walls. We had an Inupiaq language newsletter that went out monthly at Iḷisaġvik, and one of the best places it was put was on the bathroom stall doors! I tell you, I learned a lot of new words that way!

One of the most effective approaches to language revitalization is to support multiage and community-based language programs at the school rather than focusing on very young learners. Linguist and Alaska Native Language Preservation and Advisory Council member Roy Mitchell commented:

A common problem, with only a few [E]lders as fluent speakers, is thinking that first priority is putting the [E]lders into elementary classrooms for several minutes a day in each class. This cannot lead to fluency for learners quickly enough. Rather, master-apprentice language teams are the best practice when the only fluent speakers are 70+ years old; make new, fluent, L2 speakers ages 20–60 as quickly as possible! The new, fluent speakers can then effectively 1) train their own apprentices and 2) teach children and families in organized classes. So which generations speak your language in your community? (Alaska Native Language Preservation and Advisory Council, 2022, p. 72)

Are there ways you or the school can support multiage language teams or classes at school, perhaps in the evenings? Can you provide comfortable space, resources, and coffee? Assingaq Janet Johnson, Yupik language and culture director for the LYSD, noted, "The cool thing about [language revitalization efforts] is not only are the students regaining their language; the teachers are also learning as well. We're seeing more and more teachers addressing students using the language that they're learning" (Alaska Department of Education & Early Development, 2021). Remember, we are bridging worldviews, not having one replace the other. How can you, as the leader, make sure language is honored within your educational setting? What are you doing in this area?

What Is There to Do?

Open up your doors, make room for the community, respect the history your community members bring to the education of all students. Make the local language visible and audible throughout the school.

MODELS FOR PLACE-BASED CURRICULA

Place-based teaching in its simplest terms means connecting curricula to the place where students live. There are many proven models for adapting curricula to make them more place based. One such model, called *S Term* (for subsistence), became part of the North Slope Borough School District's curriculum in 2004. Dr. Pearl Kiyawn Nageak Brower explained S Term this way:

> It was like a three-week period at the end of school, in which high school students could choose different tracks, different areas of focus that they could embark upon as school closed out. [One] reason they did this is that the last weeks of school always coincided with spring whaling. You would always lose all these students who were going out to whale with their families' whaling crews. They designed this "S term" so that students actually could go out and finish up a curriculum as a part of that whaling process, or cultural activity process, and still get credit for the work that they did.
>
> In particular for the whaling piece, they created this really cool notebook that students would take with them and complete different tasks or reflect on different activities they were doing. And the notebook was something that got turned in for a grade. You really could be thoughtful about the curriculum side, while also incorporating culture and heritage and tradition.

As the S Term program developed, it spread to all schools within the North Slope Borough School District. The S Term became a one-credit course for all high school students. Members of the community would substantiate work done by students by making notes in student notebooks. Besides whaling, course selections expanded to include activities such as cooking Indigenous foods, maintaining subsistence clothing and equipment, preparing celebration feasts, and other community-involvement activities.

Dr. Brower described another example of place-based curriculum, which is from the only Tribal college in Alaska, Iḷisaġvik College, in Utqiaġvik:

> Iḷisaġvik College created a construction camp, and the students built houses for the playgrounds around the community. Because it's awfully windy and it does get cold . . . it was just a place . . . for kids at the playgrounds to be able to sit down or get out of the wind now and again.
>
> In another of the camps, they would participate in cultural activities like the spring whaling festival, Nalukataq, or with a whaling crew who had been successful in catching a whale. So the students, through these camps, serve the community.

The culture camps demonstrated respect for the culture while teaching students about giving back to their communities. At the same time, they earned academic credit with the standards embedded. This is a win-win arrangement. Assingaq Janet Johnson commented,

> In allowing our schools to bring culture and the way of life of the Yup'ik people into the school system's values and honoring the language, we're beginning to see more and more support from outside entities and businesses. It's a really good feeling not only for the students, the parents, and the communities, but also the school itself. (Alaska Department of Education & Early Development, 2021)

What Is There to Do?

Listen to and act upon ideas from others for adapting curricula. You can embed the values of the culture into lessons and, at the same time, develop skillsets with academic credit. Partner with the community on projects.

GROWING YOUR OWN: DEVELOPING TEACHERS FROM WITHIN

Real estate professionals will tell you there are three things to know about quality real estate: location, location, and location. In education there are three things to know about quality instruction: teachers, teachers, and teachers. Teacher recruitment and retention are crucial for maintaining quality instruction.

Our starting point in rural Alaska is admittedly a bit bleak. Some schools in rural Alaska have demonstrated annual teacher turnover rates of 30% to 50%, year after year. A majority of teachers hired in Alaska come from Outside. Turnover rates for teachers trained Outside are double that of teachers prepared in Alaska. Indigenous teachers currently make up only about 5% of the teaching workforce in the state.

Yet the averages mask some promising models in rural Alaska. Several school districts have developed programs to encourage local people to become teachers and school leaders, including the Lower Kuskokwim School District. The district's Teach Program, developed in the 1980s, has produced the highest percentage of Indigenous, certified teachers in the state, and it is one that is stable and effective.

Current and former administrators with LKSD all credit long-term commitments by the school board and district leaders for the successes of the Teach Program. Over more than four decades, the district has put its money where its mouth is, allocating millions of dollars in direct district subsidies and grant supports. The original intent of the Teach Program was to get more Indigenous teachers into the school district. According to Carlton Kuhns,

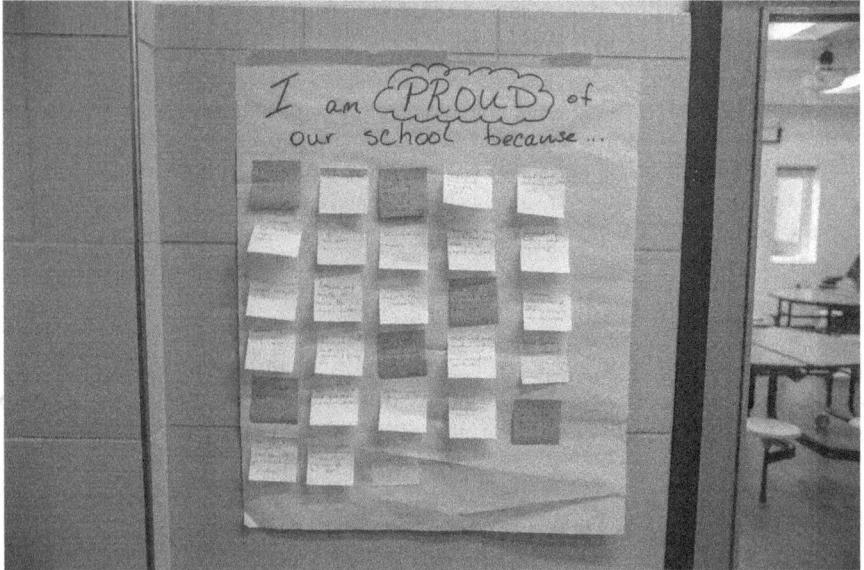

Figure 11.3. Poster in Qalirneq (Koliganek), Alaska. *Courtesy of Emily Hendricks.*

retired Lower Kuskokwim School District (LKSD) principal and assistant superintendent, as recently as 2011, up to 20% of teachers in the district were Indigenous (more than four times the state average!), and most were products of the Teach Program.

In the 2000s LKSD added an Ed Leadership Program, available to any qualified teacher in the district. This program includes assistance with tuition and attaining a Type B credential. It also involves internships where candidates serve as assistant principals in district schools. By 2020, half of all LKSD site administrators had earned their credentials through this program. At the time of this writing, six out of seven senior leadership personnel in the district office are products of the Ed Leadership Program.

What Is There to Do?

Investigate ways to encourage and support Indigenous paraprofessionals and others in the community to become teachers and administrators.

HOW DOES THE TEACH PROGRAM WORK?

First, we must note that these programs were developed and administered by the district, as are most successful school-improvement systems.

Cookie-cutter, imported approaches are rarely successful, although much can be learned from the efforts of others. You can either work with your district or school to begin supporting a grow-your-own program, or you can work to enhance a current program. Studying the LKSD program to learn of their long-term successes, challenges, and adaptations is a good place to start.

Barbara Angaiak, a recent coordinator of the Teach Program, attributes the success of the program not only to district-level support but also to the support of local school leaders and communities. Each community in LKSD, including each advisory school board, signed off on letters of support. Commitment is a term that comes up often when Barbara talks about the program.

Participants in the Teach Program must sign off every semester to show that they understand that this is a commitment not only to the program but to the district as well. Once certified, they are expected to repay the district and their communities by teaching in LKSD. In return, the district pays for tuition, fees, books, and travel, plus room and board when they are away from home.

Commitment by participants is long-term. Most of the people in the Teach Program are full-time paraprofessionals working in local schools. They also have families to attend to and are involved in community activities, such as church, Tribal organizations, and subsistence activities. Many participants are only able to take one or two courses per semester. This makes it a years-long commitment to complete the program and become a certified teacher.

In an effort to help participants maintain their commitment and handle difficulties, the district assembles cohorts of students who can support one another. This support comes in the form of remote video meetings, conference calls, and some in person get-togethers. Teach Program participants are encouraged to work together on projects or lessons. Because of the long-term nature of the program, flexibility is also built into the program to account for circumstances where a student may have to take a break once in a while but then continue at a later time.

A partnership with the University of Alaska Fairbanks (UAF) has worked well for the Teach Program. Barbara Angaiak described these efforts as making sure that courses needed by students are offered at crucial times. There has been an increase in summer school offerings, especially for classes that work better in person, such as those involving labs and collaborative projects. The university has developed a matrix for course offerings so that small groups of students can work together. They have also made a dormitory available each summer at the satellite campus in Mamterilleq (Bethel).

LKSD has added a path to the Teach Program called Two and Done. This addition is for students who have only two more semesters left, plus student teaching, to complete their certification requirements. Since UAF requires a full year of student teaching, the Two and Done program covers the final two years of their program. In order to make this work, carefully selected students receive a two-year sabbatical, including their full salary and payment for all expenses, in order to complete the final steps for earning a teaching credential.

What Is There to Do?

Understanding that employees must take care of families while taking classes is important to any grow-your-own program's success. Start by encouraging paraprofessionals to pursue a teaching career, especially those who already have some college credits. Have discussions with other leaders in your district about ways to support staff with college applications, tuition reimbursement, books and other expenses, and/or release time.

WHY DOES THE TEACH PROGRAM WORK?

It all begins with leadership. Carlton Kuhns explained that there has always been a long-term, proud commitment to local leadership in LKSD. Consistent support from the regional school board over 40-plus years, in addition to the community support of participants, has been key for the Teach Program. The successes of Yugtun language immersion programs using Indigenous speakers as teachers has only increased support for the Teach Program in many communities.

Hiring local people who are locally trained improves retention, which is good for students. Another benefit of local hiring, especially the hiring of Indigenous teachers, is that locally raised teachers do not need to learn nearly as much as people from Outside to be effective with students. Embedding local cultures and languages into lessons may be second nature. Local teachers are also tightly connected to students and communities. Some of the adjustment challenges Outside people face in coming to rural Alaska are simply not there.

Developing local teachers requires resources and long-term commitments. You can begin programs in your school or district by taking pieces of what others have done and get something started. The LKSD Teach Program continues to adapt and change. Your programs will do so as well. As administrators come and go, they will emphasize different aspects of a program. Persistence is needed, along with openness to change.

The fruits of efforts such as the Teach Program in LKSD do not come easily or overnight. School improvements are tied to long-term efforts and support from multiple people in multiple positions both inside and outside of the school building. The grow-your-own Teach Program in LKSD is one shining example. It supports the now well-known belief about the three things that contribute to quality instruction: teachers, teachers, and teachers.

What Is There to Do?

Consider starting a grow-your-own program, knowing it will require patient, persistent work. The benefits are worth the efforts.

> "[Teaching in a rural school in Alaska] is a deeper mission than teaching in a typical [US] neighborhood school. It is a way of life."
> —Carlton Kuhns, retired LKSD principal and assistant superintendent

RETENTION AND RECRUITMENT

Any experienced rural educator will tell you that turnover can make it next to impossible to implement even the best plans. Below, we take a look at some creative practices the Lake and Peninsula School District has adopted to improve teacher retention and recruitment.

Retention

In rural Alaska schools, people stay in places where they are connected to communities, feel effective, and enjoy their jobs. Former Lake and Peninsula teacher, site leader, and district leader Rick Luthi shared,

> You know, we build a real community [in Lake and Peninsula School District], and I think people feel valued. It's beyond money. I mean, money is a factor. It always is, but it's more than money. It's people feeling that they're valued. And that they're respected and they're wanted.
> There are practical issues that can help teachers feel valued. We make sure the housing is very good. We take care of those basic needs the very best we can. We subsidize all of our housing, which most districts do. We subsidize travel, we give people more flights. Our insurance—our business manager frets about it all the time—but we've got a health insurance package that people value. And it's little things. Like bringing in [a person] to talk to folks about how they can take care of themselves financially. We do longevity bonuses for folks. So it's just, you know ... a lot of pieces.

Take good care of your teachers' basic needs. Below, we outline three longer-term approaches to teacher retention that have worked in the Lake and Peninsula School District (LPSD), and that might be useful to adapt in your district or school. All were described by Ty Mase, former superintendent.

Partnering With Universities

The superintendent of Bristol Bay and [I] met with UAA [University of Alaska Anchorage] and designed a master's in Culturally Responsive Teaching, an MEd [Master of Education] program. The idea is that these teachers that come out and live in villages . . . there is no way in any class or university to teach what they're learning by being immersed [in a rural school setting]. So that was what we were really shooting for: an experience-based master's program. Teachers have to take 15 course credits at UAA, and then if they teach three years in one of our Southwest partner districts [Aleutians East, Bristol Bay, Dillingham, Lake and Peninsula, or Southwest Region], then the superintendents or the Experiential Learning Committee can award 15 additional college credits. And they earn their master's degree. So basically, for teaching in rural Alaska, it's about a half-price master's.

Right off the bat, we introduced this program, and I had a young couple sign up for it, which basically cements them in our district for three more years. That was a fist-pumping moment—that this works! We found recruiting young teachers too—especially ones that aspire to get a master's degree—it's really appealing to [them as well]. So what we're finding is most educators are coming to us right now with three-year plans at a minimum, which hopefully helps curtail the one-hit wonders, you know? Just the one year and out.

Partnering with Tribes

We're partnering now with our Native Corporation's Education Foundation and are excited about the possibilities and support that they can bring to the program. They're already strengthening the [master's] program through financial support, assisting with an external evaluation and, if possible, in the future, with scholarships for the MEd candidates. The idea is when these young educators sign a contract for the fourth year, at that point, a scholarship program kicks in, and the tribal entity—the corporation—then picks up their tuition for the previous three years. And in Lake and Peninsula's situation, we have a five-year longevity bonus that would kick in. We have teachers say, "Well, I'm going to do one more year, get my master's paid for." And then there's a $10,000 teacher retention bonus on year five. Three years is great. If you can get them for five years, that's knocking it out of the park.

RETENTION BONUSES

We have retention bonuses for teachers. When we were negotiating [teacher contracts], it just seemed like a good place to put the money. It's out there—the idea of retention bonuses—but it's not real common. There is still a mind-set, which is shocking, that when teachers stay too long, they get too expensive. You know, in this day and age, I don't really care what it costs! A really good teacher at $100,000 [who's] going to stay five or six years is better than, you know, some kid coming in for a year and washing out. That's just a big hole in our students' education.

What Is There to Do?

Take care of the little things that make a place more inviting. Make efforts to support teachers and make them feel valued. Find creative ways to fund and provide programs that provide real incentives for teachers to stay.

IMPROVE SCHOOL AND DISTRICT VISIBILITY

In order to hire someone from Outside, you need to help them find you. And they need to be able to imagine what life would be like working in rural Alaska. Alaska Teacher Placement (www.alaskateacher.org) is the most common landing point for prospective hires looking for jobs, but it's a clearinghouse for everyone. Candidates also need to be able to find information specific to the district and the school on their own. The online presence of the school matters—not just during hiring season. Ty Mase commented,

> We're trying to really increase our presence on Instagram. We're finding with a lot of the teachers that they're looking at all of their friends and their family [on social media], you know, posting and having these incredible moments [while in our villages]. We put a lot of thought into our Instagram and our presence [on social media] and what we're doing there.

In recruiting Outside teachers, as in just about everything else, success is built on relationships. LPSD administrator Rick Luthi explained how they approach recruitment—paying attention not just to individual candidates but also to college personnel as key parts of a broader strategy:

> We're all in competition for that small pool [of teachers who will come to teach in rural Alaska]. Over the years, I built a real relationship with universities Outside, like Western Oregon, University of Montana, a lot of universities back [in the East and in the Midwest] because they were turning out more teachers

than they had places for. We really had some inroads with [several smaller colleges]. Great teachers! We got a lot of our tutors and teachers from these smaller places.... We also flew a bunch of those university faculty up [to visit Alaska]. "Hey, I'm back! I'm down here seeing you. Come on up!" It gave us dividends. And it was the right thing to do. I mean, if you're going to send your graduates up, come see what we're getting them prepared to do.

What Is There to Do?

Improve and maintain a quality presence on social media. Build professional relationships with recruitment centers. Smaller universities may be more productive than larger ones.

CREATE TUTORING OR TEACHER ASSISTANT PROGRAMS

One creative approach that Lake and Peninsula started years ago was the Instructional Tutor program. Each fall the district recruits student teachers graduating in May or December to work as *intervention specialists* (tutors), formally hiring them as classroom aides for most of the spring semester. The Instructional Tutor program came out of a need to spend grant dollars—and one school principal who just needed an extra set of hands. Ty Mase recalled:

> We had improvement monies for our schools, and our principal at Nondalton was really dragging his feet at spending its monies. I called him—he was a veteran principal—and we were tussling back and forth a little bit. I was like, "We have to spend these monies, or we're going to lose them!" And he told me, "Ty, I don't need fancy curriculum, I don't need furniture for my library, I don't need . . ." and he went through the list of everything else the other principals were doing. He said, "What I really need is just an extra set of hands. That's what I want, and I don't know how to do it." I told [the principal], "Well, let's figure this out a little bit. Let me call you back. Maybe we can do something." And that's when the whole tutoring idea started. It seemed like there were plentiful teachers and educators back East, and we started recruiting December graduates at that point [for tutoring positions]."

The "something" that Lake and Peninsula ended up doing was hiring recent graduates to work from January through April as instructional tutors. The district provides tutors with free transportation and housing and pays them a reasonable salary. Ty Mase explained how tutors are used in schools:

It's that extra set of hands. It's focused intervention strategies, looking at kids who are struggling. Basically, we come up with a game plan for each tutor when they go out. "This is going to be your schedule; these are going to be your kids. This is what we want you to hit." It's a breath of excitement into the village, into the school, [and into] the kids. It's pretty wonderful.

Beyond support for students—the key mission of the program—the Instructional Tutor program is another on-ramp for recruitment. Rick Luthi explained,

> The tutor program is also a teacher recruitment strategy. I mean, they come out, they see us, they get to know us. It was so good for the schools to have those people coming in. [And now] somebody's in Nondalton, [saying,] "Hey, we're going to have an opening. . . ." We've watched those people. We know what they're like. They know us. There's no question.

Ty Mase added,

> After a couple of years, [tutors] stay and . . . take teaching jobs. And new teacher induction just gets easier and easier, because 90% of those faces looking at you have been in the district before. It just was an absolute no-brainer. We kind of stumbled into it but kept taking steps to enhance what we did.

What Is There to Do?

Look for grants or other funding mechanisms to support innovative programs. If you can find a way, bring in potential recruits for teaching or tutoring positions.

It takes time and commitment to build programs like these that are now common practice in Lake and Peninsula. Getting there requires creativity and long-term support from district leaders and school boards. What ideas can you borrow, adapt, or create on your own? Recruiting and keeping good teachers is a key to success in any school. It's worth the effort, and there are lots of ways to get started.

SOVEREIGNTY AND THE ROLE OF TRIBES

Here we return to a topic essential for school leaders to understand: sovereignty and Tribes. There are over 500 federally recognized Tribes within the United States of America today; more than 200 of these Tribes have jurisdiction over lands and people in Alaska. Each is its own sovereign nation. Each has the right to govern itself and its people. Each can pass laws, such as those that determine citizenship, child custody, voting rights, housing, the distribution of benefits, and hunting and fishing regulations.

Tribal citizens, like citizens of any nation, have rights that vary and which are different from the rights of non-Tribal citizens. As the leader of a school in rural Alaska, you must therefore understand that you will work and live with people who have sovereign rights that may be very different than your own.

Sovereignty can be complicated to define. Here's one definition from Qanglaagix Ethan Petticrew, who is Unangax and from the Aleutian Islands: "Tribal sovereignty, to me, means that we are in control of our own destiny. That we are not dependent upon any foreign government ([the United States] included) for providing essential services to our Tribal members. To me, those services would include health and education."

Qanglaagix's definition of sovereignty may not be universal, yet his suggestion that Tribes should be in control of their own destiny is perhaps the key point. The actions of school leaders should flow, whenever possible, *from* decisions made by the Tribal citizens rather than *to* them.

EDUCATE *YOURSELF* ABOUT THE LOCAL TRIBE(S)

The first step is to be aware of the Tribe(s) where you serve. The easiest way to do this is to do some research on the Tribe(s) and region. Two potentially useful resources are as follows:

- US Bureau of Indian Affairs: Tribal government and leadership contact information for all Tribes in Alaska. www.bia.gov/regional-offices/alaska/tribes-served
- Alaska Federation of Natives: largest statewide Alaska Native organization; promotes sovereignty, cultural and language education, and economic development. Organizes a large convention annually. www.nativefederation.org

Once in the village, attend tribal meetings. Observe and listen. Next, learn about laws, regulations, and rules that have been established by the Tribe in your area and that may impact your work in the school or with families and children. Share these with your staff, and listen to your local staff and community members, especially Elders. These tribal members have much knowledge that can benefit your leadership.

EDUCATE *STAFF* ABOUT THE LOCAL TRIBE(S)

As a school leader in rural Alaska, you have the responsibility to make sure your staff is informed about Tribe(s) and sovereignty. This responsibility includes making sure the staff understands the unique relationship between Tribes and local, state, or federal governments. Developing this deeper understanding will bring your staff closer to the community and allow for additional community building. Work with your staff to help them connect tribal rules and issues to school issues in order to benefit students. Tribal entities appreciate being consulted about schooling, and they often have valuable perspectives to consider. Some ideas may be different from your way of thinking about school, but openness and flexibility are key to creating successful school/community partnerships.

What Is There to Do?

Educate yourself about Tribes and sovereignty. Attend tribal meetings. Learn about tribal laws, regulations, and rules. Offer to pay community members to teach classes at in-service or to offer classes during the year (e.g., after school, with students and staff) on local history, cultural practices, or other knowledge and skills they are willing to share. Honor the Tribe with photographs or other visuals within your school building's environment.

COMMUNITIES, SCHOOLS, AND RECIPROCITY

Be aware of the give-and-take nature of people living in your community. Reciprocity is frequently an Indigenous value, and simply stated, it means you give and you take in most relationships. This includes both physical gifts and gifts of time or knowledge; the latter are the ones most often requested (even expected) by school people. What are you asking, and what are you offering?

Reciprocity invites collaboration, partnering, and mutual respect. When approaching tribal entities or community organizations, you should not go in expecting them to give you something—that is, their time, their money, and/ or their knowledge. Enter these situations with a giving attitude. Talk about what the school can do for them, and ask for ways to partner with them for the benefit of everyone.

Remember to acknowledge the land upon which you lead as well as the people—it is the correct thing to do. Your district may have adopted formal wording, or it may be evolving. One good set of resources was developed by the Anchorage Museum (www.anchoragemuseum.org/major-projects/

projects/land-acknowledgement). Remember: Tribes in Alaska have been educating young people for millennia; the school building in its modern form and purposes is new.

What Is There to Do?

Discuss with teachers—and community members—what reciprocity means and how they can demonstrate it in their work. Find ways to share school resources with the community. Begin meetings and celebrations with a land acknowledgement appropriate to the district, school, and community.

TRIBAL COMPACTING

Tribes outside of Alaska have operated public schools for many years under contracts, or compacts, with states or the federal government. The federal government has directly funded tribally operated schools outside Alaska for decades (including Washington state) under the Education Amendments Act of 1978 (Pub. L. No. 95-561; Bureau of Indian Education, 2022), and some of these compact schools have demonstrated substantial improvements over their non-tribal predecessors. As of this writing, the state of Alaska is exploring compacting for schools in Alaska. The Alaska Department of Education & Early Development has provided a brief definition of the approach it could take in the years ahead:

> Compacting is a process through which the State of Alaska and an Alaskan Native Tribal entity reach an agreement that formally recognizes a Tribal entity's authority to operate and oversee K–12 schools. These State Tribal Education Compact Schools (STECs) would be public schools open to all students and would offer a unique, culturally rich combination of Western and millennia-old tribal educational models. (Alaska Department of Education and Early Development, 2020a)

The State of Alaska and several Tribes are currently developing the first State Tribal Education Compact Schools, so the idea remains a work in progress. Funding, leadership, accreditation, reporting, and a range of operational details need to be determined; the idea of compacting with Tribes to run schools provides evidence of how thinking about schooling in Alaska continues to evolve. It is essential that school leaders in rural Alaska stay current on evolving issues, trends, and relationships and that they keep staff advised as well.

EMBRACE WORKING WITH INDIGENOUS PEOPLES

As an educational leader in rural Alaska, you need to be respectful of the sovereignty of the nations and peoples with whom you live and work. If you did not grow up in the community where you work, you are a guest; follow the laws established by the Tribes governing that region. Learn to incorporate Indigenous ways of being, traditions, languages, and local cultures into school operations, curricula, instruction, policies, and student success.

What does consideration of Tribes and sovereignty mean for you as a school leader? It means clearly understanding that you serve Indigenous communities in your work. It means showing respect by learning as much as you can about the people you serve. And it means that a part of your charge includes exercising voice and influence during a time when relationships between Tribes, school districts, and the state of Alaska remain works in progress. Any time decisions about schooling are made, you can always ask, Who is represented here? Who is not? And ultimately: How can I shape my school in ways that recognize tribal sovereignty and meet the needs of young people in this community?

TAKEAWAYS

- Create a welcoming environment in the school by adapting curricula and connecting to local cultures, languages, and place.
- Make Indigenous languages visible and audible throughout the school.
- Create or support pathways for Indigenous paraprofessionals and others to become teachers and administrators.
- Find creative ways to recruit and retain teachers, as well as to make teachers feel valued.
- Educate yourself and all school staff about Tribes and sovereignty in rural Alaska.

Epilogue

At this point we hope one of our big claims—that there's no such thing as a "typical" rural Alaska school—is clear. Maybe you've already experienced this, watching the thermometer drop in the school office during a cold snap, waiting for the sun to come up for the first time in weeks, or laughing with parents at a basketball game. Or maybe you're still looking ahead to all of it.

Each school in rural Alaska is unique based on who and what surrounds it. Rural Alaska schools are small, are embedded in communities with strong social ties, and serve families with deep cultural, language, subsistence, employment, and living skills that can support young people as they grow. It's true that schools in rural Alaska (like schools anywhere) face challenges. But it's also true that (paraphrasing Suzzuk Mary Huntington) one could not imagine a better setup to do well with kids than in rural Alaska.

The job of a rural Alaska school leader, whether in a district office or in a small community well off the road system, is demanding. You will be required to do things not required in most other school situations. While you may not feel like an expert in many areas, you're almost guaranteed to get practice doing just about everything, from making breakfast to fixing the public-address system and buying party supplies for graduation.

One element we hope you understand is that rural Alaska is Indigenous Alaska. This means that schools in rural Alaska must serve the needs of Indigenous peoples. They must do so in ways that make possible the futures of Indigenous communities as a whole, as well as the chosen futures of young people in rural Alaska.

Of course, schools in rural Alaska must also answer to Western bureaucratic requirements that carry value (e.g., teaching students to read in English at grade level). Your job as a school leader is not to choose winners and losers among competing demands; it is to integrate Indigenous and non-Indigenous knowledge systems in ways that strengthen school-community connections and improve student outcomes.

Your best starting point is to engage with, listen to, and act respectfully toward members of the community. One of the clear advantages to leadership in rural Alaska is that relationships with students, staff, and families are more intimate and rich than those in other contexts. That human, relational knowledge can help you make grounded decisions that shape your specific school's future. Small schools like we have in rural Alaska highlight the need to nurture relationships and collaborate on virtually all things.

Another takeaway we hope we made clear is that schools in rural Alaska must connect to the knowledge, cultures, and languages of students and families—and must reflect them in lessons, activities, and routines. Teachers and school leaders must learn about the community where they live—not *any* community but *this specific* community. A good starting point is to participate in village life beyond the school. It's best to observe before talking, to learn how to show and give respect, to ask questions instead of talking about your views, and to ensure that you build relationships based on reciprocity and trust.

Several chapters in this book discuss teaching and learning. It's true that when judged by test scores alone, many rural Alaska schools have a long way to go. Students in rural Alaska deserve excellent instruction, full stop. Poor test scores are a symptom you need to address. Yet we also suggest that school leaders in rural Alaska should define academic success according to local standards as well. Schools in rural Alaska need to provide students with the knowledge and skills needed for fulfilling and productive lives. We encourage you to find ways to value (perhaps measure) successes defined by the community your school serves. Can graduates take care of themselves and their families? Can they find and keep work or go to college if they choose? Two specific areas where we recommend that schools expand opportunities are in subsistence and career and technical education. Both provide engaging, meaningful opportunities for young people to be successful in the years after they leave school.

You will need to adapt curriculum to meet the needs of students in rural Alaska. Nearly all commercial curricula fail to meet the needs of rural Alaska schools. If you need evidence, look at your test scores. Some of the most important adaptations schools can make at any grade level or subject are those that provide additional practice, that ensure teachers teach all necessary subskills, and that improve cultural relevance. Culturally relevant instruction must be embedded in every classroom. As far as we know, the only way you can help ensure the school makes effective cultural connections is to make meaningful human connections. Spend time in the community, invite shared decision making, and try to develop a deep understanding of the place where you work and of the families you serve.

How you lead—how you create a context where people are able to do and be recognized for good work—has a profound influence on the school. If you supervise well, promote collaboration, and empower others, people will get better at their jobs and will stay longer. Retention of good staff is good for your school. No question. If you create a welcoming environment and work to bring the community into the school, this will strengthen the school and produce better outcomes. We pointed out that rural Alaska needs more Indigenous teachers and leaders. The more you can support pathways that enable local people to become teachers and future leaders, the better.

We hope you're arriving at the conclusion of this book with some clear ideas about what you might do next. We've tried to share stories that show how people, schools, districts, programs, Tribes, communities, and agencies can expand the work any of us might be able to do on our own. And we hope we've been clear that the work of school leadership is done by building trust, by showing respect, and in partnership with others. Which, we suppose, is our major takeaway: what we're telling you is you don't need to figure all of this out on your own. And you shouldn't try. Pick up the phone, walk down the hallway, make a connection with someone who knows more than you. That's progress. What's the good news? Everyone in rural Alaska can teach you something—maybe even that guy skipping his snowmachine over open water (*don't*).

We wish you well with what lies ahead. Thank you, on behalf of young people, for the work you do in rural Alaska schools!

Acknowledgments

This book's origin story is probably not one for Marvel. But to those Alaska State System of Support coaches who were there at the Atwood Building on a cold December morning years ago, thank you. You were instrumental in your encouragement and willingness to help. Per Tonio, *this might be it*. Thank you to Carl Chamblee, Charlie Crangle, Melissa Linton, Leanne Mahalak, Pat McDonald, Lesa Meath, Tonio Nguyen, Laurie Schoenberger, Carol Thompson, and Evelyn Willburn. Also, thank you to Karen Melin and Tamara Van Wyhe for sharing space and time at a key moment: No you? No book.

To the authors, thank you for your wisdom and words. And for your willingness to trust us to share what you've given with respect. It's one thing to talk about rural Alaska schools with a colleague or friend—and another thing entirely to do so in public. You have been a joy to work with.

To the range of experienced colleagues and friends who consistently made our writing and thinking better, we meant to thank you for your specific contributions with words like "Thanks for reviewing chapter 5, actually thanks for the whole *idea* of chapter 5!" But when we tried to list everything, you kept showing up over and over again, and it was all going to embarrass everyone. So we'll just say thank you this one time. Just know that what we mean is "Thank you for all the many times you've helped—with writing, ideas, interviews, chapter reviews, edits, stories, and laughter." What you do is, we hope, somewhere in the heart of this book: Brad Billings, Gguitka Sperry Ash (Sugpiaq), Jerry Covey, Nita Yurrliq Prince Rearden (Yup'ik), Dr. Pearl Kiyawn Nageak Brower (Iñupiaq/Armenian), Rick Luthi, Ronalda Cadiente Brown, Aantooxu.aat (Teikweidí, Brown Bear clan of the Tlingit and Ilocano), Susan Hubbard, Suzzuk Mary Huntington (Kigiqtaamiu Inupiaq), and Ty Mase.

Acknowledgments

To the Alaska school leaders who spoke with us as the book emerged and whose words appear in the text, thank you. The book is better because of your generosity, wisdom, and insight into what schools in rural Alaska can be: Barb Angaiak, Carlton Kuhns, Lyle Melkerson, Qanglaagix Ethan Petticrew (Unangax), Roger Franklin, and Terri Walker, Aviññaq (Iñupiaq).

To the rural Alaska educators who spoke with us and whose words appear in the text, thank you. It is your work with young people in schools—as teachers, paraprofessionals, counselors, and other school staff—that most immediately makes a school a vibrant community where each student can find out what they will become: Barb and Skip Winslow, Suaqpak Tunualak Edna Ahmaogak (Inupiaq), Emma Melkerson (do not stab Lyle in the eye), Eva Thomas Churchwell (Athabascan), Jessica Angalkuruk Mark (Yup'ik), Josh Purkeypile, Julie Vasquez, Karla Edenshaw, Lisa Cates, Luke Rowley, Mae Pitka, and Okalena Arnaq Morgan.

To the community leaders in rural Alaska who spoke with us and whose words appear in the text, thank you. Your work connecting communities and schools makes them better, and your willingness to share how this works in rural Alaska has made for a better book: Tatianna Andrew (Yup'ik), Dorothy Wonhola (Yup'ik), Ken Yates (Haida), Matushka Pauline Askoak (Yup'ik), and Mike Williams Sr. (Yupiaq).

Not quoted but critical to the book were the people who shared ideas, explained what things are or were, or helped us clarify our thinking about rural Alaska schools and leadership. Thank you for sharing your experiences and knowledge: Brad Allen, Sheila Box, Jerry Schoenberger, John Pingayak (Cup'ik), LeAnn Young, LoAna Benton, Sue McIntosh, and Teri Cothren.

Writing is difficult. We often found substantial distance between what we meant and what we wrote. To all of you who reviewed chapters in this book, you've saved us from a substantial amount of poor writing, vague ideas, and unsupported claims. All of the remaining errors and dubious ideas are entirely ours. You tried, and we are grateful: many listed above, Arnaq Esther A. Ilutsik (Yup'ik), and Elizabeth Will. We are also grateful to the University of Alaska Fairbanks, Alaska Native Language Center. We consulted the Alaska Native Place Names list regularly when writing.

Words rarely do rural Alaska justice. To Emily Hendricks, Seth Adams, Kathy Turco, the A-CHILL program, and the Alaska State Library, thank you. Your photography has made this book more beautiful, and if a picture is worth a thousand words, you have saved readers from many, many pages of text. An especially warm thanks to Elizabeth "Putt" Clark, who graciously put up with our many asks for graphic support. Thank you, too, to the University of Alaska Fairbanks' K–12 Outreach program and the Alaska Statewide Mentor Project for sharing photography but, much more significantly, for the work you do in supporting K–12 schools and teachers in rural Alaska.

Special thanks to Ron Dalby, who took our manuscript (and its potentially record-breaking volume of text boxes, em dashes, and overwriting) and made it substantially better. Also, it has been such a pleasure to work with the friendly, professional staff at Rowman & Littlefiel/Bloomsbury. Thanks go to Megan DeLancey, Jasmine Holman, and Carrie Brandon for their attention to detail, expert assistance, and helpful responsiveness to our questions. Also, thanks to the production staff for turning our rough draft into a professional looking manuscript that makes us proud to be associated with Rowman & Littlefield/Bloomsbury.

Jan: Thank you to the many K–8 students of the Mt. View community, Dgheyaytnu (Anchorage), for starting me on this life's journey to equitable instruction for all children. Thank you to Drs. Adams and Parker-Webster for holding my wrinkled hand while guiding my research on teaching through culture. And loving thanks to family—Ted, Gabriel, Jason, Isabella, Diana, Statia, Kaden, and Richard—who each cheered me on, provided much laughter, and never took me too seriously. And to Bob and Chris, coeditors, you two have set the bar high for what it means to be a team player and thought partner in this shared labor of love. Finally, thanks to the many Indigenous folks in my life who have opened my Western eyes to another way of knowing—you matter.

Bob: There are many people important to me who have encouraged and supported me in the effort to get this book ready for publication. High on the list are Janice Littlebear and Christian Wilkens, both of whom have had unflinching dedication, consuming passion, and necessary good humor throughout this project. Rick Luthi, a mentor, colleague, and good friend, has continually offered encouragement while I attempt to absorb a small part of his wisdom and experience. Of course, most important of all is Carol, who lifts me up on a daily basis and unselfishly offers her love, support, and good humor to my life, as well as to my son, Jesse, who has an uncanny ability to be insightful on a plethora of topics and was most helpful with the section on critical thinking, at which he is an expert.

Chris: Thank you to the State University of New York Brockport for work space, research support, and a professional home over the years. It remains a surprise that you keep sending me paychecks for work I love anyway. To Bob Thompson and Jan Littlebear, this project has brought joy during some hard years. I am looking forward to our work on *When Bob Almost Died*. To Julie, Rowan, and Cal, you are the best people in my life. Thank you for being you and for not judging me too harshly despite the trail of coffee mugs all over the house. And for your laughter, your love, and the ever-evolving backstory of Izzy.

Appendix A
Tribes in Alaska by Location

NOTES

- Tribes in Alaska are not a static set of governments. Below are Tribes recognized by the United States Department of the Interior, Bureau of Indian Affairs, as of January 30, 2020: http://www.bia.gov/regional-offices/alaska/tribes-served.
- Here is the contact information for Tribes in Alaska:
  - US Bureau of Indian Affairs (search by map or download a directory): www.bia.gov/service/tribal-leaders-directory
  - National Congress of American Indians: www.ncai.org/tribal-directory
- This is the list of Indigenous place names from the University of Alaska Fairbanks, Alaska Native Language Center, Alaska Native Place Names: www.uaf.edu/anla/collections/map/names. (In some cases, there may be disagreement or local variation in the pronunciation of names or spelling.)
- Elsewhere in the book, we first list Indigenous place names with English names in parentheses. Below, we list English language place names in the left column; our intent is only that readers be able to easily find places on (typically English-name) maps and Tribes of interest.

Place Name (English)	Indigenous Place Name	Tribe
Akhiok	Kasukuak	Kaguyak Village
Akhiok	Kasukuak	Native Village of Akhiok
Akiachak	Akiacuar	Akiachak Native Community
Akiak	Akiaq	Akiak Native Community
Akutan	Achan-ingiiga	Native Village of Akutan
Alakanuk	Alarneq	Village of Alakanuk
Aleknagik	Alaqnaqiq	Native Village of Aleknagik

Appendix A

Place Name (English)	Indigenous Place Name	Tribe
Allakeket	Alaasuq	Alatna Village
Allakeket	Aalaa Kkaakk'et	Allakaket Village
Ambler	Ivisaappaat	Native Village of Ambler
Anaktuvuk	Anaqtuuvak	Village of Anaktuvuk Pass
Anchorage	Dgheyaytnu	Ivanof Bay Tribe
Anchorage	Caniqaq	Native Village of Chenega (Chanega)
Anchorage	Dgheyaytnu	Native Village of Georgetown
Anchorage	Paimiut	Native Village of Paimiut
Anchorage	Ohgsenakale	Portage Creek Village (Ohgsenakale)
Anchorage	Dgheyaytnu	Ugashik Village
Angoon	Aangóon	Angoon Community Association
Aniak	Anyaraq	Village of Aniak
Anvik	Gitr'ingith Chagg	Anvik Village
Atka	At xˆ a xˆ	Native Village of Atka
Atmautluak	Atmaulluaq	Village of Atmautluak
Atqasuk	None listed	Native Village of Atqasuk
Beaver	Ts'aahudaaneekk'onh Denh	Beaver Village
Bethel	Mamterilleq	Native Village of Napaimute
Bethel	Mamterilleq	Orutsararmiut Traditional Native Council
Bettles Field	Kk'odlel T'odegheelenh Denh	Evansville Village (Bettles Field)
Brevig Mission	Sitaisaq	Native Village of Brevig Mission
Buckland	Kaŋiq	Native Village of Buckland
Cantwell	Yidateni Na'	Native Village of Cantwell
Chalkyitsik	Jałgiitsik	Chalkyitsik Village
Chefornak	Cevv'arneq	Village of Chefornak
Chevak	Cev'aq	Chevak Native Village
Chignik	Cirniq	Chignik Bay Tribal Council
Chignik	Cirniq	Native Village of Chignik Lagoon
Chignik Lake	Igyaraq	Chignik Lake Village
Chitina	Tsedi Na'	Native Village of Chitina
Chuathbaluk	Curarpalek	Native Village of Chuathbaluk
Chugiak	Idlughet	Eklutna Native Village
Circle	Danzhit Khànląįį	Circle Native Community
Clarks Point	Saguyaq	Village of Clarks Point
Copper Center	Tl'aticae'e	Native Village of Kluti Kaah
Cordova	Igya'aq	Native Village of Eyak
Craig	Sháan Séet	Craig Tribal Association
Crooked Creek	Qipcarpak	Village of Crooked Creek
Deering	Ipnatchiaq	Native Village of Deering
Dillingham	Curyung	Curyung Tribal Council
Dillingham	Curyung	Native Village of Ekuk
Diomede	Imaqłiq	Native Village of Diomede (Inalik)
Eagle	Tthee T'äwdlenn	Native Village of Eagle
Eek	Ekvicuaq	Native Village of Eek
Egegik	Igyagiiq	Egegik Village

Place Name (English)	Indigenous Place Name	Tribe
Ekwok	Iquaq	Native Village of Ekwok
Elim	Neviarcaurluq	Native Village of Elim
Emmonak	Imangaq	Chuloonawick Native Village
Emmonak	Imangaq	Emmonak Village
Fairbanks	Łiteet'aii	Birch Creek Tribe
Fairbanks	Mendees Cheeg	Healy Lake Village
Fairbanks	Kelt'aaddh Menn'	Village of Dot Lake
False Pass	Isanax̂	Native Village of False Pass
Fort Yukon	Gwichyaa Zheh	Native Village of Fort Yukon
Gakona	Ggax Kuna'	Cheesh-Na Tribe
Gakona	Ggax Kuna'	Gulkana Village Council
Gakona	Ggax Kuna'	Native Village of Gakona
Galena	Notaalee Denh	Galena Village (Louden Village)
Gambell	Sivuqaq	Native Village of Gambell
Glennallen	None listed	Native Village of Tazlina
Golovin	Cingik	Chinik Eskimo Community (Golovin)
Goodnews Bay	Mamterat	Native Village of Goodnews Bay
Grayling	Sixno' Xidakagg	Organized Village of Grayling (Holikachuk)
Haines	Deishú	Chilkat Indian Village
Haines	Deishú	Chilkoot Indian Association
Holy Cross	Ingirraller	Holy Cross Tribe
Hoonah	Xunaa	Hoonah Indian Association
Hooper Bay	Naparyaarmiut	Native Village of Hooper Bay
Hughes	Hut'odlee Kkaakk'et	Hughes Village
Huslia	Ts'aateyhdenaadekk'onh Denh	Huslia Village
Hydaburg	Higdáa Gándlaay	Hydaburg Cooperative Association
Igiugig	Igyaraq	Igiugig Village
Iliamna	Illiamna	Village of Iliamna
Juneau	Dzánti K'ihéeni	Central Council of the Tlingit & Haida Indian Tribes
Juneau	Dzánti K'ihéeni	Douglas Indian Association
Kake	Ḵéex'	Organized Village of Kake
Kaktovik	Qaaktuġvik	Kaktovik Village (Barter Island)
Kalskag	Qalqaq	Village of Kalskag
Kalskag	Qalqaq	Village of Lower Kalskag
Kaltag	Ggaał Doh	Village of Kaltag
Karluk	Kal'ut	Native Village of Karluk
Kasigluk	Kassigluq	Kasigluk Traditional Elders Council
Kenai	Shk'ituk't	Kenaitze Indian Tribe
Kenai	Shk'ituk't	Salamatof Tribe
Ketchikan	Kichx̱áan	Ketchikan Indian Community
Ketchikan	Gasa'áan	Organized Village of Kasaan
Ketchikan	Kichx̱áan	Organized Village of Saxman
Kiana	Katyaaq	Native Village of Kiana
King Cove	Agdaaĝux̂	Agdaagux Tribe of King Cove
King Cove	Agdaaĝux̂	Native Village of Belkofski

Place Name (English)	Indigenous Place Name	Tribe
King Salmon	None listed	King Salmon Tribe
Kipnuk	Qipnek	Native Village of Kipnuk
Kivalina	Kivaliñiq	Native Village of Kivalina
Klawok	Lawaak	Klawock Cooperative Association
Kobuk	Laugviik	Native Village of Kobuk
Kodiak	Sun'aq	Lesnoi Village
Kodiak	Agw'aneq	Native Village of Afognak
Kodiak	Sun'aq	Sun'aq Tribe of Kodiak
Kodiak	Sun'aq	Tangirnaq Native Village
Kokhanoik	Qarr'unaq	Kokhanok Village
Koliganek	Qalirneq	New Koliganek Village Council
Kongiganak	Kangirnaq	Native Village of Kongiganak
Kotlik	Qerrulliik	Native Village of Hamilton
Kotlik	Qerrulliik	Village of Bill Moore's Slough
Kotlik	Qerrulliik	Village of Kotlik
Kotzebue	Qikiqtaġruk	Native Village of Kotzebue
Koyuk	Kuuyuk	Native Village of Koyuk
Koyukuk	Meneelghaadze' T'oh	Koyukuk Native Village
Kwethluk	Kuiggluk	Organized Village of Kwethluk
Kwigillingok	Kuigilnguq	Native Village of Kwigillingok
Larsen Bay	Uyaqsaq	Native Village of Larsen Bay
Levelock	Liivlek	Levelock Village
Manley	Too Naaleł Denh	Manley Hot Springs Village
Manokotak	Manuquutaq	Manokotak Village
Marshall	Masserculleq	Native Village of Marshall (Fortuna Ledge)
Marshall	Urr'agmiut	Village of Ohogamiut
McGrath	Tochak'	McGrath Native Village
Mekoryuk	Mikuryar	Native Village of Mekoryuk
Mentasta	Mendaesde	Mentasta Traditional Council
Metlakatla	Maxłakxaała	Metlakatla Agency
Metlakatla	Maxłakxaała	Metlakatla Indian Community, Annette Island Reserve
Minto	Menhti Xwghotthit	Native Village of Minto
Mountain Village	Asaacaryaraq	Asa'carsarmiut Tribe
Naknek	Nakniq	Naknek Native Village
Nanwalek	Nanwalek	Native Village of Nanwalek (English Bay)
Napakiak	Naparyarraq	Native Village of Napakiak
Napaskiak	Napaskiaq	Native Village of Napaskiak
Napaskiak	Napaskiaq	Oscarville Traditional Village
Nelson Lagoon	Niilsanam Alĝuudaa	Native Village of Nelson Lagoon
Nenana	Toghotili	Nenana Native Association
New Stuyahok	Cetuyaraq	New Stuyahok Village
Newhalen	Nuuriileng	Newhalen Village
Newtok	Niugtaq	Newtok Village
Nightmute	Negtemiut	Native Village of Nightmute
Nightmute	Negtemiut	Umkumiut Native Village

Place Name (English)	Indigenous Place Name	Tribe
Nikiski	Hekdichen Hdakaq'	Lime Village
Nikolai	Nikolai	Nikolai Village
Nikolai	Tilayadi	Telida Village
Nikolski	Chalukax^	Native Village of Nikolski
Ninilchik	None listed	Ninilchik Village
Noatak	Nuataam Kuuŋa	Native Village of Noatak
Nome	Ugiuvak	King Island Native Community
Nome	Sitŋasuaq	Native Village of Council
Nome	Sitŋasuaq	Nome Eskimo Community
Nome	Sitŋasuaq	Village of Solomon
Nondalton	Nundaltin	Nondalton Village
Noorvik	Nuurvik	Noorvik Native Community
Northway	K'ehtthiign	Northway Village
Nuiqsut	Nuiqsat	Native Village of Nuiqsut
Nulato	Noolaaghe Doh	Nulato Village
Nunam Iqua	None listed	Native Village of Nunam Iqua
Nunapitchuk	Nunapicuar	Native Village of Nunapitchuk
Old Harbor	Nuniaq	Alutiiq Tribe of Old Harbor
Ouzinkie	Uusenkaa	Native Village of Ouzinkie
Palmer	Nay'dini'aa Na'	Chickaloon Native Village
Palmer	None listed	Knik Tribe
Pedro Bay	None listed	Pedro Bay Village
Perryville	Perry-q	Native Village of Perryville
Petersburg	Séet Ká	Petersburg Indian Association
Pilot Point	Agisaq	Native Village of Pilot Point
Pilot Station	Tuutalgaq	Pilot Station Traditional Village
Platinum	Arviiq	Platinum Traditional Village
Point Hope	Tikiġaq	Native Village of Point Hope
Point Lay	Kali	Native Village of Point Lay
Port Graham	Paluwik	Native Village of Port Graham
Port Heiden	Masrriq	Native Village of Port Heiden
Port Lions	Masiqsirraq	Native Village of Port Lions
Quinhagak	Kuinerraq	Native Village of Kwinhagak (Quinhagak)
Rampart	Dleł Taaneets	Rampart Village
Red Devil	None listed	Village of Red Devil
Ruby	Tl'aa'ologhe	Native Village of Ruby
Russian Mission	Iqugmiut	Iqurmiut Traditional Council
Sand Point	Uĝnaasaqax^	Native Village of Unga
Sand Point	Sanaĝax	Pauloff Harbor Village
Sand Point	None listed	Qagan Tayagungin Tribe of Sand Point
Savoonga	Sivunga	Native Village of Savoonga
Scammon Bay	Marayaarmiut	Native Village of Scammon Bay
Selawik	Siiḷivik	Native Village of Selawik
Seldovia	Angagkitaqnuuq	Seldovia Village Tribe
Shageluk	Edixi	Shageluk Native Village
Shaktoolik	Saktuliq	Native Village of Shaktoolik

Place Name (English)	Indigenous Place Name	Tribe
Shishmaref	Qigiqtaq	Native Village of Shishmaref
Shungnak	Isiŋnaq	Native Village of Shungnak
Sitka	Sheet'ká	Sitka Tribe of Alaska
Skagway	None listed	Skagway Village
Sleetmute	Cellitemiut	Village of Sleetmute
South Naknek	Qinuyang	South Naknek Village
St. George Island	Anĝaaxchaluxˆ	Saint George Island
St. Mary's	Negeqliq	Algaaciq Native Village (St. Mary's)
St. Mary's	Negeqliq	Pitka's Point Traditional Council
St. Mary's	Negeqliq	Yupiit of Andreafski
St. Michael	Taciq	Native Village of Saint Michael
St. Paul Island	Tanaxˆ Amixˆ	Saint Paul Island
Stebbins	Tapraq	Stebbins Community Association
Stevens Village	Denyeet	Native Village of Stevens
Stony River	K'qizaghetnu	Village of Stony River
Takotna	Tochotno'	Takotna Village
Tanacross	Taats'altęy	Native Village of Tanacross
Tanana	Hohudodetlaatl Denh	Native Village of Tanana
Tatitlek	Taatiilaaq	Native Village of Tatitlek
Teller	Tala	Native Village of Mary's Igloo
Teller	Tala	Native Village of Teller
Togiak	Tuyuryaq	Traditional Village of Togiak
Tok	Teełąy	Native Village of Tetlin
Toksook Bay	Nunakauyaq	Nunakauyarmiut Tribe
Tuluksak	Tuulkessaaq	Tuluksak Native Community
Tuntutuliak	Tuntutuliaq	Native Village of Tuntutuliak
Tununak	Tununeq	Native Village of Tununak
Twin Hills	Ingricuar	Twin Hills Village
Tyonek	Qaggeyshlat	Native Village of Tyonek
Unalakleet	Uṉalaqłiit	Native Village of Unalakleet
Unalakleet	Uṉalaqłiit	Qawalangin Tribe of Unalaska
Utqiagvik	Utqiaġvik	Inupiat Community of the Arctic Slope
Utqiagvik	Utqiaġvik	Native Village of Barrow Inupiat Traditional Government
Venetie	Vashrąįį K'o̧ o̧	Arctic Village
Venetie	Vįįhtąįį	Native Village of Venetie Tribal Government
Venetie	Vįįhtąįį	Village of Venetie
Wainwright	Ulġuniq	Village of Wainwright
Wales	Kiŋigin	Native Village of Wales
Wasilla	None listed	Native Village of Kanatak
White Mountain	Nasirvik	Native Village of White Mountain
Wrangell	Shtax'héen	Wrangell Cooperative Association
Yakutat	Yaakwdáat	Yakutat Tlingit Tribe

Appendix B
Alaska Standards for Culturally Responsive Schools

Alaska Native Knowledge Network. (1998). *Alaska standards for culturally responsive schools.* ankn.uaf.edu/Publications/culturalstandards.pdf

Standards	Pages
Students	5–8
Educators	9–12
Curriculum	13–16
Schools	17–20
Communities	21–24

Below are listed the standards only; each includes multiple indicators (not listed) for how these standards could be met. Readers are encouraged to read the full standards document.

CULTURAL STANDARDS FOR STUDENTS

A. Culturally knowledgeable students are well grounded in the cultural heritage and traditions of their community.

B. Culturally knowledgeable students are able to build on the knowledge and skills of the local cultural community as a foundation from which to achieve personal and academic success throughout life.

C. Culturally knowledgeable students are able to actively participate in various cultural environments.

D. Culturally knowledgeable students are able to engage effectively in learning activities that are based on traditional ways of knowing and learning.

E. Culturally knowledgeable students demonstrate an awareness and appreciation of the relationships and processes of interaction of all the elements in the world around them.

Figure B.1. Courtesy of Alaska Native Knowledge Network. *Reprinted with permission.*

CULTURAL STANDARDS FOR EDUCATORS

A. Culturally responsive educators incorporate local ways of knowing and teaching in their work.
B. Culturally responsive educators use the local environment and community resources on a regular basis to link what they are teaching to the everyday lives of the students.
C. Culturally responsive educators participate in community events and activities in an appropriate and supportive way.
D. Culturally responsive educators work closely with parents to achieve a high level of complementary educational expectations between home and school.
E. Culturally responsive educators recognize the full educational potential of each student and provide the challenges necessary for them to achieve that potential.

CULTURAL STANDARDS FOR CURRICULUM

A. A culturally responsive curriculum reinforces the integrity of the cultural knowledge that students bring with them.

B. A culturally responsive curriculum recognizes cultural knowledge as part of a living and constantly adapting system that is grounded in the past but continues to grow through the present and into the future.
C. A culturally responsive curriculum uses the local language and cultural knowledge as a foundation for the rest of the curriculum.
D. A culturally responsive curriculum fosters a complementary relationship across knowledge derived from diverse knowledge systems.
E. A culturally responsive curriculum situates local knowledge and actions in a global context.

CULTURAL STANDARDS FOR SCHOOLS

A. A culturally responsive school fosters the ongoing participation of Elders in all aspects of the schooling process.
B. A culturally responsive school provides multiple avenues for students to access the learning that is offered, as well as multiple forms of assessment for students to demonstrate what they have learned.
C. A culturally responsive school provides opportunities for students to learn in and/or about their heritage language.
D. A culturally responsive school has a high level of involvement of professional staff who are of the same cultural background as the students with whom they are working.
E. A culturally responsive school consists of facilities that are compatible with the community environment in which they are situated.
F. A culturally responsive school fosters extensive ongoing participation, communication, and interaction between school and community personnel.

CULTURAL STANDARDS FOR COMMUNITIES

A. A culturally supportive community incorporates the practice of local cultural traditions in its everyday affairs.
B. A culturally supportive community nurtures the use of the local heritage language.
C. A culturally supportive community takes an active role in the education of all its members.
D. A culturally supportive community nurtures family responsibility, a sense of belonging, and cultural identity.
E. A culturally supportive community assists teachers in learning and utilizing local cultural traditions and practices.
F. A culturally supportive community contributes to all aspects of curriculum design and implementation in the local school.

ADDITIONAL RESOURCES TO HELP IMPLEMENT

Alaska Department of Education & Early Development. (2012, May). *Guide to implementing the Alaska cultural standards for educators.* https://www.asdn.org/wp-content/uploads/Implementing-AK-cultural-standards-1.pdf

Southeast (Alaska) Regional Resource Center. (2015). *Culture in the classroom: Standards, indicators, and evidences for evaluating culturally responsive teaching.* Project create. aasb.org/wp-content/uploads/Culture-in-the-Classroom-No-AK.pdf

Appendix C
Alaska Indigenous Languages Map

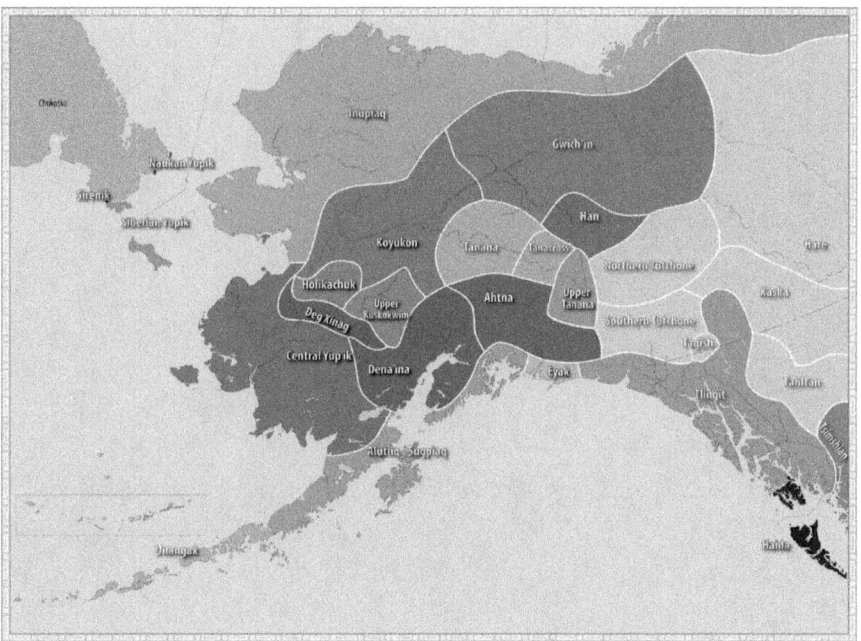

Figure C.1. Indigenous peoples and languages of Alaska. *Courtesy of Alaska Native Language Center, University of Alaska Fairbanks and Institute of Social and Economic Research, University of Alaska Anchorage. Copyright ©2011. Reprinted with permission.*

Glossary

advisory school board (ASB): locally elected boards for individual schools that represent the interests of the community and communicate those interests to the regional school board and administration. Required under Alaska statute for regional school boards, permitted for borough school districts.

aide: see paraprofessional.

Alaska Career Information System (AKCIS): a free career guidance system for K–12 students and educators in Alaska that provides information and career exploration tools. The information populating AKCIS comes from the University of Oregon's College of Education and the Alaska Department of Labor.

Alaska Department of Education & Early Development (DEED): state of Alaska agency responsible for distribution of public school funding and general implementation of Alaska law and regulation concerning the operation of public schools.

Alaska National Interests Land Conservation Act (ANILCA): 1980 federal law that created most of the national parkland in Alaska; provided the definition for "subsistence uses" that is foundational for subsistence activities management in Alaska today.

Alaska Native: a more precise term than Indigenous but used interchangeably in this book; a term in general use in Alaska (2024) that includes multiple Indigenous peoples and nations across the state. Best used in writing as an adjective and in plural (e.g., Alaska Native peoples) to clearly indicate diversity within the broad term. Avoid incorrect usage (e.g., Native Alaskan or Alaskan Native).

Alaska Native Claims Settlement Act (ANCSA): federal legislation that (partially) resolved longstanding Indigenous land claims in Alaska; a direct result of advocacy by the Alaska Federation of Natives (AFN) following the discovery of significant oil deposits on the North Slope (building the Trans-Alaska Pipeline System, or TAPS, required a clear title to the land between the Slope and Valdez). ANCSA established for-profit Alaska Native corporations (12 regional and 200+ Village Corporations); established 12 regional nonprofit corporations; conveyed land title for roughly 44 million acres to the newly created corporations; and allocated nearly $1 billion in compensation for stolen lands to the newly created corporations.

Alaska Native Corporation: General term for the for-profit corporations established in 1971 by the Alaska Native Claims Settlement Act (ANSCA). May refer to a regional corporation or to a village corporation. Issues stock and distributes dividends to enrolled Indigenous shareholders, as well as holds title to (and manages) roughly 44 million acres of land across Alaska. Corporate structure differs significantly from the lower-48 reservation and land-trust arrangements with the federal government. See also Alaska Native Claims Settlement Act, regional corporations, regional nonprofit organizations, and village corporations.

Alaska Native Science and Engineering Program (ANSEP): University of Alaska programs intended to "provide an excellent education and a life of unlimited possibilities for every Alaskan." Operates elementary, middle, high school, and university programs at several campuses (including Mamterilleq [Bethel] and Qikiqtaġruk [Kotzebue]), as well as partners with multiple school districts across the state. Perhaps most well-known for summer middle- and high-school programs that bring students from across the state to Fairbanks to live in dorms and do STEM education.

Alaska Performance Scholarship: state of Alaska–funded scholarship for high school graduates attending college or career training in Alaska. Has three levels with varying eligibility criteria and funds awards.

Alaska Standards for Culturally Responsive Schools: standards developed in 1998 as a complement to content standards. Provide guidance on how to engage students in learning through the local culture. Organized around five components of schooling: students, educators, curriculum, schools, and communities. A required component for teacher evaluations.

Alaska State Troopers: state of Alaska police agency. Responsible for statewide law enforcement; often serve as the major police force in rural Alaska. Posts are often in hubs like Sitŋasuaq (Nome); rural villages may experience significant wait times when requesting State Trooper support, given the varying travel conditions.

Alaska Statewide Mentor Project (ASMP): statewide mentoring program operated by the University of Alaska. Focuses on providing experienced mentor teachers at no or low cost to early career teachers (first- and second-year teachers) across Alaska.

Alaska Type M certificate: special teaching certificate for those without a bachelor's degree who can demonstrate special competency in Indigenous languages or cultures, military science, or vocational/technical education. Must be requested by a school board through the superintendent.

assimilation(ist): the process by which the values, behaviors, and/or beliefs of Indigenous peoples come to resemble those of Western peoples. Can be forced (as in residential schools that banned Indigenous languages and traditions) or through active choice (as in the replacement of dog teams with snowmachines). *Assimilation* is a verb; *assimilationist* is used as an adjective (e.g., assimilationist beliefs) or a person. Carries substantially negative connotations.

bilingual: the use of two languages. Often used in Alaska as an adjective (bilingual program or bilingual aide) to specify funding source (such as federal Title III funding). In rural Alaska schools, most bilingual programs focus on teaching Indigenous languages and cultures. The structure, goals, and grade levels of bilingual programs in rural Alaska vary widely; a commonly limited resource in many villages is the availability of fluent language users.

Boarding Home Program: operated by the state of Alaska (1966–1986), it sent rural Indigenous high school students to urban schools in Alaska (primarily Anchorage and Fairbanks); students lived with (typically non-Indigenous) host families during the school year.

boarding school: a school established by Western peoples for Indigenous children, it operated in or outside Alaska; students lived exclusively at the school, outside their communities. The first in Alaska was established in Sitka in 1878 by Presbyterian missionaries; many more were established in Alaska and the lower 48 by governmental agencies during the Assimilation era (1887–1934). Typically operated with the explicit purpose of eliminating Indigenous languages, beliefs, and traditions via English-only language policies; uniforms and harsh behavioral codes. Abused and traumatized generations of Indigenous children and families; many hid abuses and deaths from parents. Most in Alaska were closed by the early 1980s. Should be distinguished from modern residential schools in Alaska, such as Mt. Edgecumbe High School, Galena Interior Learning Academy, and Nenana City School, which operate as secular district schools in Alaska.

building plant operator (BPO): an operations and maintenance position in many rural Alaska schools. Responsible for the building "plant," including heating and ventilation, electrical, water, alarm, and fire suppression systems, as well as general maintenance and upkeep. Distinct from a custodian (who cleans); requires creative troubleshooting of a wide variety of building problems in rural schools with limited access to parts and equipment. Wise school leaders take good care of talented BPOs.

Bureau of Indian Affairs (BIA): a federal agency within the Department of the Interior that is responsible for implementing federal laws and policies impacting Indigenous peoples in the United States.

Bureau of Indian Education (BIE): an office within the Bureau of Indian Affairs (BIA) responsible for various Tribal-serving schools and school programs.

bush: often used interchangeably with *village* in Alaska; indicates communities off the road system. Acceptable when used as an adjective (e.g., bush plane) but to be avoided as a noun (e.g., he lives in the bush) due to negative connotations and common alternatives (e.g., rural, remote, village, off the road).

career and technical education (CTE): classes or experiences that prepare students for careers. In Alaska, emphasis is generally in areas that do not require college degrees. See also vocational education (older term).

certified staff: includes teachers and administrators certified by the state of Alaska.

classified staff: includes all school staff other than certified teachers and administrators: paraprofessionals, cooks, custodians, and building plant/maintenance personnel.

culturally relevant education: an approach to education that recognizes the importance of including students' cultural backgrounds, interests, and lived experiences in all aspects of teaching and learning.

culture camp: In the context of schools, a week-long (occasionally longer) summer orientation for new staff, operated by school districts in partnership with Tribal members. Beyond school contexts, many Tribes also operate culture camps for young people; they are of various lengths and formats, with a general goal of sharing cultural knowledge, skills, and/or languages.

dual enrollment: enrollment at the university level in a class or classes that can yield both K–12 and university credit. Available at most colleges and universities in Alaska. Format varies. Can include regular university courses or early college/middle college courses taught by university faculty members. Can also include courses taught by K–12 teachers with agreement/approval by the universities.

Elder: A term of respect, includes those who carry and transmit cultural, language, or other knowledge valued by an Indigenous people. Does not denote a specific age group (not all older people in a community are Elders). Indigenous peoples decide who is accorded the title Elder, and this varies by community. Always capitalize to avoid confusion with age descriptor.

Eskimo: Although still used in Alaska, carries colonial/explorer roots and is not an Indigenous term. Preferred term is *Inuit* and/or to specify the

peoples or nations discussed. *Do not use* unless this is your background or you're quoting directly from a source (and then provide context).
fetal alcohol spectrum disorders (FASD): a brain-based disability caused by prenatal alcohol exposure. Common across Alaska. May impact behavior, judgment, memory, learning, emotions, attention, impulse control, understanding cause and effect, and more. Early diagnosis and intervention is useful; the state of Alaska funds a statewide multidisciplinary FASD team. Also described as fetal alcohol effect (FAE) and/or fetal alcohol syndrome (FAS). *Do not* suggest that students may have FASD; it is diagnosed by others and is a deeply sensitive topic in rural Alaska.
fish camp: river- or oceanside summer camp primarily for subsistence fishing and processing (cleaning, drying, smoking, etc.). In rural Alaska, families may go to fish camp for weeks at a time, returning to the same location annually. These can serve as a base for other subsistence activities such as hunting or berry picking; may have permanent structures like cabins, sheds, and racks or may involve temporary structures like tents.
Great Sickness: in 1900, an outbreak of measles in rural Alaska, which, in combination with an overlapping influenza outbreak (the Great Death), killed an estimated one-quarter to one-half of Yup'ik and Inupiat peoples in western Alaska.
health clinic: the sole medical provider in many rural Alaska villages, often staffed by a community health aide. May have a physician assistant or nurse practitioner. Provides primary care services for residents, often in coordination with hub clinics and hospitals.
heritage language: language(s) learned at home or in community settings. In rural Alaska these are typically Indigenous languages. May not be fully developed. May also be a language a person does not speak or understand but identifies with culturally.
Honda: general term for all-terrain vehicles (ATVs), or four-wheelers, in rural Alaska.
hub/hub city: a population center in Alaska that serves multiple outlying villages, often with businesses and services not available in individual villages, such as government offices, hospitals, restaurants, hotels, and so forth. Definitely includes Qikiqtaġruk (Kotzebue), Utqiaġvik, Mamterilleq (Bethel), and Curyung (Dillingham). Maybe includes Dgheyaytnu (Anchorage), Fairbanks, and Dzánti K'ihéeni (Juneau). Although these latter three certainly serve multiple outlying villages, they have additional non–hub city identities (big city, government center, military town, etc.).
immersion camp: see culture camp.
Indian: Although still used in Alaska to refer to specific peoples (most commonly, Athabascan peoples in the Interior and Tlingit and Haida peoples in Southeast), this term has colonial roots and often stereotypes more than

enlightens. Preferable is the term Indigenous, perhaps Alaska Native, and/ or to specify the peoples or nations discussed. *Do not use* unless this is your background or you're quoting directly from a source (and then provide context).

Indian Child Welfare Act (ICWA): 1978 federal law that governs the removal and out-of-home placement of Indigenous children. Requires Tribes and families to be involved in child welfare cases.

Indigenous: Preferred term throughout the book to include Alaska Native peoples, including Inupiat, Yupik, Aleut, Eyak, Tlingit, Haida, Tsimshian, and a number of Northern Athabaskan peoples. Also includes non–Alaska Native peoples, such as First Nations peoples in Canada and Native peoples in the lower 48. Best used as an adjective (e.g., Indigenous peoples). Always capitalize.

in-service: school-district provided professional development for staff. Often provided for several days or a week before the school year starts, typically organized by the district office and conducted at hub-school sites.

itinerant (teachers, principals, or specialists): a district employee who travels to various school sites during the year. May spend a day or multiple days at each school. Typically lives in the district hub (e.g., Mamterilleq [Bethel]), flies out to rural schools, and stays in itinerant housing.

K–12 generalist: a teaching position common in rural Alaska schools, especially one- or two-teacher sites. Requires teachers to teach multiple grade levels and subjects during the day.

Kasayulie settlement: a 2011 settlement of a 1997 lawsuit over funding rural schools in Alaska (*Kasayulie et al. v. State of Alaska*). The Kasayulies were parents of children in Akiacuar (Akiachak); their coalition pointed out that funding for rural schools in Alaska was unfair and racially discriminatory because rural, primarily Indigenous communities could not levy taxes to fund schools as could urban communities. In the settlement the state agreed to change the school construction funding mechanism and pay millions of dollars to build new schools in five communities.

language revitalization: complementary to *language preservation*. Efforts to halt or reverse the decline of an Indigenous language in Alaska.

lead teacher: A teaching position in small-enrollment rural Alaska schools. Includes teaching duties through most or all of the school day. Generally designated at school sites that have itinerant principals (who travel between multiple sites, often spending one or two weeks at each site per month). See also principal/teacher.

local advisory board: see advisory school board.

missionary: a member of a religious group sent into an area to promote their faith. In Alaska these missionaries were Christian; the earliest (Russian Orthodox) mission in Alaska was established at Sun'aq (Kodiak) in 1794.

Often served as de facto agents of settler colonialism in the years before the district (1878), territory (1912), and eventually the state (1959) of Alaska were organized. The legacies of missionary work remain strong in parts of rural Alaska, including Orthodox, Lutheran, Presbyterian, and Quaker ("Friends") churches. Carries substantially negative connotations, given colonial roots.

Molly Hootch: a 1976 consent decree ending a lawsuit (*Tobeluk v. Lind*) signed by the state of Alaska and a coalition of 27 teenagers in Alaska who pointed out that requiring village students to attend boarding schools was discriminatory. The state of Alaska signed a consent decree with the plaintiffs in 1976, agreeing to build high schools in every community with at least fifteen high school–aged children. Molly Hootch, a sixteen-year-old from Imangaq (Emmonak), was the first named plaintiff; the consent decree is often informally called the Molly Hootch case or settlement. This settlement was the major impetus for building new village schools throughout rural Alaska.

multigrade classroom/multiage classroom: a classroom assigned to a single teacher that includes students of various ages or grade levels. For example, a K–2 classroom may include a mix of students from three different grade levels. Common in small rural schools where there are fewer than 10 students in a given grade level.

Native: acceptable for use in the specific term "Alaska Native" and for specifying entities that use the term (Native Village of Kivalina, Alaska Native Land Claims Settlement Act). Avoid as a general adjective (e.g., Native worldview) or as a stereotypical, negative colonial word (e.g., the Natives are restless); falling out of use beyond Alaska. Preferred term is Indigenous and/or to specify the peoples or nations discussed.

Native American/American Indian: Although used in the lower 48 and on some bureaucratic forms (i.e., Census and school reporting), these terms are not used in Alaska and risk subsuming/stereotyping a wide range of peoples. Preferred term is Indigenous, perhaps Alaska Native, and/or to specify the peoples or nations discussed. *Do not use* unless this is your background, or you're quoting directly from a source (and then provide context).

Native dance (also dances of various groups; e.g., Yup'ik dance): Traditional style of dancing, performed with songs (in Indigenous languages) and often a drum (or drums). Typically choreographed, it includes traditional dress and may involve masks and specific roles/styles by gender. Both Yup'ik and Iñupiaq dance may also be called Eskimo dance—*do not use* this latter term if it is not your background.

Native Youth Olympics: annual youth athletics competition sponsored by the Cook Inlet Tribal Council (since 1986). Emphasizes Indigenous skills contests, such as the Alaskan high kick, seal hop, and wrist carry.

Nelson Act: a 1905 federal law that established a segregated system of education for Indigenous and non-Indigenous students. Gave the Bureau of Indian Affairs (BIA) nearly exclusive control over Indigenous schooling in Alaska until well after statehood (1959).

North Slope / the Slope: geographically, the region of Alaska on the northern slope of the Brooks Range. In general use, refers to Prudhoe Bay and other oil fields (e.g., He works on the Slope). Also, a borough government and school district based in Utqiaġvik.

Office of Children's Services (OCS): state of Alaska agency responsible for fielding and acting upon reports of child abuse or neglect. Also oversees foster care in Alaska.

on the road/off the road: one of the more important geographic traits of a location in Alaska; also has economic, cultural, and language significance. Our book primarily discusses schools off the road system. Being off the road system means relying on planes, boats, four-wheelers (Hondas), and/or snowmachines. Off-the-road communities are more likely than others to have subsistence economies, Indigenous language speakers, high interconnectedness among residents, and limited access to/higher costs for public and private goods and services.

Orthodox Church: may refer to Eastern Orthodox or Russian Orthodox churches. Among the oldest established churches in Alaska with roots in the era of Russian colonization.

Outside: a general geographic term, meaning beyond Alaska. Used as a noun (e.g., She's from Outside); generally refers to the contiguous 48 states. Interchangeable with *lower 48* and *down South*.

paraprofessional: person not required to have a professional license or certification. Provides instructional or other educational support to students under the supervision of a teacher or other professional educational service provider. See also certified staff, aide.

Perkins funding/Carl D. Perkins funding: federal funding for CTE programs administered by the Alaska Department of Education & Early Development.

Permanent Fund Dividend (PFD): an annual payment to all residents of the state of Alaska from the state's Alaska Permanent Fund; established as a repository for oil revenues in 1976. Historically, the PFD has averaged $1,600 per resident (adjusted to 2019 USD).

principal/teacher: a combined teaching and administrative position in small-enrollment rural Alaska schools. Generally involves teaching duties through most or all of the school day, with additional administrative duties completed after school or during release time. See also lead teacher.

regional corporation: for-profit corporations established in 1971 by the Alaska Native Claims Settlement Act (ANCSA). Issue stock and distribute dividends to enrolled Indigenous shareholders; they hold the title to (and manage) nearly 27 million acres of land in Alaska. There are currently 12 regional corporations in Alaska. A 13th regional corporation was established in 1975 (in Seattle, Washington) to represent people no longer residing in Alaska; the 13th regional corporation was dissolved in 2013. Regional corporations regularly rank among the largest employers and most profitable businesses in Alaska.

regional nonprofit corporation: established in 1971 by the Alaska Native Claims Settlement Act (ANCSA) to provide social services and health care for Indigenous peoples in Alaska. There are currently twelve Alaska Native regional nonprofit corporations providing services throughout the state. Specific objectives of each nonprofit vary but generally focus on health, cultural, and educational opportunities.

relocation: describes efforts of some rural communities in Alaska to move due to climate-related threats. Acceptable to use when discussing village or school efforts to move themselves geographically. Use with caution due to possible associations with colonialist displacement/relocation—just be clear who is behind relocation efforts and what roles participants play.

remote: a geographic indicator of a school or community (e.g., Anĝaaxchalux̂ [St. George] is a remote village in the Aleutian chain), implies an off-the-road system location, or one limited by irregular Alaska Marine Highway (ferry) service. More specific/narrow than using the term *rural* in Alaska; often used interchangeably with bush.

residential school: see boarding school.

rural: preferred term throughout the book. Primarily a geographic indicator (as in rural Alaska schools), but in Alaska, it also generally means an off-the-road system and implies a small population (in Southeast Alaska, Yaakwdáat [Yakutat] is rural; Dzánti K'ihéeni [Juneau] is not). Possible confusion with broad use of term *rural* in the lower 48.

School Climate and Connectedness Survey: an annual survey administered by the Alaska Association of School Boards (AASB) to Alaska students, staff, and families. Solicits perceptions of school climate, relationships, social and emotional learning, and risk behaviors at school and school events.

school leadership team: generally an informal group in rural schools, including a principal (or principal/teacher or lead teacher) and other staff on some identified basis (long service at the school or a position such as counselor). Meets regularly to plan, identify, and resolve problems, as well as to respond to student or other school issues.

secondary generalist: teaching position common in rural Alaska schools. Requires teachers in grades 7–12 to teach multiple grade levels and subjects during the day.

shareholder: an owner of stock in an Alaska Native corporation (regional or village) under the Alaska Native Claims Settlement Act (ANCSA; 1971).

snowmachine: preferred term for vehicles generally called snowmobiles outside of Alaska. Sometimes also called *snow-go* in rural Alaska.

sovereignty: in general, the power, authority, and right of a people to govern themselves. A noun that is often used as an adjective (e.g., sovereign rights). Sovereignty is not granted by external authority but is a human right (as are, for example, life and liberty). The *exercise* of sovereignty is often influenced by external factors. In Alaska, Tribal sovereignty remains an evolving concept. For example, Tribes have successfully exercised sovereign rights in some areas (membership, marriage, adoption, inheritance, and divorce) but less successfully in others (criminal justice, education, and business). Although the US federal government has recognized the sovereignty of 229 Tribes in Alaska for many years, the state of Alaska only recently affirmed some aspects of Tribal sovereignty in 2017 (via a letter from then attorney general Jahna Lindemuth).

Spanish flu: an outbreak of influenza from 1918 to 1919 that killed an unknown percentage of people in Alaska; disproportionately deadly among Indigenous peoples. Some villages saw mortality rates of more than half (in Brevig Mission 72 out of 80 residents died); following the Spanish Flu, some villages were abandoned, and many orphaned children were relocated to residential boarding schools.

specialists: general term in rural Alaska that includes counselors, speech pathologists, physical and occupational therapists, and other personnel, many of whom deliver related services for students with individual education programs (IEPs).

subsistence: an economic and cultural term, defined in both Alaska and federal law as "customary and traditional uses" of wild resources for food, clothing, fuel, transportation, construction, art, crafts, sharing, and trade. Subsistence links people to the land and to others, including ancestors. How subsistence is done matters a great deal, and its successful practice can be critical for both physical and cultural survival. Primarily an adjective (e.g., subsistence activities or subsistence calendar), often used in contrast with *the cash economy*.

subsistence calendar: an adjusted school-year calendar intended to reduce conflicts between school days and subsistence activities such as hunting, gathering, or fishing. May involve longer-duration school days (or school year), along with designated "subsistence days," where school is not in session.

teaching through culture: pedagogical approach that seeks to promote standards mastery by grounding teaching and learning practices in the cultural practices, values, and norms specific to communities in Alaska. Related approaches are described as *place-based education* and *culturally responsive education*.

time immemorial: extending beyond the reach of memory or record. A phrase used by Iġġiaġruk William L. "Willie" Hensley in his 1966 paper, *What Rights to Land Have the Alaska Natives?: The Primary Question*. Hensley was describing how long Indigenous peoples have lived on the land now called Alaska.

Tobeluk v. Lind: see Molly Hootch.

tote: large plastic storage bin with a lid, typically used in rural Alaska for shipping goods on bush planes. Preferred over suitcases or cardboard boxes because they are inexpensive and waterproof.

traditional foods: generally, these are foods acquired through subsistence activities and/or with longstanding cultural roots among Indigenous peoples.

traditional knowledge: knowledge, skills, and practices developed, sustained, and passed from generation to generation among Indigenous peoples in Alaska, often forming part of cultural and spiritual identities. Includes (but is not limited to) knowledge of subsistence, technologies, medicine, navigation, ecology, and cultural expressions, such as languages, stories, spiritual practices, and law. Many aspects of traditional knowledge have been developed through empirical observation and interaction with the environment.

Tribal police officer (TPO): a trained police officer employed by a Tribe. The qualifications, training, and duties of Tribal police officers vary and are defined by Tribes, not the state or municipalities.

Tribe/Tribal: acceptable for use in specifying an entity (such as Tribal police officer) or, when capitalized, in naming a political entity (e.g., the Knik Tribe). To be avoided as a general adjective due to negative connotations and stereotyping (e.g., tribal politics). It would be preferred to name the people(s) discussed (e.g., the Native Village of Kivalina) or the use of better descriptors (people, nation, society).

urban: in Alaska, primarily refers to the areas around the Big 5 school districts—Anchorage, Juneau, Fairbanks, the Matanuska-Susitna Borough, and the Kenai Peninsula. Can also refer to smaller cities such as Kichx̱áan (Ketchikan), Sheet'ká (Sitka), and Sun'aq (Kodiak). Unclear usage for hubs like Qikiqtaġruk (Kotzebue), Utqiaġvik, Mamterilleq (Bethel), and Curyung (Dillingham).

village: a term with multiple meanings, it is primarily used to suggest communities with small population sizes off the road system in Alaska (though not exclusively; e.g., Teełąy [Tetlin] is a village on the road system). Term also suggests a primarily Indigenous population (Aangóon [Angoon], a predominantly Tlingit community, is generally described as a village, while K'udeis'x̱'e [Pelican], a predominantly Caucasian community, is not). Can be used as an adjective (e.g., village English) or a noun (e.g., heading back to the village), though be advised that these can carry negative connotations.

village corporations: for-profit corporations established in 1971 by the Alaska Native Claims Settlement Act (ANCSA). Issue stock and distribute dividends to enrolled Indigenous shareholders; they hold the title to and manage roughly 17 million acres of land surrounding villages in Alaska. There are roughly 200 village corporations in Alaska.

village English: widely used term for the English spoken (and that influences the writing) in Alaska Native villages; distinguished from academic or "standard" English. Often uses grammar and syntax rules rooted in Indigenous languages (e.g., I always/You never). The term *village English* has both geographic and dual-language roots; it suggests where the language is used and its origins as a contact language. Speakers of village English often code switch between settings (family vs. school). Acceptable term when discussing language or academic supports. Use with caution in any context due to negative connotations. An acceptable goal in schools could include improved biliteracy skills—but *not* replacing or suppressing village English.

village police officer (VPO): a trained police officer employed by a state or municipal police department. Has the authority to arrest and issue citations, detain suspects, and conduct investigations.

village public safety officer (VPSO): a public safety position in rural Alaska that provides community policing, fire protection, emergency medical services, and search and rescue coordination. Employed by regional corporations, regional nonprofits, and/or municipalities. VPSO funding is allocated by the state of Alaska. Can enforce Alaska laws but must do so in coordination with direction from the state Department of Public Safety.

vocational education: see career and technical education (CTE).

Western: indicates origins outside Alaska, generally with historic connections to regions or nations in Europe or areas whose populations have had a large presence of particular European ethnic groups. Used as an adjective (e.g., Western world or Western orientation); does not necessarily imply any specific geography.

Yuuyaraq: the Yup'ik way of being. Also the title of a much-read 1988 book by Harold Napolean, *Yuuyaraq: The Way of the Human Being*. Additionally, a seventh- and eighth-grade curriculum developed by the Lower Kuskokwim School District that is described as "a set of well-defined cultural values, rules and roles 'to live a full and fruitful life without doing harm to oneself, others and nature with all it brings.'"

References

Alaska Business. (2020). *2020 Top 49ers.* www.akbizmag.com/the-2020-top-49ers
Alaska Department of Education & Early Development. (2012, May). *Guide to implementing the Alaska cultural standards for educators.* https://www.asdn.org/wp-content/uploads/Implementing-AK-cultural-standards-1.pdf
Alaska Department of Education & Early Development. (2020a). *What is Tribal compacting of education in Alaska?* https://education.alaska.gov/compacting
Alaska Department of Education & Early Development. (2020b). *Who are Alaska's CTE students?* www.akleg.gov/basis/get_documents.asp?session=31&docid=59407
Alaska Department of Education & Early Development (2023, August). *Alaska's teacher retention and recruitment.* https://education.alaska.gov/trr
Alaska Department of Education & Early Development. (n.d.). *Lower Yukon School District walrus hunt strengthens community bonds and teaches life skills.* https://education.alaska.gov/information-exchange-blog/lysd-walrus-hunt-strengthens-cultural-bonds-and-life-skills
Alaska Department of Fish and Game. (2022). *Subsistence in Alaska.* www.adfg.alaska.gov/index.cfm?adfg=subsistence.main
Alaska National Interest Lands Conservation Act, Publ. L. No. 96-487, 124 Stat. (1980).
Alaska Native Knowledge Network. (1998). *Alaska standards for culturally responsive schools.* https://uaf.edu/ankn/publications/guides/alaska-standards-for-cult
Alaska Native Language Preservation & Advisory Council. (2022). *2022 Biennial Report to the Governor and Legislature.* The Great State of Alaska, Division of Community and Regional Affairs. https://www.commerce.alaska.gov/web/dcra/AKNativeLanguagePreservationAdvisoryCouncil.aspx?TSPD_101_R0=
Amarok, Barbara QasuGlana. (2014). *An indigenous vision of 21st century education in the Bering Strait region.* [Doctoral dissertation, University of Alaska Fairbanks]. https://scholarworks.alaska.edu/handle/11122/5117
ANCSA Regional Association. (2022). *Economic impacts.* https://ancsaregional.com/economic-impacts

Association for Career and Technical Education. (2022). *Why CTE?* www.acteonline.org/why-cte

Barker, J. H. (1993). *Always getting ready / Upterrlainarluta: Yup'ik Eskimo subsistence in southwest Alaska.* University of Washington Press.

Barnes, M. (2018). Alaska's teachers are leaving at much higher than the national average. Here's what's being done about it. *Juneau Empire.* www.juneauempire.com/news/alaskas-teachers-are-leaving-at-much-higher-than-the-national-average-heres-whats-being-done-about-it

Barnhardt, R. (2005). Culture, community and place in Alaska Native education. *Democracy & Education, 16*(2), 44–51.

Barnhardt, R. (1977). Administrative influences in Alaskan Native education." In R. Barnhardt (ed.), *Cross-cultural issues in Alaskan education.* Center for Northern Educational Research.

Barnhart, R., & Kawagley, O. (Eds.). (2010). *Alaska Native education: Views from within.* Alaska Native Knowledge Network.

Barry, J. M. (2004). *The great influenza: The story of the deadliest pandemic in history.* Penguin.

Brown, D. (1970). *Bury My Heart at Wounded Knee.* Holt, Rinehart, & Winston.

Bureau of Indian Education. (2022). *About BIE.* U.S. Department of the Interior. https://www.bia.gov/bie

Carter, S. [mcspankenplatter]. (2008, October 10). *Mary Huntington on Inupiaq language.* [Video]. YouTube. www.youtube.com/watch?app=desktop&v=dIc8l7Xa5pE

Chingos, M. M., & Peterson, P. E. (2011). It's easier to pick a good teacher than to train one: Familiar and new results on the correlates of teacher effectiveness. *Economics of Education Review, 30*(3), 449–65. https://doi.org/10.1016/j.econedurev.2010.12.010

Darnell, F., & Hoem, A. (1996). *Taken to extremes: Education in the far north.* Scandinavian University Press North America.

Dauenhauer, R. (1980). *Conflicting visions in Alaskan education.* University of Alaska, Center for Cross-Cultural Studies.

DeFeo, D. J., Fallon, S., Hirshberg, D., & LeCompte, C. (2014). *Alaska career pathways: A baseline analysis.* University of Alaska Anchorage, Institute of Social and Economic Research. https://pubs.iseralaska.org/media/2d7ea661-265b-41e9-829e-a9cb42ddee23/2014_06-AKCPPoS.pdf

DeFeo, D. J., & Hirschberg, D. (2020a, March 20). *CAEPR researchers testify about teacher turnover to the Alaska Legislature.* University of Alaska Anchorage, Center for Alaska Education Policy Research. https://iseralaska.org/2020/03/caepr-researchers-testify-about-teacher-turnover-to-the-alaska-legislature

DeFeo, D. J., & Hirschberg, D. (2020b). *Teacher retention & recruitment in Alaska.* University of Alaska Anchorage, Center for Alaska Education Policy Research. www.akleg.gov/basis/get_documents.asp?session=31&docid=61361

DeFeo, D., & Tran, T. C. (2019). Recruiting, hiring, and training Alaska's rural teachers: How superintendents practice place-conscious leadership. *Journal of Research in Rural Education, 35*(2), 1–17. https://eric.ed.gov/?id=EJ1213138

DeFeo, D. J., Tran, T., Hirshberg, D., Cope, D., & Cravez, P. (2017). *The cost of teacher turnover in Alaska.* University of Alaska, Anchorage, Institute of Social and Economic Research. https://iseralaska.org/static/legacy_publication_links/2017-CostTeacher.pdf

DeFeo, D., & Tran, T. (2019). *Dual enrollment in Alaska: A 10-year retrospective and outcome analysis.* University of Alaska, Anchorage, Institute of Social and Economic Research. https://iseralaska.org/publications/?id=1754

Dittmar, J. (2018, October). Harnessing change: Sled dog care and mushing program leads children into the future." *Alaska.* https://alaskamagazine.com/tag/george-attla

Dunbar-Ortiz, R. (2015). *An Indigenous peoples' history of the United States.* Beacon Press.

Edge, J. (2017, June 15). *Longevity crucial to teachers' impact in classroom.* Alaska Public Media. www.alaskapublic.org/2017/06/15/longevity-crucial-to-teachers-impact-in-classroom

Emekauwa, E. (2004). *The star with my name: The Alaska Rural Systemic Initiative and the impact of place-based education on Native student achievement. The case for place-based rural trust white paper on place-based education.* Rural School and Community Trust. https://eric.ed.gov/?id=ED484828

Engelmann, S., & Silbert, J. (2004). *Expressive Writing 1 (Student Workbook).* McGraw Hill.

First Alaskans Institute [firstalaskansinstitute3753]. (2018, November 3). *2018 Social Justice Summit—Day One Keynote by Ernestine Saankalaxt Hayes* [Video]. YouTube. https://www.youtube.com/watch?v=mPcGZvEVKfU

Fitch Ratings. (2020, April 9). *Fitch Affirms McGraw-Hill's IDR at "B+"; Outlook Revised to Negative.* Fitch Ratings. www.fitchratings.com/research/corporate-finance/fitch-affirms-mcgraw-hill-idr-at-b-outlook-revised-to-negative-09-04-2020

García, E., & Weiss, E. (2019, April 16). *U.S. schools struggle to hire and retain teachers.* Economic Policy Institute. www.epi.org/publication/u-s-schools-struggle-to-hire-and-retain-teachers-the-second-report-in-the-perfect-storm-in-the-teacher-labor-market-series

Goldsmith, S. (2008). *Understanding Alaska's remote rural economy.* University of Alaska Anchorage, Institute of Social and Economic Research. https://iseralaska.org/publications/?id=1186.

Gómez, & Gómez. (2022). *Gómez and Gómez Dual Language Training Institute.* https://www.dltigomez.com.

Green, J. R. (2010). *Investigating a Yup'ik immersion program: What determines success?* [Master's thesis, University of Alaska Fairbanks]. https://scholarworks.alaska.edu/handle/11122/8562

Hamilton, L. (2017, May 3). *Lake and Peninsula School District switches to "subsistence calendar."* KDLG 670 AM. www.kdlg.org/education/2017-05-03/lake-and-peninsula-school-district-switches-to-subsistence-calendar

Haupt, R., Smith, N., Jones, P., Marks, L., Bradley-Klug, K., & Hermetet-Lindsay, K. (2020). Forming Effective Partnerships between School and Community Service Providers. *Communique, 49*(1), 17–19.

Hays, Lydia. (2019). *Alaska Native Tribes, ANCSA corporations, and Tribal organizations.* Publication Consultants.

Heifetz, R., & Linsky, M. (2002, June). A survival guide for leaders. *Harvard Business Review,* 65–73. https://hbr.org/2002/06/a-survival-guide-for-leaders

Hensley, W. I. (1966). *What rights to land have the Alaska Natives?: The primary question.* Alaskool. www.alaskool.org/projects/ancsa/wlh/WLH66_1.htm

Hensley, W. I. (2010). *Fifty miles from tomorrow: A memoir of Alaska and the real people.* Picador.

Hill, A., Hirshberg, D., & Kasemodel, C. (2014). *Will they stay, or will they go? Teacher perceptions of working conditions in rural Alaska.* University of Alaska Anchorage, Center for Alaska Education Policy Research. https://scholarworks.alaska.edu/handle/11122/8966

Hill, A., Hirshberg, D., & Shaw, D. G. (2013). *Why aren't they teaching? A study of why some University of Alaska teacher education graduates aren't in classrooms.* University of Alaska Anchorage, Center for Education Policy Research. https://scholarworks.alaska.edu/handle/11122/8970

Hill, F., Kawagley, O., & Barnhardt, R. (2006). *Alaska Rural Systemic Initiative: Final report, phase II, 2000–2005.* National Science Foundation. www.uaf.edu/ankn/publications/collective-works-of-ray-b/AKRSI-Final-Report.pdf

Hillman, A. (2016, June 15). *LKSD dual language program helps students succeed in Yupik and English.* Alaska Public Media. www.alaskapublic.org/2016/06/15/lksd-dual-language-program-helps-student-succeed-in-yupik-and-english

Hirshberg, D. (2019, February 21). *Retention and turnover of teachers in Alaska: Why it matters* [PowerPoint presentation]. Alaska Municipal League, Juneau, Alaska. https://scholarworks.alaska.edu/handle/11122/11108

Holloway, S. (n.d.). *History of Alaska education policy series: Origins of the Children's Cabinet and quality schools initiative.* Alaska Association of School Boards. https://aasb.org/history-of-alaska-education-policy-series-origins-of-the-childrens-cabinet-and-quality-schools-initiative

Hull, M. (2002). "Place-based Education in Russian Mission." *Sharing Our Pathways, 7*(5). http://ankn.uaf.edu/SOP/SOPv7i5.html

Institute for Education Sciences. (2017). *Writing.* National Assessment of Educational Progress. https://nces.ed.gov/nationsreportcard/writing

Kawagley, A. O. (1992, Spring). A Native view of culturally relevant education, an invited essay. *Arctic Research of the United States, 6.* www.uaf.edu/ankn/publications/collective-works-of-angay/Native-View-of-Cultu1819F5.pdf

Kawagley, A. O. (1993). *A Yupiaq worldview: Implications for cultural, educational, and technological adaptation in a contemporary world.* [Doctoral dissertation, University of British Columbia]. https://open.library.ubc.ca/media/download/pdf/831/1.0098864/1

Kawagley, A. O. (2006). *A Yupiaq worldview: A pathway to ecology and spirit* (2nd ed.). Waveland Press.

Kellie, C. Q. (2017, July 3). *I always, you never: A celebration of village english.* Nalliq. https://nalliq.com/2017/07/03/i-always-you-never-a-celebration-of-village-english

Kim, G. (2019). *Dunleavy pursuing educational compact with Alaska tribes.* Alaska Public Media. www.alaskapublic.org/2019/12/09/dunleavy-pursuing-educational-compact-with-alaska-tribes

Klnl, T., & Podolsky, A. (2016, June 3). *Does teaching experience increase teacher effectiveness? A review of the research.* Learning Policy Institute. https://learningpolicyinstitute.org/product/does-teaching-experience-increase-teacher-effectiveness-review-research

Ladson-Billings, G. (1995). Toward a theory of culturally relevant pedagogy. *American Education Research Journal, 32*(3), 465–91. https://doi.org/10.3102/00028312032003465

Lebrón, E. L. R. (2021, Spring). A formula for success: Teaching Native American community college students math—and to believe in themselves. *American Educator.* www.aft.org/ae/spring2021/lebron

Lemov, D., Driggs, C., & Woolway, E. (2016). *Reading Reconsidered: A Practical Guide to Rigorous Literacy Instruction.* Wiley.

Lindemuth, J. (2017, October 19). *Re: Legal status of tribal governments in Alaska.* Legal opinion, letter to governor of Alaska. https://law.alaska.gov/pdf/opinions/opinions_2017/17-004_JU20172010.pdf

Lipka, J. (2019). Going to Egg Island: Adventures in grouping and place values. In *Math in a Cultural Context.* University of Alaska Fairbanks. CC BY NC 4.0.

Lower Kuskokwim School District. (2022). *Ayaprun Elitnaurvik.* https://ayaprun.lksd.org/about/ayaprun_elitnaurvik

Maclean, E. (1986). *Culture and change for Iñupiat and Yupiks of Alaska."* Alaskool. www.alaskool.org/native_ed/articles/EMaclean-CC.htm

Marzano, R. J. (2020). *Teaching basic, advanced, and academic vocabulary: A comprehensive framework for elementary instruction.* Marzano Resources.

Masters, R. (2014). You be the jury. In *Journeys Common Core, grade 3, vol. 1* (pp. 74–75). Houghton Mifflin Harcourt.

Napoleon, H. (1996). *Yuuyaraq: The way of the human being.* Alaska Native Knowledge Network, University of Alaska Fairbanks.

National Congress of American Indians. (2019). *Becoming visible: A landscape analysis of state efforts to provide Native American education for all.* www.ncai.org/policy-research-center/research-data/prc-publications/NCAI-Becoming_Visible_Report-Digital_FINAL_10_2019.pdf

National Park Service. (2022). *Subsistence in Alaska: An enduring way of life.* Story Maps. www.nps.gov/gis/storymaps/cascade/v1/index.html?appid=42e0af0fd1ab485596a0475d186a0919

National Science Foundation. (2021). *Bachelor's degree holders in the labor force.* Science and engineering state indicators. https://ncses.nsf.gov/indicators/states/indicator/bachelors-degree-holders-in-labor-force

Nelson Act (Alaska Roads, Schools, and Insane), §§ 277-33-616 (1905).

Nesteroff, K. (2021). *We had a little real estate problem: The unheralded story of Native Americans & comedy.* Simon & Schuster.

Neuman, S. B., Kaefer, T., & Pinkham, A. (2014). Building background knowledge. *The Reading Teacher, 68*(2), 145–48. https://doi.org/10.1002/trtr.1314

O'Malley, J. (2017, July 17). The teenage whaler's tale: Internet death threats hound a young Alaskan after a successful hunt. *High Country News.* www.hcn.org/issues/49.12/tribal-affairs-a-teenage-whaler-pride-of-his-alaska-village-is-haunted-by-trolls

Orvik, J. M. (1975, August). An overview of Alaska Native bilingual education. *Topics in Culture Learning, 2,* 1–17. https://eric.ed.gov/?q=ED120273

Papay, J. P., & Kraft, M. A. (2015). Productivity returns to experience in the teacher labor market: Methodological challenges and new evidence on long-term career improvement. *Journal of Public Economics, 130,* 105–19. https://doi.org/10.1016/j.jpubeco.2015.02.008

Pember, M. A. (2021, November 24). A history not yet laid to rest. *The Atlantic.* www.theatlantic.com/ideas/archive/2021/11/native-american-boarding-schools/620760

Pingayak, John. (1998). *The Cup'ik people of the western tundra: A curriculum.* University of Alaska, Institute for Social and Economic Research. https://files.eric.ed.gov/fulltext/ED448943.pdf

Roehl, R. F., II. (2010). *Correlation between teacher turnover rates in the state of Alaska and standardized test scores in the area of mathematics on the standards based assessments/high school qualifying exam.* [Doctoral dissertation, University of Alaska Fairbanks]. https://scholarworks.alaska.edu/handle/11122/9039

Rose, W. (2014). *Rural Alaska teacher's moving guide: What to expect on the last frontier.* CreateSpace.

Sakakibara, C. (2020). *Whale snow: Iñupiat, climate change, and multispecies resilience in arctic Alaska.* University of Arizona Press.

Sampson, R. (2002, Summer). Native languages in Alaska, part II. *Sharing Our Pathways, 7*(3). http://ankn.uaf.edu/sop/SOPv7i3.html

Sealaska Heritage [Shininstitute]. (2020, September 1). *My life in education as a Native teacher: With Shgen George* [Video]. YouTube. www.youtube.com/watch?v=H6WtQz40rN0

Seventh International Conference of America States. (1933). *Convention on Rights and Duties of States adopted by the Seventh International Conference of American States.* Ministry of Foreign Affairs, Uruguay. https://treaties.un.org/doc/Publication/UNTS/LON/Volume%20165/v165.pdf

Sharp, S., & Hirshberg, D. (2005). *Thirty years later: The long-term effect of boarding schools on Alaska Natives and their communities.* University of Alaska Anchorage, Institute of Social and Economic Research. https://scholarworks.alaska.edu/handle/11122/8972

Southeast (Alaska) Regional Resource Center. (2015). *Culture in the Classroom: Standards, indicators and evidences for evaluating culturally responsive teaching.* Project create. https://aasb.org/wp-content/uploads/Culture-in-the-Classroom-No-AK.pdf

Tetpon, B., Hirshberg, D., Leary, A., & Hill, A. (2015). Alaska Native-focused teacher preparation programs: What have we learned? *Alaska Native Studies Journal, 2,* 88–100. https://scholarworks.alaska.edu/handle/11122/11105

Thalheimer, W. (2010, November 5). K–12 Classrooms: Research Review of Multigrade, Multiage, Combination Classrooms. *Work-Learning Research.* www

.worklearning.com/2010/11/05/k-12-classrooms-research-review-of-multigrade-multiage-combination-classrooms

Tobeluk v. Lind, 72 U.S. 2450 (1976), Superior Court for the State of Alaska, Agreement of Settlement. www.alaskool.org/native_ed/law/tobeluk.html

Treuer, David. (2019). *The heartbeat of Wounded Knee: Native America from 1890 to the present*. Penguin Random House.

Vazquez Cano, M., Bel Hadj Amor, H., & Pierson, A. (2019). *Educator retention and turnover under the midnight sun: Examining trends and relationships in teacher, principal, and superintendent movement in Alaska*. Education Northwest, Regional Educational Laboratory Northwest. https://eric.ed.gov/?q=ED598351&id=ED598351

Wallace Foundation. (2013). *The school principal as leader: Guiding schools to better teaching and learning*. www.wallacefoundation.org/knowledge-center/pages/the-school-principal-as-leader-guiding-schools-to-better-teaching-and-learning.aspx

Will, M. (2016, May 18). Teachers of color pay an "invisible tax" that leads to burnout, ed. sec. writes. *Education Week*. www.edweek.org/teaching-learning/teachers-of-color-pay-an-invisible-tax-that-leads-to-burnout-ed-sec-writes/2016/05

Willingham, D. (2006, Spring). How knowledge helps: It speeds and strengthens reading comprehension, learning—and thinking. *American Educator*. http://www.aft.org/periodical/american-educator/spring-2006/how-knowledge-helps

Willingham, D. (2010). *Why don't students like school?* Jossey-Bass.

Yazzie-Mintz, T. (2000). *Holding a mirror to "Eyes Wide Shut": The role of Native cultures and languages in the education of American Indian students*. Office of Educational Research and Improvement, US Department of Education. https://eric.ed.gov/?id=ED444778

Younging, G. (2018). *Elements of Indigenous style: A guide for writing by and about Indigenous peoples*. Brush Education.

Index

Page references for figures are italicized

academic success: beyond school, 125; continuous improvement, 129–32; critical thinking, 111, 136–37, *138*; data, 16, 23–24, 40, 81–83, 124–26, 149, 164, 191; data, student outcomes, 15, 63, 169; data, text proficiency, *17*; data, using data, 126; high expectations, 69, 107–8, 127, 172–73; leadership role, 123, 135, 138–39, 220; leadership that drives change, 123; rural disadvantage, 127; school improvement, 32, 69, 129, 133–34, 148–49, 169, 180, 208; school improvement, practical suggestions, 130–31; school improvement, reading improvement goal, 131–32; student outcomes, 15, 63, 169. *See also* data; utilizing

advisory school boards, 51, 156, 164, 207, 239

AFN. *See* Alaska Federation of Natives; Native organizations

Ahmaogak, Edna, 224

AKCIS. *See* Alaska Career Information System; career and technical education

AKRISE. *See* Alaska organizations; Alaska Rural Innovation and Student Engagement Network

AKRSI. *See* Alaska organizations; Alaska Rural Systemic Initiative

Alaska Department of Education and Early Development (DEED), 16, 23, 95, 98–99, 109, 113, 149, 152, 166, 169, 216; M Limited certification, 95; suicide prevention, 171

Alaska education, history of: missionary schools, 115, 245; Molly Hootch, 8, 107, 245; superintendent Foster, 5. *See also* Alaska Native Claims Settlement Act; boarding schools; Native corporations

Alaska geographic regions: Aleutian Islands, 214, 247; Annette Islands Reserve, 20; Northwest Arctic, 91, 96, 101, 119, 135, 155; Prudhoe Bay, 20, 246; Tanana River, 87; Tuluksak River, 47–48. *See also* Tribes; Tribes in Alaska by Location, Appendix A

Alaska government: Department of Fish & Game, 11, 23, 47–48, 89; Department of Health and Social Services, 41, 158, 169; Department of Public Safety, 175; Division of Community and Regional Affairs, 24; Office of Children's Services, 166–67; State Board of Education,

259

71; State System of Support Coaching Program, 148–49. *See also* Department of Education and Early Development

Alaska health services, 13; Bristol Bay Health Services, 171; Care Crisis and "Warm" Line, 159; fetal alcohol spectrum disorders (FASD), 243; Mental Health Trust, 176; Native Health Consortium, 41, 93; Native Tribal Health Consortium, 13, 171; School Counselor Association, 176; Suicide Prevention Resource Center, 243; Tribal Health Consortium, 13, 171

Alaska Indigenous peoples, history of: boarding schools, 5, 6, 7, 38, 50, 106–7, 115, 241, 245, 248; Great Sickness, 5, 243; Spanish flu of 1918-1919, 5, 248; *Tobeluk vs. Lind*, 7–8, 107, 245; United States Bureau of Indian Affairs (BIA), 5–6, 24, 50, 95, 214, 242, 246; Wrangell Institute, 5–6. *See also* Alaska laws; Alaska Native Claims Settlement Act; Indigenous culture; Native corporations

Alaska laws: Alaska National Interest Lands Conservation Act (ANILCA), 87, 239

Alaska Native Claims Settlement Act (ANCSA), 13, 20–21, 239–40, 246–50; legal issues, in Alaska education, 18, 22; State Tribal Education Compact Schools (STECS), 216

Alaska Native corporations. *See* Native corporations

Alaska Native organizations. *See* Native organizations

Alaska Native peoples. *See* Alaska Indigenous peoples, history of

Alaska organizations: Alaska Association of Elementary School Principals, 39–40; Alaska Association of Secondary School Principals, 39–40; Alaska Rural Innovation and Student Engagement Network (AKRIS), 150; Alaska Rural Systemic Initiative (AKRSI), 109–10; Alaska Staff Development Network (ASDN), 39, 41, 150; Alaska Statewide Mentor Project (ASMP), 144, 149, 224, 240; Amundsen Educational Center, 103; ANCSA Regional Association, 20; Artists in Schools, 151; Association for Career and Technical Education, 89, 95; Center for Alaska Education Policy Research, 23; Center for Cross-Cultural Studies, 260; Community Genealogy Project, 58; Council of School Administrators, 18, 23, 39–40, 158, 182, 192; Institute for Social and Economic Research (ISER), 10, 23; Orthodox Church, 112–13, 120, 244–46; Sealaska Heritage Institute, 45, 150, 173, 191; Southeast Regional Resource Center (SERRC), 9, 23

Alaska Permanent Fund Dividend, 13, 246

Alaska place names: Alakanuk (Alarneq), 31, 38; Anchorage (Dgheyaytnu), 16, 19, 96, 108, 241, 243, 249; Angoon (Aangóon), 45, 249; Aniak (Anyaraq), 71; Anvik (Gitr'ingith Chagg), 259; Black River (Qip'ngayak), 106; Craig (K'aaws Tlaay), 151; Deering (Ipnatchiaq), 261; Dillingham (Curyung), 9, 25, 53, 172, 210, 243, 249; Fairbanks, 16, 91, 105, 168, 241, 243, 249; Hooper Bay (Naparyaarmiut), 49; Huslia (Ts'aateyhdenaadekk'onh Denh), 85–86; Hydaburg (Higdáa Gándlaay), 151, 154; Juneau (Dzánti K'ihéeni), ix, 16, 243, 247, 249; Kake (K̲éex̲'), ix; Kalskag (Qalqaq), 76; Kiana (Katyaaq), 95; Kivalina (Kivaliñiq), 2–3, 14, 77, 179,

184–85, 187; Kobuk (Laugviik), 95; Kodiak (Sun'aq), 138, 244, 249; Kotzebue (Qikiqtaġruk), ix, 2, 8, 95–97, 101, 155, 240, 243, 249; Kuskokwim River (Kusquqvak), 47, 120; Kwethluk (Kuiggluk), 108; Metlakatla (Maxłakxaała), 19–20; Nanwalek, 138; Nenana (Toghotili), 96, 102; New Stuyahok (Cetuyaraq), 33, 52, 54, 171; Port Heiden (Masrriq), 189; Russian Mission (Iqugmiut), 110–11; Shungnak (Isiŋnaq), 55, 57, 195–99; Sitka (Sheet'ká), 6, 241, 249; St. Paul Island (Tanax̂ Amix̂), 1; Tanana (Hohudodetlaatl Denh), 86–87; Tanana River (Tth'iitu' Niign), 87; Tetlin (Teełąy), 19–20, 33, 142; Toksook Bay (Nunakauyaq), 119; Twin Hills (Ingricuar), 25, 144; Unalaska (Iluulux̂), 1; Utqiaġvik (formerly Barrow), 9, 95, 103, 204, 243, 246, 249; Wainwright (Ulġuniq), 83, 127; Wales (Kiŋigin), ix; Yukon River (Kuigpak), 90, 120, 173

Alaska public safety, 12; State Troopers, 166; village police officer (VPO), 166, 250

ANCSA. *See* Alaska laws; Alaska Native Claims Settlement Act

Andrew, Tatianna, 33–34

Angaiak, Barbara, 207

ANILCA. *See* Alaska laws; Alaska National Interest Lands Conservation Act

ANSEP. *See* Alaska Native Science and Engineering Program; post-secondary education

Arnaq, Esther Ilutsik, 65–66

ASDN. *See* Alaska organizations; Alaska Staff Development Network

Ash, Sperry Gguitka, 10, 138, 170–71, 175

Askoak, Matushka Pauline, 33–34

ASMP. *See* Alaska organizations; Alaska Statewide Mentor Project

assessment, 2, 61, 66, 74, 81, 83–84, 94, 98–99, 125–26, 129, 132–33, 198, 235; Alaska Career Information System (AKCIS), 94, 102, 239; National Assessment of Educational Progress (NAEP), 8, 16, 78; School Climate and Connectedness Survey, 152, 247; WorkKeys, 99

Athabascan, 33, 86–87, 243

Attla, George Jr., 86, 89–90

Barnhardt, Ray, 4, 69, 110

BIA. *See* Bureau of Indian Affairs; United States organizations

Blackjack, Ada, 71

boarding schools, 5–7, 38, 50, 106–7, 115, 245, 248. *See also* Alaska education, history of

boroughs: Bristol Bay Borough, 102, 171, 210; Kenai Peninsula Borough, 16, *17*, 249

Brower, Pearl Kiyawn Nageak, 201–2, 204

Cadiente Brown, Ronalda, Aantooxu.aat, 35, 169, 200

Career, Technical, and Subsistence Education, 85, 87–89, 91–94, 97–100

Career and Technical Education (CTE), 85, 87–103, 136, 154–55, 220, 242; Alaska Association for Career and Technical Education, 95; Alaska Career Information System (AKCIS), 94, 102, 239; Alaska CTE history, 132–35; Bristol Bay Regional Career and Technical Education, 102; career clusters, 97, 99; career pathways, 97–98, 102; career plans, 94, 99; Carl D. Perkins Career and Technical Education Act, 97, 246; curriculum, 88–90, 93, 96, 99; hiring CTE teachers, 95–96; job knowledge, 91, 93, 95; King Career Center,

96; Kusilvak Career Academy, 102; Northwest Alaska Career and Technical Center (NACTEC), 96, 102–3; partnerships, with careers, schools, universities, 85, 92, 94, 99, 100, 103; programs, school, A-CHILL, examples of, history of, 85–92, 95–97, 102–3; rural CTE, 87–92; things to do, 98–99; think local, 88–89, 93–95, 98–99; transitions, to work, 93, 97; WorkKeys, 99. *See also* Alaska Native Science and Engineering Program; Career, Technical and Subsistence Education

Cates, Lisa, 153

community: activities, 4, 34, 53–54, 58, 118, 120–21, 147–48, 204; celebrate success, 132; in classrooms, 16–18, 55, 77, 110–11, 117–18, 151; connections with, 10, 15, 18, 28–30, 39, 47, 51, 56, 107, 162–63, 195–99; employment, 12; empowered community, 16, 49, 139, 202; engagement with, 14, 27, 31–34, 50–52, 54, 71, 88, 91, 98, 113, 134, 159, 172, 201, 220–23; knowledge of, 149, 152, 165, 170, 214–15; life in, 52, 58–59; local talent, and knowledge, 55–56, 144, 150, 155; Slaaviq, 113, 120. *See also* Alaska government; Division of Community and Regional Affairs

Covey, Jerry, 95, 100–101

cross-cultural instruction: cross-cultural learning, 32, 43, 52, 77, 147, 174; culturally relevant instruction, 46, 82, 103, 137, 186, 220, 242; culturally responsive curricula, 71, 83, 113–14, 186; culturally responsive instruction, 9, 46–47, 70, 77, 109–10, 115, 117, 192, 201, 210; culturally responsive school, 9, 45–47, 50, 56, 59–60, 163, 170–73, 233–36, 240; culturally responsive teacher, 9; cultural relevance, 65, 220; cultural standards, 8–9, 23, 64, 71, 84, 113, 173, 233–36; integrating culture in the classroom/school, 46, 55, 57, 60, 132; *Math in a Cultural Context*, 72, 84; place-based curricula, 199, 204; place-based teaching, 109–11, 137, 139, 172–73; *Quyurramta* (All of Us Together), 77; Rural School Project, 105; S term, 204; systemic integration, 8; teaching through culture, 105, 107, 109, 114, 119, 174, 248; tribal compacting, 216; *Uksuum Cauyai: The Drums of Winter*, 105. *See also* cultural standards

CTE. *See* Career and Technical Education

cultural standards: Alaska Standards for Culturally Responsive Schools, 9, 46, 60, 71, 77, 84, 113, 172–73, 240; Alaska Standards for Culturally Responsive Schools, Appendix B, 233–36; *Guide to Implementing the Alaska Cultural Standards for Educators*, 71, 84, 236

curriculum, 23, 28, 60, 63–64, 84, 93; academic standards, 74; academic vocabulary, 76; adapting, for culture, 57–59, 71–72, 109, 201, 205, 250; adapting, for students, 61, 67, 69, 77, 186; Alaskool, 77, 84, 90; alternate texts, 80; assessment, 66, 74, 83–84, 91, 125–26, 129, 132–33, 198, 235; ease of use, 64; evaluating curriculum, 45, 63–64, 81–82, 165; fidelity to curriculum, 17, 69; grade level issues, 16, 69, 74, 117, 124–25, 131, 144–46, 219; grade level texts, 68–69, 74; integrating science and math, 46, 48; Lexiles, for reading, 68, 84; math, 16–17, 46, 54, 57, 61–63, 66, 67, 89, 100, 111, 136, 143, 145; oral language, 63, 74–75; reading, also ELA, 16–17, 67–69, 73–74, 78, 81, 83, 124,

126–27, 131–32, 143–45; relevance, cultural, 46–47, 57, 65; relevance, of adopted curriculum, 16–17, 45; science, 16, 46–48, 56, 76–77, 89, 91, 97, 100, 111, 136, 143–44, 155; SRA *Expressive Writing*, 78, *80*; start small, 60, 81; student practice, 63, 66, 72–75, 78, 81–82, 84, 137, 155, 220; subsistence-based, 88–89; subskills, teaching, 73–74, 82, 220; systemic integration, 8; text complexity, 68, 84; vocabulary, 66–68, 74, 76, 78, 82; writing, also ELA, 16–17, 74–75, 78, *80*, 81–82, 111, 143–45. *See also* Alaska Native Knowledge Network; Alaska Standards for Culturally Responsive Schools; cross cultural; cross-cultural instruction; cultural standards; leadership

data, utilizing, 16, 23–24, *28–29* , 81, 124, 126, 165, 191; student outcomes, 15, 63, 83, 125, 169; student proficiency, 16, *17*, 18, 59, 63, 69, 74, 78, 116, 125, 135, 168–69, 174. *See also* assessment
DEED. *See* Alaska Department of Education and Early Development

Edenshaw, Karla, 151, 154
Elder, Sarah, 105
Elders, 3, 5, 7, 15, 27, 29, 31, 53, 55, 57, 165, 196–99, 235, 242; in classrooms, 56–57, 117–19, 162–63, 201; local knowledge, 38, 47, 54, 63, 88, 114, 202, 214; sharing knowledge, 8, 58, 77, 89, 98
Emekauwa, Emeka, 109
English Language Learners (ELL), 3, 80, 114, 116; academic English, 65–66, 74–75, 82, 117; ELL Activity Guide, 67; village English, 65, 250
Eskimo Olympics. *See* extra-curricular; Native Youth Olympics

extra-curricular, 29, 153; co-curricular, 54, 139, 148, 153, 204; Native Youth Olympics (NYO), 155; small schools, 155

Franklin, Roger, 195–99

George, Shgen, 45, 173
Gregory, Joe Cikigaq, 106

Hayes, Ernestine Saankalaxt, 6
Heidelberger, Michael, 139
Hensley, Willie, 249
Hill, Frank, 110
Hubbard, Susan, 161, 168
Hull, Mike, 110–11
Huntington, Suzzuk Mary, 65, 127, 182, 185–86, 219

Indigenous cultures: calendars, subsistence, 11, 112–13; ceremonies, 118–21; cultural relevance, 45, 47, 59, 65, 217, 220; Iñupiat, 56, 196–99, 244; local knowledge, 47, 49, 55, 110, 125; oral history, 111; preserving culture, 4, 7, 58, 65; Tlingit, 201, 243; traditions, 11, 51, 57, 77, 87–88, 97–98, 119–21, 125, 136, 165, 197–99, 204, 217, 249; Yupiaq, 49, 56, 58; Yuuyaraq, 49, 250. *See also* cross-cultural instruction; culturally responsive school; cross-cultural instruction, place-based teaching; cross-cultural instruction, teaching through culture; cultural standards; Elders; subsistence
Indigenous languages, 114, 174, 243; Alaska Indigenous Languages Map, Appendix C, 237; Alaska Native Language Center, 9, 23, 114, *237*; Alaska Native Language Preservation and Advisory Council, 114, 203, 251; bilingual programs, 116, 241; dual language, 117;

Indigenous languages, history of, 5; instruction of, 4, 18, 142, 202–3; Iñupiaq, 2–3, 16, 142; language loss, 114–15; revitalization, 8, 55, 89, 116–17, 174, 203, 244; vocabulary, 76, 117, 162; Xaad Kil, 142; Yugtun, 208; Yup'ik, 77, 114–15, 142, 200, 205. *See also* schools; Indigenous immersion

Indigenous peoples, in Alaska, history of, 4–5, 170; boarding schools, 5, *6*, 7, 38, 50, 106–7, 115, 241, 245, 248; Spanish flu of 1918-1919, 5, 17–18, 248; *Tobeluk vs. Lind*, 7–8, 107, 245; United States Bureau of Indian Affairs (BIA), 5–6, 50, 115, 214, 242, 246; Wrangell Institute, 5, *6*

Indigenous teachers, 70, 185–86, 190–91, 193, 205; from paraprofessionals, 187, 208; Teach Program, 205–8

instruction: adverse childhood experiences, 153; background knowledge, 66–69, 76, 82, 136, 173; bias, 170; blended instruction, 145–46; critical thinking, 111, 136–38; direct instruction, 73, 143; distance delivery, 92, 99, 154; dual language, 117; grouping students, 131, 133, 144–46; integrated instruction, 9, 58, 136, 199; online instruction, 94, 111, 124, 145–46, 154; reading goals, 131; skills practice, 73, 80, 82; social-emotional learning, 130, 152, 169; subskills, teaching, 73–74, 82, 220; text complexity, 68, 84; Trauma-Informed Instruction, 168–70, 176. *See also* cross-cultural instruction; curriculum

interventions: English Language Learners, 3, 67, 80, 114, 116; Multi-Tiered System of Supports (MTSS), 29, 80, 134; Response to Intervention (RTI), *29*, 80, 134; Sheltered Instruction Observational Protocols (SIOP), 117. *See also* instruction; social-emotional learning; Trauma-Informed Instruction

ISER. *See* Alaska organizations; Institute for Social and Economic Research

John, Mark, 119
Johnson, Assingaq Janet, 203, 205

Kamerling, Leonard, 105
Kasayulie settlement, 244
Kawagley, Oscar Angayuqaq, 49–50, 56, 58, 110, 137
Kuhns, Carlton, 126–27, 205, 208–9

Ladson-Billings, Gloria, 46
language: academic English, 65–66, 74–75, 82, 117; bilingual education, 1, 30, 77, 98, 116, 174, 241; dual language, 117; preserving language, 58–59, 116–17, 174, 203, 245; village English, 65, 250. *See also* Alaska Native Language Center; Alaska Native Language Preservation and Advisory Council; Indigenous languages; Indigenous immersion; schools

leadership, evaluations: Danielson Framework, 180, 186; evaluations, of staff, *29*, 46, 82, 113, 173, 180–81, 184–85; Marzano model, 180

leadership, supervision, 152, 156, 166, 168, 192, 221; *Culture in the Classroom*, 9, 192; effective supervision, 178–82, 184–85; supervision: improving, recruiting and keeping good teachers, 177; teacher placement, in classrooms, 190

leadership, training: Ed Leadership Program, 206; leadership development, 18, 39, 150, 191–92. *See also* Alaska Association of Elementary School Principals; Alaska Association of Secondary School

Principals; Alaska organizations; Alaska Staff Development Network; universities; University of Alaska, Anchorage; University of Alaska, Fairbanks; University of Alaska, Southeast
leadership: cross-cultural issues, 32, 43, 45, 59, 174; development, 190–92; district handbooks, *28*, 166–68; longevity, 38–40, 52, 209–10; other duties, 36, 45, 141, 154, 156; shared leadership, 35–36, 55, 156, 164, 175, 182, 220–21; shared responsibility, 134, 139, 248; time in classrooms, 27, *29*, 82–83, 180–81, 185; who to call, getting help, 158. *See also* self-care
Lindemuth, Jahna, 19–20, 248
local advisory board. *See* advisory school boards
Luthi, Rick, 46, 125, 179, 209, 211, 213

Mark, Jessica Angalkuruk, 144, 149, 154
Mase, Ty, 178, 187, 189–91, 210–13
Melkerson, Emma, 184
Melkerson, Lyle, 180, 185, 187
Miller, Gayle, 116
Mitchell, Roy, 203
Moen, Jason, 110
Morgan, Okalena, 71, 76
MTSS. *See* instruction; Multi-Tiered System of Support

NACTEC. *See* Career and Technical Education; Northwest Arctic Career and Technical Center
NAEP. *See* assessment; National Assessment of Educational Progress
Nageak, Roy, Sr., 77
Napoleon, Harold, 49
national organizations: National Association of Secondary School Principals (NASSP), 260; National Congress of American Indians, 17, 227; National Science Foundation, 72
Native corporations, Alaska Native Corporations, 13, 20–21, *21*, 55, 57, 59, 91, 93–94, 99, 149, 192, 240; Alaska Native Village Corporation Association, 20; Native Corporation Education Foundation, 210; regional corporations, 20, 53, 93, 246–47; regional non-profit corporations, 2, 247; shareholders, 248; village corporations, 20, 93, 250
Native organizations: Alaska Federation of Natives (AFN), ix, 23, 109, 214, 240; Alaska Native Justice Center, 176; Alaska Native Knowledge Network, 4, 18, 23, 46, 60, 90, 233, *234*
new directions: learning from others, 195

Ongtooguk, Paul, 1
orientation: accountability partners, 36; being new, 25; Before First Day of School, *28*; Camp Nu-Na-Hak, 108; culture camps, 57, 65, 119–20, *120*, 174, 188, 202, 204, 242; developing teachers, 14, 150, 185, 187, 189, 205–9; First Week of School, *29*; First Month of School, *29–30;* mentors, 39, 144, 148–49, 188, 240; new leaders, advice for, 33–35, 141, 182; new teachers, 32, 76, 107, 118–19, 188, 213; Umkumiut, culture camp, 119. *See also* Alaska organizations; Alaska Statewide Mentor Project

paraprofessionals, 3, 52, 91, 144, 149, 152, 154, 156, 158, 168, 173, 182, 206–8, 246; aides, classroom, *143*, 143–44. *See also* Indigenous teachers; from paraprofessionals
partnering, 27, 31, 94, 113, 152, 164, 173, 202, 205, 215; with districts, 85, 99–100, 210; reciprocity, 215;

with Tribes, 92, 109, 169, 210; with universities, 77, 207, 210
Peratrovich, Elizabeth, 151
Petticrew, Qanglaagix Ethan, 214
Pitka, Mae, 110
post-secondary education: Alaska Native Science and Engineering Program (ANSEP), 100, 240; Alaska Performance Scholarship, 91, 240; dual credit, for college, 93; Ilisaġvik College, 94–95, 103, 201, 203–4; programs, 74, 95–97, 102–3, 189, 193; student aid, 99. *See also* universities
professional development, for teachers, 18, 39, 70, 76, 95, 115, 131, 148–49, 163, 169, 192, 244; collaboration, 110, 121, 139, 148; community, learning about, 113, 149, 165; instructional tutors, 212–13; organizations, for professional development, 150; orientation, 31, 57
Purkeypile, Josh, 31, 38

Rearden, Nita Yurrliq Prince, 8, 15, 112, 200
recruitment: Alaska Teacher Placement, 153, 211; master's program, 191, 210; outside teachers, 147, 189, 211–12; student teachers, 188–89; teacher recruitment, 179, 209; teachers, recruiting from within, 205; Teach Program, 205–8; Tutor Program, 189–90, 212–13
relationships, 15, 20, 27, 30, 56, 121, 144, 153, 165, 173–74, 178; community, life in, 52, 54, 148; community engagement, 16, 32; connections, with community, 18, 31, 50–51, 58, 106–9, 147, 159, 162, 197–99; partners, 36; reciprocity, 71, 107–8, 118–19, 215–16, 220; shared responsibility, 55; volunteers, 150. *See also* community; Indigenous cultures; school climate

retention: bonuses, 211, 221; mentors, 149; teacher retention, 12–14, 178–79, 183–85, 192, 205, 208–10; teacher turnover, 14–15, *14*, 64, 70, 178, 205, 209. *See also* master's program; recruitment; Teach Program; teacher recruitment; Tutor Program
Rowley, Luke, 55, 57, 59
RTI. *See* instruction; Response to Intervention
rural Alaska, about, viii, 2, 4–5, 9–10, 18–20, 22, 32, 50, 55, 65, 70, 87, 121, 147, 159, 218, 247; families, 7, 10, 22, 50, 52, 58, 106, 112, 127, 152–53, 159, 170, 173, 186, 198; market economies, 11, 87, 89, 97; subsistence economies, 11, 89, 246; teacher supply, 13; transfer economies, 13

Sampson, Ruthie, 139
school climate, *28–29*, 139, 152, 161–64, 174, 183, 195–96, 247; personalizing school, 134–36; school, as a host, 27, 37, 118, 164, 166, 168; school climate, safety, and learning, 161; welcoming environment, 16, 34, 50, 117–18, 162–66, 174, 201, 221. *See also* community; engagement; school safety
school districts: Alaska Gateway School District, 85, 89, 102, 142, 155; Aleutians East School District, 210; Anchorage School District, 96, 102; Bering Strait School District, 96, 102–3; Chugach School District, 96, 101–2, 129; Dillingham City School District, *53*, 102, *172*, 210; Fairbanks North Star School District, 16, *17*; Galena City School District, 96, 102, 241; Hydaburg City School District, 151, 154; Lake and Peninsula School District, 102, 112, 178–79, 187, 189, 209–10, 212–13;

Lower Kuskokwim School District, 9, 77, 96, 102, 116, 119, 187, 193, 205, 250; Lower Yukon School District, 96, 102, 173; Matanuska-Susitna Borough School District, 16, *17*; Nome City School District, 96, 102–3; North Slope Borough School District, 9, 204; Northwest Arctic Borough School District, 91, 96, 101–2, 119, 135, 155, 195–99; Southeast Island School District, 155; Southwest Region School District, 102, 155, 210; Yukon-Koyukuk School District, 85, 89, 102; Yukon Kuskokwim School District, 9, 103; Yupiit School District, 6, 102, 109

school improvement, 32, 69, 129, 133–34, 148–49, 169, 180, 208; action plans, 130; coaching, 74, 148–49, 158, 191; continuous improvement, 18, 129, 132; practical suggestions, 130–31; reading improvement goal, 131–32; school improvement system, 133–34, 206; school turnaround, 129; student outcomes, 15, 63, 169. *See also* data

school programs: Alaska Care and Husbandry Instruction for Lifelong Living (A-CHILL), 85–89, *90, 97*; aviation, 91, 114; Frank Attla Youth and Sled Dog Care Mushing Program, 85; Galena Interior Learning Academy, 102, 241; It's a 'WE'™, 196–97, 199; Quality Schools Initiative, 129; Sheltered Instruction Observational Protocols (SIOP), 117; Weekly Parent Attendance Program, 197. *See also* Career and Technical Education

schools, Indigenous immersion: Ayaprun Elitnaurvik in Mamterilleq (Bethel), 114, 116; Nikaitchuat Ilisaġviat Iñupiaq (Utqiaġvik), 9; Ya Ne Dah Ah (Chickaloon), 9

schools: Alak School, 127–28, 139; Chief Ivan Blunka School, 33; Hopson Middle School, 259; Jimmy Huntington School, 85; McQueen School, 179; Northway School, *90*; Nulato School, *86*; Shungnak School, 55, 57, 195–99; Tetlin School, 19, 33, 142, 249; Togiak School, *13, 92, 108, 128* ; Tuluksak School, 48

school safety: child abuse, 22, 166, 175, 246; code of ethics, 166; counseling, social work, 37, 158, 176, 191, 248; crisis management, 159, 166, 169, 175; health clinics, 12, *28*, 166, 243; student supports, 20, 39, 63, 66, 74, 80, 83, 98–100, 106, 108, 125, 134, 152, 162, 166, 219; suicide prevention, 166, 171

self-care, 148, 157, 200

SERRC. *See* Alaska organizations; Southeast Regional Resource Center

small schools, 31, 96, 133, 141, 155, 182, 220; advantages, 153, 159–60; blended instruction, multiage classroom, 145–46; conflict and climate, in small schools, 152; curricular, co-curricular, and extra-curricular opportunities, in small schools, 153, 155; multiage classroom, teaching tips, 143–44, 159, 203, 245; multigrade and multi-age classrooms, 142–43, 145–46, 245; online learning, 154; other duties as assigned, 156; paraprofessionals, 146, 149, 154; personalizing school, 150; social-emotional needs, 152

STECS. *See* Alaska laws; State Tribal Education Compact Schools

student success, 126, 162–63, 171, 178, 180, 201–2; high expectations, 17, 69, 108, 127, 172–73. *See also* academic success

subsistence, 11, 23, 34, 47, 57–58, 85, 87–89, 91, 97–98, 112–13, 119, 127,

150, 200, 204, 220, 239, 248–49; things to do, 98–99. *See also* Alaska Career; Indigenous cultures; Technical and Subsistence Education
suicide prevention, 166, 171; Alaska Department of Education and Early Development, suicide, 175; Alaska Native Tribal Health Consortium, suicide, 176; Suicide Prevention Resource Center, 176. *See* Alaska health organizations; school climate; school safety

technology, *28–30* , 136; distance delivery, 92, 99, 145–46, 154, 158; online visibility, of school programs, 211. *See also* Career and Technical Education
Thomas-Churchwell, Eva, 33–34
TLPI. *See* Tribal Law and Policy Institute; Tribal organizations
Topkok, Sean Asikłuk, 1
Trader, Mary Maacuar, 105
trans-Alaska pipeline, 21, 240
Tribal organizations: Cook Inlet Tribal Council, 21, 155, 245; Metlakatla Indian Community, 20; Tribal Law and Policy Institute (TLPI), 150
Tribes, 18–19, 21–22, 24, 41, 84, 112, 210, 213–17, 244, 249; sovereignty, 2, 18–20, 23, 213–17, 248; Tribal, Tribes, aspects of, viii, 10, 19–20, 22, 24, *28*, 32, 59, 68, 77, 93, 103, 150, 166, 176, 210, 215–17; Tribal compacting, 216; Tribes in Alaska by Location, Appendix A, 227. *See also* Alaska laws; Alaska Native Claims Settlement Act; Metlakatla Indian Community; State Tribal Education Compact Schools; Tribal organizations

United States government: Bureau of Indian Affairs (BIA), 5–6, 50, 115, 214, 242, 246; Bureau of Indian Education, 216, 242; Department of Education, 72, 77, 97; National Park Service, *21*, 239; National Science Foundation, 72, 90; United Nations Declaration of the Rights of Indigenous Peoples, ix
United States laws: Indian Child Welfare Act, 22, 176, 244; Nelson Act, 5, 246
universities: Alaska Pacific University, 93, 189, 192; Iḷisaġvik College, 93–95, 103, 204; University of Alaska, 10, 14, 72, 77, 84, 93, 95, 100, 102, 109, 189, 193, 240; University of Alaska, Anchorage, 24, 210; University of Alaska, Fairbanks, 23, 114, 207, 227; University of Alaska, Southeast, 35, 169, 187, 191, 200; University of Puget Sound, 45

Vasquez, Julie, 153
Veniaminov, John, 1

Waghiyi, John, 88
Waker, Kateri, 7
Walker, Terry Aviññaq, 91, 135
Waska, Raymond Iraluq, 107
Waska, Stanley Cakicenaq, 105
Williams, Mike, 6
Winslow, Barbara, Skip, 105–9, 121
Wonhola, Dorothy, 33–34

Yates, Ken, 151
Yazzie-Mintz, Tarajean, 47
Younging, Gregory, *Elements of Indigenous Style*, viii
Yuuyaraq, 490, 250

About the Editors and Contributors

Janice DeVore Littlebear taught for 15 plus years, then mentored early career teachers across Alaska, traveled the globe working with teachers, brought cultural pedagogical practices to the Alaska Statewide Mentor Project, and directed the Teacher Education K–8 Certificate program at Alaska Pacific University until he retired, in 2021.

Robert S. (Bob) Thompson has served as a teacher and principal in urban and rural Alaska for the last 35 years. He started his career in the Matanuska-Susitna Borough School District in 1986. In 2002 he and his wife began work in rural Alaska, including in Alak School in Ulġuniq (Wainwright), Hopson Middle School in Utqiagvik, and later, at Chief Ivan Blunka School in Cetuyaraq (New Stuyahok). He has been involved with the State System of Support Coaching program since its inception and served as the managing director of the program for four years. He now continues his consulting work from his home in Palmer, Alaska.

Christian P. Wilkens is associate professor at the State University of New York Brockport. He taught in Dzánti K'ihéeni (Juneau), Alaska, and worked briefly for the Alaska Department of Education. He has served as a school improvement coach in Kivaliñiq (Kivalina), Teełąy (Tetlin), Gitr'ingith Chagg (Anvik), and Qalqaq (Lower Kalskag), and he consults with rural school districts in special education and teacher recruitment.

* * *

Sean Asikłuk Topkok is Iñupiaq, Sámi, Kven, Irish, and Norwegian. His parents are the late Clifford and Aileen Topkok, both from Iiġalugniagvik (place to go fishing), the original name of Teller. Previously, Asikłuk worked as the Indigenous curriculum specialist for the Alaska Native Knowledge Network, and he is currently an associate professor at the University of Alaska Fairbanks in the Center for Cross-Cultural Studies.

Robin Jones was born and raised in Dgheyaytnu (Anchorage) and is the principal of Iditarod Elementary School. She served for many years as the principal of "Chief" Ivan Blunka School in Cetuyaraq (New Stuyahok), Alaska. She was selected by her peers as the Alaska Association of Secondary School Principals (AASSP) Region 7 Principal of the Year in 2017 and 2020 and, most recently, as the Alaska Principal of the Year in 2021.

Meghan Redmond is the principal of Homer Middle School. She previously served as the lead teacher at Ingricuar (Twin Hills) for six years and as the assistant principal of Chief Ivan Blunka School in Cetuyaraq (New Stuyahok) for five years, where she was named the 2019 NASSP National Assistant Principal of the Year.

Carol Thompson is an elementary school educator and a reading/curriculum specialist. She has worked in both urban and rural Alaska and served rural schools as a State System of Support coach for the Alaska Department of Education & Early Development for seven years. She currently continues her work as a private consultant to school districts in Alaska.

Abby Qirvan Augustine was born in Kwiguk, Alaska, and grew up in nearby Imangaq (Emmonak) on the Yukon delta. Abby is a retired Yup'ik language immersion teacher and one of the two founding teachers of Ayaprun Elitnaurvik Yup'ik Immersion School in Lower Kuskokwim School District, Mamterilleq (Bethel).

Benjamin Glover is currently a middle school science teacher at Susquenita Middle School. He served as principal of Tetlin School in Teełąy (Tetlin) and principal of Hydaburg City School in Higdáa Gándlaay (Hydaburg). He has also served as dean of vocational education and workforce development for Iḷisaġvik College.

Deidre Jenson, EdD has served as a teacher and administrator in several locations in Alaska—mostly rural—since 2005. She was principal in

Ipnatchiaq (Deering) in the Northwest Arctic Borough School District for four years and recently returned to Southeast Island School District to be the area principal/state and federal programs manager.

Evelyn J. Willburn is an educator who has worked in many of the state's rural schools for the past 33 years. Her experience includes multigrade teaching and work as an elementary school principal. For the last seven years, she has worked as a consultant/coach and long-term substitute for schools around the state.

Lesa Meath grew up, taught, and lives in Fairbanks, Alaska (the territory of the original inhabitants, the Tanana Khwt'ana). An Alaskan educator for over 30 years and a national board certified teacher, Lesa's experience includes working as a consultant to schools in both rural settings and on the road system, for three years as a State System of Support coach, and for six years with the Alaska Statewide Mentor Project. She has had the privilege of working with fellow educators and students in over a dozen Alaska districts.

www.ingramcontent.com/pod-product-compliance
Lightning Source LLC
Chambersburg PA
CBHW050434240426
43661CB00055B/2377